IRMA

Life Lessons from
the Worst Storm
in Atlantic History

MARK R. WILSON

IRMA

IRMA

Life Lessons from
the Worst Storm
in Atlantic History

MARK R. WILSON

Cover and interior design by Tabitha Lahr
Published 2019

Dedicated to all the people
whose lives were affected by Irma

In memory of Chris Davies, friend and employer
at Octopus Divers, Saint Martin, for all too short a time

CONTENTS

Introduction

T he catalyst for this story is without question Hurricane Irma, but the full story did not reveal itself to me in its entirety until Graeme ignited the spark in January 2018. Graeme, my brother Ian, and I were talking about Irma when Graeme said he had the answer to a question—a question which, at the time, was actually more a thing to be pondered than a true question. All the same, he was on to something. The idea for the story was born, and I felt compelled to write it.

My story begins at Irma's peak, at a time when I had given up and was resigned to my fate and to ending my days in the middle of what turned out to be the worst storm in Atlantic history. It then rewinds twenty-one years to 1996 and a day out in Cornwall, UK, which awakened a fascination for sharks and for the ocean. Over the following years, an ever-deepening connection with the ocean became a passion. This eventually led to the decision to study and work toward a career in marine conservation.

We all make decisions all the time, good and bad. Some are simple to make, some are harder, and some turn out—somewhat unexpectedly—to be monumental. The way I see it, there are different types of decisions. Quick, spur of the moment ones where we act with little or no regard for the outcome; and the ones where we already have a desired outcome in mind and act accordingly to achieve it. When we make decisions in the moment, the outcome will surely follow; sometimes it will be positive, sometimes not. If we make a decision with a desired outcome in mind and subsequently act accordingly to achieve it, we would hope to be on a path toward it.

Perhaps you believe the decisions we make and the actions we take keep our fates or destinies in constant flux and that nothing in life is certain. Or you might believe in fate, and that everything in life happens for a reason, and that in the grand scheme of things, we are all powerless, regardless of our path, and will fulfill our destinies written in the stars. How about the experiences in life we have no control over and would not have chosen for ourselves? How do these experiences affect our psyche and how important are they to our decisions, to understanding our self and our subsequent path through life?

Prologue

I know what true fear is. I have given up. Pandora's box is truly empty now, and I am waiting for the worst, the end. The single-story house we are in is being ripped apart and surely won't last much longer.

Screaming into my ear over the terrifying cacophony, Jenn asks, "Are we going to die?"

I truly believe we are, and I'm sure she does too. I look into her eyes momentarily and see my fear reflected back. I want to be strong, I want to be positive, but I answer rather feebly, "I hope not."

Some will ask me later, did I find a new faith in God at this time? Did I pray? No, quite simply, no such thoughts entered my mind. Petrified and cowering in the corner of the room with the storm raging all around and with what can only be described as buckets of seawater being hurled in my face, I closed my stinging eyes, tried to block out Irma's terrifying two-hundred-mile-per-hour howl and wondered, *How did I get here?*

One

Basking Sharks Summer 1996

"Y ou can't go out there! You can't swim, you idiot."
This is very true, I can't. Still, I have to go out and see the two basking sharks swimming long lazy circles in the bay up close; I just have to. We are at Kennack Sands on the Lizard Peninsula in Cornwall on a warm, sunny June afternoon. The surrounding rugged Cornish cliffs are cloaked in green and gradually slope away to sea level, revealing the small, sheltered, little-known sandy bay. The tide is low, exposing the compacted dark wet sand that the next incoming tide will soon reclaim. Further up the beach is the warm dry fluffy sand favoured by the few outstretched sun seekers at this secluded Cornish gem. The shimmering, pale green sea is gently rolling in soft waves that break just offshore into a calm, white froth that lazily flows in to massage the sand and fringing rocks.

I strip to my shorts and make numerous, tentative attempts to summon the courage to enter the inviting but chilly water. I manage to make it no further than thigh deep in the frothy white surf. The courage, of course, is required to face the water, not—as perhaps others might need—to face the huge but harmless sharks. I am becoming increasingly frustrated at my shortcomings in the swimming department as I wade in and out of the surf, only to be encouraged back to safety by Jo every time. Then I experience an aha moment. There is a small beach hut in the car park selling buckets and spades and all the usual beach paraphernalia.

"Let's go to the beach hut; they might sell body boards," I say excitedly.

With a groan, a roll of the eyes, and in a tone you might use when giving in to a child's persistent demands for ice cream, Jo replies, "Come on then."

Yes yes yes! They do indeed sell body boards. I quickly exchange a twenty-pound note for a brightly coloured polystyrene ticket into basking shark territory. I don't know how to use this either, of course, but it floats doesn't it? I'll be fine.

We make our way across the nearly empty car park and back to the beach where I scamper past the scattered outstretched sun bathers waiting for the ultraviolet light to trigger the melanin in their skin into action. Then, upon reaching the flat wet sand, my trot accelerates to a run until I get to the water's edge. As soon as I reach the water, I attach the leash to my ankle and excitedly make my way to the water.

Jo has caught up with me now and announces loudly and with a wry smile, "It goes around your wrist, stupid."

"Oh, does it?" I reply in a sheepish, slightly inquiring tone. "Thanks."

I correct my rookie error, smile, and off I go wading through the white surf, with purpose this time. The water quickly reaches my chest, so it's time to get atop my new seagoing companion. I manage to board quickly but just as quickly fall off the other side with a *whoops*. I am not out of my depth, but I cling to my inanimate new best friend gratefully. My second attempt at boarding is made with slightly less enthusiasm. I'm wobbly but I'm on. I commence paddling, first with one arm at a time and then both together. Neither feels overly effective, but I am less wobbly when I use both arms simultaneously, so off I go rowing my way toward the waiting sharks with all the grace and agility of a windup bath toy.

The sharks are approximately three hundred feet from the beach, and after a few strokes of my favoured rowing action, I am actually making good progress, albeit still slightly wobbly. Once within a few yards of the sharks, I begin to appreciate their size. The dark triangular dorsal fins stand proud above the surface of the water, and rather than appearing ominous, they beckon me closer while providing a clue as to the size of the harmless, plankton-feeding leviathans swimming below. Both sharks are swimming in large circles and seem to be following the same path. I keep moving carefully with the intent of positioning myself in their path while at the same time doing my utmost not to intrude. Each time they pass, I get a tantalising glimpse, not only of the sharks, but—though I don't yet know it—also of the future. Suddenly one of them rises higher out of the water and moves closer, revealing its entire dorsal fin, tail, and snout. This enables me to estimate its size, and it truly is huge, easily fifteen feet long. I want to see them under the water too.

"Dammit," I say aloud, thinking I should have bought a mask or swimming goggles as well. I slip from the board anyway and, despite the attached leash, I take care to keep one hand firmly gripping my small refuge like a climber clinging to a rock face. Without the necessary eyewear, it is difficult to see the sharks clearly under the water. I do, however, see a very large blurry shark shape.

Sharks are not the only blurred thing in my life at this time. Despite being twenty-seven years old, I have no clarity or direction in life, and as for girlfriends—well that's the most confused thing of all. I like Jo, we get on very well, we have had two or three petty fallings out, but these are always easily remedied too; although Jo has always instigated our making up. Aside from knowing I like her, am comfortable around her, and enjoy her company, I am unable to take it any further or express any feelings whatsoever. I have no idea what she means when she tells me how she feels about me. I experience a sense of dread and completely clam up every time the subject is broached. Something that is not blurry in this regard is being utterly convinced I will not have a happy, healthy, longstanding relationship. How does someone reach this conclusion, and so young? Is it somehow programmed in? I just don't believe happy, healthy, long-term relationships are for me.

Is it sometimes simply easier for us to dismiss things we don't understand than to make the effort to try?

Unlike understanding feelings, slipping from the board for the blurry view of the sharks is easy, but getting back on is quite another matter. Now that I cannot jump off the sand, mounting the board is even more ungainly than it was at the beach. After numerous attempts, I make it, but somehow I am sideways. I could attempt to move around for the remainder of my time like a crab, but I'm not sure this will be very efficient. So, after fidgeting and wobbling about, I am now parallel to the board once more. Now that I am safely aboard and facing in the right direction, I elect to stay on rather than risk looking like a fool in front of the graceful sharks. Besides, the clear water penetrated by the early afternoon sun reveals almost the complete shark to me while I remain high and almost dry on my floating platform.

Occasionally, I look toward the beach to check my bearings and see Jo patiently standing there clutching an oversized beach towel. Despite being what should be well outside of my comfort zone, I feel calm, relaxed, and very much at home while also feeling privileged to be welcomed and accepted into the company of these two magnificent creatures. I could stay here all afternoon, but I am starting to feel cold, so it's time to head back to the beach. I turn to face the shore and start paddling. It doesn't take long before I start to feel a little tired. A quick glance to the beach and the realisation that Jo has become no larger tells me I have made no progress whatsoever. I pause and can feel myself slowly slipping out to sea. Could this be a reflection of my relationship? My life? Will I soon slip away from Jo? Is this what I want, to avoid the complications of relationships?

At the time, I did a good job of ignoring the finer points of our relationship and Jo's dissatisfaction, but I realise now that Jo was becoming increasingly frustrated with my total inability to express my feelings. I was, without a doubt, a rubbishy boyfriend in this regard. I don't believe that younger version of myself was totally useless though. In many ways, I behaved as a good boyfriend should. I helped her whenever she needed help, wasn't normally mean, wasn't rude, nor did I raise my voice in anger or frustration. I would gladly transport her to and from work, riding my motorbike at an almost impossible fifteen miles an hour when she rode pillion because she was afraid to go faster. After many very slow rides, one day I realised both her knees were dug into my hips, like a woman on horseback. It was only then I sped up.

Teaching Jo to drive the trusty old Opel Kadett in the Tesco parking lot or the Park and Ride on warm, dry summer evenings provided laughs for both of us. Like the time she forgot to steer and took the elderly but trouble-free car beyond the boundaries of the car park and partway into a grassy ditch. I enjoyed her company a great deal. I know that much. She made me laugh and was so silly sometimes it was brilliant. At times she was perfect in her silliness, naivety, and gullibility.

One particular example of how adorable she was came on one of our regular lazy Sunday afternoons of fresh-bread cheese sandwiches, my favourite salt-and-vinegar crunchy stick crisps that had to be eaten in a very specific way, and TV.

After being engrossed in the computer-generated show recreating the life of woolly mammoths, Jo exclaimed, "Wow, I thought mammoths were extinct."

Immediately I seized the opportunity to invent a story about their rediscovery some years earlier and explained how they were thriving in the very high arctic. She, of course, absorbed everything without question as I grinned broadly, at least on the inside.

I mentioned not normally being mean, but once I was horribly so. It was during one of those petty fallings-out, after Jo had walked some three or four miles across Exeter to my house in the pouring rain to patch things up. On hearing a knock on the door, I peered from the upstairs window to see a soggy Jo standing there in her favourite green cardigan that was almost the same colour as the fetid, uncared for, lifeless pond beside her.

"Hello," she said, as she looked up in my direction with a smile that transcended her drowned-rat appearance and made her glow. I don't know exactly why, but I was in no mood for a conversation.

"What are you doing here now?" I enquired in a sour tone.

"Come down and let me in," she said, flapping her sodden cardigan-cloaked arms to her side, with sleeves extending well beyond her hands.

"I don't want to talk now," I insisted as I turned and closed the window. She knocked on the door again, but I made no attempt to speak to her through the window or otherwise. She knocked with a renewed vigour and in disbelief at my attitude. I had no intention of letting her into the house, soaked to the bone or otherwise.

It would seem abundantly clear to anyone that I was being stubborn and cruel. But I would realise later that the cruelty was a side effect of something more. It was my way of avoiding conflict, at least in part. At the time I knew I was definitely stubborn and didn't want to talk to her. But looking back, now I'm not sure if my mindset was careless, or if I told myself I didn't care less.

For close to half an hour, Jo knocked on the door repeatedly, and in between I took a few sneaky looks from the window to see if she was still there. Eventually she gave up and walked all the way back home in the pouring rain. I would soon learn that, even if I wanted to avoid an argument, this was an extremely cruel and hurtful way to treat someone who cares about you, and no way to behave in any relationship.

Looking back now, I seem to have been performing badly in an audition for a part I would never play, a part in something I truly didn't understand or want to. So was it horribly selfish of me to try out, knowing I didn't actually want the part?

I'm paddling harder now, and to monitor progress, I look to my left and find a reference point on the towering—from this perspective at least—cliffs that surround me. After being head down and paddling hard for half a minute or so, a quick look left informs me that I am still in the same position. Something clicks, and I suddenly realise why it was so easy to paddle out. I was going with the current. Now, of course, I'm going against it, or trying to. Despite my predicament, I don't feel stressed at all. I do feel short of breath, but still very much at ease in the water. Now I must really work hard. After a further half-minute or so of intense effort, I look to the beach once more. Jo is bigger now, I'm sure of it. I take a tentative look left and behind, hoping to see my point of reference, but damn, I can't. Where is it? I keep looking but it is difficult to make out from a different angle. Then I find it, and yes it is behind me. Good. I'm making progress.

My huffing and puffing closely mimics the loud exhales of surfacing whales, and despite my aching lungs and arms, I continue forward with renewed vigour. A few minutes later, I can finally stand and begin wading toward the beach while looking forward to the towel that Jo is holding. Wait. She's not holding it. I can see it on the sand, the wet sand revealed by the retreat of the tide. She bends down and grabs it for me, and I can tell by her face that she realises what I already know: the towel is very wet, far too wet to provide any comfort.

She looks at me sheepishly while I enquire, somewhat miffed, "Why did you put it on the wet sand?"

"Um … because I didn't know the sand was wet," she replies, lowering her head, peering up at me, and speaking ever more slowly with each passing word. She turns equally slowly to face the warm dry sand just a few feet away.

"Jo," I say as I shiver, "this flat dark compacted sand is wet." I moan as I scuff it with the bottom of my foot, "The fluffy sand there is dry," I add sarcastically while pointing just ahead.

We are soon in the ever faithful Kadett, towel incident forgotten and heater blowing welcome warmth while I excitedly relay details of my first experience with sharks. Why have I not done anything like this before? I was so at home and must do it again. I have no idea how significant today is and where it will eventually lead. Sometimes we just have to act in the moment.

A few weeks have passed since I swam with the basking sharks. It's Friday night, and Claire, Jo's housemate, is having a birthday gathering at their house with a *Pulp Fiction* theme. Most of the girls are wearing wigs in the style of Uma Thurman's character in the movie. Claire and I are practicing self-defense moves recently taught to me by a work colleague in the dimly lit living room, much to the amusement of the others. After five or ten minutes of slightly drunken shenanigans and unconvincing displays of prowess on both sides, I make a further attack on Claire and she quickly grasps an arm, twists me around, and rather convincingly sends me crashing all the way through a sash window conveniently set at hip height. I go reeling straight out into the back yard. I quickly pick myself up and turn to see Claire peering through the curtain, looking as shocked as I feel at the rather dramatic outcome. I move toward the window where she pulls the curtain aside and looks me over for cuts. Fortunately no harm whatsoever has been done, aside from the window, of course, and perhaps my pride. The heavy curtains dampened my fall through the breaking glass, much as the incident itself will soon dampen the mood.

We pull the curtain further aside and carefully pull two or three protruding shards from the bottom of the frame. Jo appears just as I climb over and back into the room, and she doesn't look happy. She unleashes a short barrage of displeasure in my direction as others slowly leave the room.

"I don't understand, what do you mean, your friends are scared of me?" I exclaim. "Claire certainly isn't." I grin. "I've never done a thing to any of them, have I?"

"No, I know you haven't," she agrees, but she still sounds unhappy.

"Have you said something to make them feel this way then?" I shrug and pull a silly face.

A drawn out "No" is her reply, "of course not."

"Well, it's their fault then; it's ridiculous and you should tell them so."

"You do something about it to make them feel better," she replies in a heightened pitch, putting the onus back on me.

"How?" I moan. "I've done nothing wrong in the first place." My voice is getting higher too, as I become more exasperated.

"Well you need to do something," she says, anger in her tone.

An hour before, I had paraded around the house wearing one of the girls' wigs atop my bald head, looking ridiculous in front of everyone, and— accepting a dare—went out to collect Kentucky Fried Chicken wearing it. When did self-ridicule become a sin? I realise this evening's antics perhaps weren't the sole impetus for Jo's friends' apparent fear of me. But it does demonstrate my nonthreatening demeanor and makes me wonder where this thinking—which to me is completely irrational—came from. Anyway, since this conversation is going nowhere, I give a subtle shake of the head and walk away without an excuse to find Pete, the other housemate.

"Sorry for smashing the window," I say with a hint of a wry smile. "I'll pay to get it fixed."

"I know someone who can replace it, so don't worry about it. We'll sort it out next week, mate," he says, as if he doesn't give a damn.

I find Jo and try to talk to her again, but she is clearly upset with me. Since I don't care to argue, I leave and go home to bed. It's hard for me to accept that someone is afraid of me when, as far as I'm concerned, I have done nothing to warrant such a thing.

In 1996 I was lifting weights regularly and was a big strong muscular lad weighing between 225 and 235 pounds. When I joined the Spartan Club gym at age eighteen, nine years earlier, I would say I had a physique of absolutely no note. An average frame, not skinny, no muscular definition, not particularly fat either—just nothing, a non-physique if there ever was such a thing. Those early months in the gym were hard work and not enjoyable. After around six months, I still didn't look like I worked out. But almost from the outset, it was apparent that I was strong and able to lift weights far in excess of what my frail body appeared to be capable of. Being strong was intriguing, so I continued to soldier on, even though it took at least a year before any physical changes were noticeable, and they were minimal. I was what gym folk call a hard gainer.

So why go to the gym in the first place? Eighteen-year-old boys frequent gyms for many reasons. Some to gain muscular weight, some to lose weight, some to get fit, some to develop big arms and chest to impress the ladies, some for the social aspect, perhaps even in the hope of meeting girls there. None of these motivated me. I went to the gym for one reason alone, to spend time with Dad. He had been a regular gym user for many years, and this provided the perfect opportunity to get together with him three or four times a week.

My parents had separated when I was just eight years old. Since this time, I had not spent nearly enough time with Dad, and I missed him. To begin with, I didn't enjoy the gym, but I did enjoy the company, very much. Eventually, squatting, bench pressing, and dead lifting impossible weights provided a mental lift as well. While there was no need to, I wanted to do well and impress Dad. So I worked hard, and after those initial first few months, I was enjoying the physical challenges and the mental boost the gym provided as much as my dad's company.

I feel annoyed and upset that Jo would side with her friends and support the idea that I behave in some way as to intimidate them. As far as I'm concerned, my appearance does nothing but reflect the effort I put in to spend time with my dad. My continued presence at the gym does not stem from any insecurity, or a desire to stand out or to intimidate. Yes, I have grown to enjoy it, and through the years I have trained harder and eaten the right food to help me along the way, but is for my own benefit, nothing else. I am good at something and I can see the evidence.

But despite this, I am not actually comfortable with being muscular and oversized. Even though I know my behaviour is not intimidating, I still don't like the fact that my appearance might be. Even when working out in the gym now with Darron, I remain covered up. In fact, in the summer I am always envious of my brother Ian who is of a more regular build and wears vests. I would like to wear a vest and cool off, and sometimes wear no shirt at all and get some sun, but I always feel a bit silly and self conscious, so remain covered up in public.

A couple of hours later, true to form, Jo turns up at my house in a taxi. She wakes me up, and we make up.

Two

Exmouth 1997

With its sprawling campus, Exeter offers all the functionality of a university in inspirational surroundings. Manicured lawns, large trees, and ponds are plentiful, providing a great atmosphere to study and for me to work.

I first came to work in the food warehouse in 1985, receiving deliveries, picking orders, and subsequently loading the delivery van with foodstuffs to be delivered to the twelve different kitchens and halls of residence. After passing my driving test in early 1987, I had the freedom of driving around and making deliveries myself in a Ford Transit van. In late 1990, a further opportunity arose, and I became the warehouse manager and assistant buyer. This meant a move to the office, a desk, and juggling two telephones. In early 1991, Andy joined the team and replaced me as the driver. Like me, Andy is a fan of rock, alternative, and heavy metal music. We soon became good friends and socialized regularly outside of the workplace on weekends at the spots favoured by rock fans, The Crown and Sceptre and Timepiece.

This particular weekend in early May 1997, we have planned a night out in Exmouth, a small seaside town not ten miles away. We spend the evening with Reese, a friend who also works at the university. It makes a change to have a night out in Exmouth, and we enjoy ourselves until the very end of the night.

The three of us are eating our burgers when Reese moves a short distance away from the burger stand to talk to someone. Very soon they are no longer talking but rather seem to be engaged in a heated exchange. As we sense the change of mood we instinctively shuffle a little closer while continuing to enjoy our burgers, still within range of the smell of frying onions and the chatter of those still waiting.

A couple of minutes later, only half paying attention, we are still none the wiser as to the source of the disagreement until I speak up in a frustrated tone and say, "Come on, Reese, let's go."

"Hang on, he's a paedophile," comes the slightly irked reply, as if questioning why I don't already know this.

"Oh, okay," I say, puzzled, "but what's that got to do with you?"

"It was in the papers; he's evil," he spits, as if tempting me to be as animated about it as he is quickly becoming. I certainly am not condoning nor do I have any sympathy for such a human being, but I don't know the accusation to be true either. What's more, it is simply not my business, or Reese's for that matter. All the while the accused stands with shoulders slightly slumped, looking not so much downtrodden but uninterested, as if he didn't give a damn what anyone thought or said about him.

"Okay, but it's still nothing to do with you, so come on," I say as I half turn away and flap an arm in our general homeward direction.

"No, everyone needs to know who he is, and he should pay, he needs sorting out," Reese says angrily. "Look, he's not denying it, we all know it's true," he continues ever louder.

True, the accused makes no attempt to deny the claims, and shrugs nonchalantly as if to say, so what. This seemingly defiant response to such an accusation still does nothing to stir me; we've finished our compulsory late night burgers and all I can really think about is heading home.

"Well, maybe so, but it's no one's business here, so let's go, come on," I insist. Exactly why Reese is taking this person to task for his alleged crimes I don't know, but he is becoming increasingly agitated. I can't speak for Andy, but I am becoming increasingly bored. The two of them now begin to exchange threats and generally bad-mouth each other in a manner befitting two drunks on a Saturday night who are looking for a physical confrontation. I, on the other hand, am growing more frustrated at the escalating scene before me.

"Come on," I drone, "pack it in; let's go."

"No," Reese yells, "he needs to pay for what he is," and he points a stabbing finger in the direction of the accused.

"Well you're not doing anything, are you?" I shout, not with intent to motivate, but more as an observation and a good reason to leave. "You're just mouthing off," I add, "so forget it, let's go."

"Well what are *you* doing?" Reese protests, perhaps with intent to goad. I don't know.

"It's nothing to do with me," I exclaim in a voice so high-pitched it almost tails off to nothing. "Jesus Christ!" I scream in frustration.

"Yeah, I see," he replies, sounding cocky and subtly nodding his head as if accusing me of something.

Then the accused turns his attention away from Reese and toward me, yelling, "What's it got to do with you, anyway?" He stands taller now, with his open hands raised out in front of him in a gesture of invitation.

"Nothing," I say defensively, "so let's forget about it and all go home."

He then takes a few paces forward, enough to close the gap between us. There is a momentary pause before he swings a punch at me, misses, and quickly runs away.

In the years that follow, I will wish many times that he had connected with a knockout punch and sent that younger fool version of me straight to the pavement in an undignified heap. I will spend the intervening years contemplating how life might have been different if this had been the case.

All that needs to be done at this point is nothing, but unfortunately, that's not what happens. After initially running, he stops a short distance away and begins goading me into a further confrontation.

"Come on then," he yells, while waving a beckoning hand.

I just shake my head as I turn to Andy and mutter, "Dickhead." Hand-waving gestures and the usual expletives used when under the influence of alcohol and spoiling for a fight continue. Still I take no notice. I don't know him either; there is no reason for me to care what he thinks of me or to be provoked.

Yet he is persistent. "Come on, asshole," he yells again.

I don't know why, but I give in to his petty goading, rise to the challenge, and run toward him. I catch up with him just as he enters a small darkened alley and punch his face that is half-turned toward me, perhaps to check my proximity to him. He falls straight to the ground. Enough's enough, time to go home, with me the victor and him with a nosebleed, bruised cheek, or blackened eye and shattered ego. But no, I crouch beside him on one knee and continue to punch him five more times as he lies prone on the pavement. Not in a wild frenzy, but in a slow and deliberate manner. After five blows I stop but remain crouched over him silent and motionless, just looking at him in the dim light of the alley.

"What have you done?" I hear Reese say in a slightly panicked tone, rousing me from my paralysed state.

I look up to see his arms slightly raised and outstretched at his sides as if exasperated with me.

"Come on, let's go!" he screams as he instantly turns and jogs off back toward the main street.

I also see Andy as I look up, but unlike Reese, he remains silent. As I rise in the darkened alley, it is now I notice some blood on his face. Others appear on the scene as Andy and I walk out of the alley to where Reese waits impatiently. We hurry away from the alley, prompted by Reese who guides us back to his house via the safety of back streets so as to evade any potential police presence.

Moments later, as we jog along the road, Andy says, "Here you go, Chief," and extends his hand toward me, offering his red-and-black checked shirt.

I regard him with a puzzled expression.

"Wipe the blood off your hand and cover it up," he says flatly. I realise instantly that he is disappointed in me, but he still helps me. Andy is a good and loyal friend.

We arrive at Reese's house ten minutes later without further incident. But unlike Andy and me, Reese is stressed, which surprises me. After all, he was the one looking for trouble. I have no idea how you are meant to feel after being the victor in such a fight, a fight that arguably wasn't much of a fight at all. I feel nothing, not tough, not triumphant, nothing. I have no idea why I did it, and I fall asleep believing that I have left him with perhaps a bloody nose and a black eye.

"You really hurt him, you know," says Reese when we get up the following morning.

"I don't think so. Sure he has a nosebleed and a black eye," I reply confidently, "but that's it." I turn to Andy for conformation.

"I don't know, Chief," he replies. "It might be a bit worse than that. He didn't look good, I'm sure his nose will be broken at the very least."

"Well, okay, perhaps it is, but you had your nose broken when that idiot head-butted you last year for no reason," I remind Andy.

"I did, yeah."

"You did look terrible, and funny, with black eyes and a swollen face but it wasn't that bad, was it? You were okay."

"Yeah, true," Andy says as he turns to Reese, who doesn't look convinced.

"It's worse than that, I'm sure," he says, while looking to Andy and me in turn.

"Oh, Reese, it's not," I interject. I'm annoyed.

"You really messed him up," he goes on.

"Bloody hell, forget about it," I say.

"If he's hurt, I guess we'll hear about it somewhere, won't we?" Andy suggests.

"Yes, exactly," I say. "Now can we leave it?"

"Sure," replies Andy.

"Okay, Reese?" I ask.

"Yeah, I guess," he says reluctantly.

"Well there's nothing else to say, is there? We could go round and round all day guessing how badly he may or may not be hurt," I say. "There's no point."

"Okay, well, we should keep it to ourselves," Andy points out.

"Yeah," I reply as I turn to Reese.

"Yeah, yeah," he says, nodding his head as if to suggest keeping it between us goes without saying.

Three days later, Reese calls me at my office and asks me to meet him outside in the service road between the supermarket and the warehouse. I walk the short distance across the black tarmac yard to where he is standing, and he immediately thrusts the local newspaper into my hand.

"Look at this," he says, pointing to a story on the second page.

I read in stunned silence as I learn the police are looking for someone in connection with a serious incident in Exmouth that left the victim unconscious and with serious facial injuries.

Reese breaks the silence when he says, "This is you, I knew it."

I hate to admit it, but I think so too. I am still struggling to process the information when I say, "Still unconscious, serious facial injuries … but I gave him a nosebleed. I can't inflict serious injuries on someone."

"You have mate, this is bad," he replies, offering no reassurance.

Despite the bright spring day and subtle warmth from the sun, I feel cold as I struggle to accept what I appear to have done. As well as feeling numb to the news, I have quickly become aware of the possible criminal repercussions and am equally concerned about police intervention.

"Just keep it between us and no one will know. It says the police are looking," I say. "They clearly don't know it's me, do they?"

An hour later, Andy, Reese, and I go to the ever-packed student dining hall for lunch and amid all the clatter of cutlery and crockery and the clatter in my head, Reese insists on bringing it up once again. "I see his bloody face every time I close my eyes," he says. "It's giving me nightmares."

This seems excessive to me. I have knots in my stomach, one for worry about the condition of the victim, and another for trying to come to terms with what it appears I have done. But why is *he* so stressed? If he has images in his mind—and why would he make it up—why don't I?

"What?" I exclaim, annoyed at what to me seems to be an extreme response. "Why would you feel like that?"

"I just do. I can't help how I feel," he says somewhat defensively.

"Well it seems over the top to me. I don't feel great about it, but I'm not having nightmares," I say. "Bloody hell."

"You went over the top, you were crazy," says Reese. "What will you do now?"

"You're talking as if I can put it right or make it go away, but I can't, can I? I wish it would go away," I say. "If we shut up about it as we said we would, then perhaps it will." I'm feeling agitated and annoyed at the same time.

"It does seem bad, Chief," adds Andy.

"I know," I say quietly with my head slightly lowered. "I'm sure he will soon be conscious and he'll be fine," I say with a half smile in an attempt to reassure Andy and myself. But I'm not sure either of us believes it.

The following day things take a turn.

I bump into Reese walking across the yard. I smile and say, "All right," in our usual greeting as we approach each other.

But something is not all right, for he lowers his head slightly as if to avoid my eye.

Before I can say anything further, he blurts out, "I've spoken to my dad about what happened."

"What!" I exclaim.

"I've told him everything."

I'm reeling from the news as the potential enormity of his sharing this quickly builds.

"Why would you do that?" I can't believe he has done this, I really can't, as the three of us agreed to tell no one.

"I had to tell someone. I've been so stressed about the whole thing," he says.

"Stressed? Why are *you* stressed? You could have spoken to me or Andy." This feels like the start of something bigger, and I soon discover what.

"No, I had to talk to my dad."

"You didn't *have* to, there was no need to involve your dad at all, mate," I say in a mild panic. "Why would you do that?"

"He's coming to see you at four anyway, when you finish work," he says while shuffling uncomfortably from one foot to another.

"What, why?" I shake my head in disbelief.

"He'll be going to the police to say I have information about the incident in the paper. He wants to give you the opportunity to turn yourself in first." He is now speaking in a very matter-of-fact way.

Why has he done this? Okay, I did wrong, of course I did, I know that, but friends don't react like this without a reason. I get very little work done for the rest of the day, and by the time his dad comes to talk to me, something is very clear to me. Reese has told him knowing full well he will go to the police. Shortly before his dad arrives, I challenge him on this.

"You knew your dad would go to the police, and that's why you told him."

"No, I didn't," he protests.

"Bullshit, Reese, you're not that stupid," I say angrily, with a full understanding of the enormity of the situation I am now faced with.

"I didn't know what he'd say," he protests again. This is a plain lie; I know it as well as he does.

"Reese, you have used telling your dad to drop me in it. I can't believe it," I say as I walk away, disappointed by what I see as a direct betrayal. But there is clearly still more to it. Why exactly has he told his dad? Does he think it's the right thing to do and I should face justice? Well, morally, of course, I *should* face justice, but how often do people make themselves known to the police in such a case? I do feel awful and try to consider if I will feel any better if I own up to my crime, but I fail to come up with an answer.

It will be months later before I realise why Reese told his dad. He was carrying some of the responsibility and felt he would, in some way, be vindicated by facilitating my arrest. I realise something else, as well. I was influenced by him that night. I am embarrassed to admit it to myself, but I have to face up to it. Yes, ultimately I acted alone, but I allowed myself to get involved in an argument of his making. I don't yet understand why. That will come much later.

Sure enough, just after four o'clock, his father turns up. I'm standing outside in the yard leaning against the wall when a car pulls up and parks at the top of the service road. I don't know the car, but when a tall figure emerges, I know it's the man I'm waiting for. He sees me and raises a hand in acknowledgement. I stand and wait as he walks the hundred feet toward me. He is somehow moving in slow motion, as if every step is taken through treacle; he is slowly bringing my new reality ever closer.

"Hello, Mark, how are you?" he asks.

"I've been much better," I reply. "Anyway, Reese tells me you intend to go to the police?"

"Yes, Mark, I do," he says without hesitation.

"You're not here to discuss it, then; you're absolutely doing it?"

"You've done a terrible thing here, Mark. This guy is in a bad way," he says, sounding ever more serious.

"I appreciate that, but none of us know the full details. I know it says serious in the paper, but you don't know what that means. He might be fine soon," I say, hoping for a sign of softening.

"If you go to the station at Heavitree Road now it will be much better for you than if I do. I'm here to give you that chance to help yourself," he says matter-of-factly, completely dismissing what I just said.

Well thanks, I think. The thought of turning myself in to the police brings up mixed feelings. I'm not at all happy with what I did, but it doesn't feel real. I am also reluctant to deal with the consequences. People get away with this sort of thing all the time, don't they? Is that acceptable? Why should I be caught—or, more to the point, betrayed by a friend? But has Reese ultimately done the right thing, whatever his motivation?

"I am going to go now, Mark, if you don't," he says.

"Bloody hell, this isn't easy, you know," I protest.

"Yeah well, how about the poor ..."

"Okay, okay," I interrupt. "I'll go, I'll go now, just give me a few minutes."

"Be sure that you do, Mark," he says as he walks away, presumably to tell Reese.

I go back to my office and call Jo to let her know the latest installment. She wishes me luck and tells me to come to her house as soon as I leave the police station.

The drive to the station from the university takes barely five minutes, giving me not much time to think about what I'm doing. I have made a quick decision that this was better than waiting for the police to turn up and arrest me. It is, of course, the right thing to do as well, but it still feels very strange. I park the car at the station, walk into the tiny reception hall, press the buzzer —which feels like pressing my own bruise—and wait for an officer. My heart begins to race as he appears and asks with a smile, "How can I help you?"

"I am the person responsible for the incident in Exmouth last Saturday evening that left someone hospitalized."

The officer looks rather bewildered and says, "Give me a minute," as he disappears for a moment or two, only to reappear with a colleague.

"So you say you are responsible for the reported assault in Exmouth last Saturday?" asks the second officer while his colleague looks on, slightly bemused.

"Yes, that's right," I say mournfully.

"Okay, wait there."

"Wait there" is this my cue to turn and run, go home, and hope it all goes away. Before I have a chance to reconsider, a door opens to my left and the same officer reappears.

"Come through and we'll sit down and sort this out," he says as he leans forward, pushing the door open wide and beckoning me to enter. Sort it out? That seems to imply it can be dealt with and wrapped up this afternoon, but something tells me we are way beyond that now. We walk a few paces along the clinical-smelling hallways where no one other than a police officer really wants to be. I am trying to quickly process what is going on. This is very unfamiliar territory to me and feels almost like a dream. Just a few short paces and we make our way into an interview room which, apart from the warm, late afternoon sun beaming through the window, is a bare, uninviting space. It holds a small rectangular table, a tape recorder, and three metal-framed chairs with minimal cushioning.

"Tell me again why you are here?" asks the officer.

"I am responsible for the assault in Exmouth last Saturday," I answer with a heavy feeling in my chest.

"Are you sure that your incident and the one in the paper are one in the same?" he asks in the same manner in which his colleague just said "Wait there" at the reception. Is this another chance to run?

Dejected, I say, "Yes, I'm quite sure."

"Where did the incident take place?" he asks.

"It was just inside a small alley right around the corner from the main town square," I reply.

"Do you know what time, approximately?"

"Well, we left the nightclub at closing time, went straight to the burger bar, and we had been there maybe ten minutes. So no later than one *thirty*."

"Okay, excuse me while I go and check that all this matches our records. I need to make sure we are indeed talking about the same incident." He delivers this in an almost reassuring tone, implying that it still might not be.

I don't believe that for a minute, and elect not to cling to a false hope. I'm in it now, there's no mistaking it. But all the same, I have to wait in limbo until everything is confirmed. I sit alone in the room while the officer does his duty, all the while wondering how on earth this will turn out.

The officer returns soon enough and announces, "Well, everything matches" with an expressionless face. "I believe we are indeed talking about the same incident."

Even though I knew it already, my heart sinks at the news.

"I'm sorry, but I am going to have to formally arrest you now. Then you will go to a custody cell until the duty solicitor is available."

All I can manage is "Okay." I am arrested and immediately led out of the interview room to a custody cell.

This is all both overwhelming and confusing, not least of all because the arresting officer is very polite and civil about the whole thing and takes me to the cell much in the manner of a porter escorting a guest to a hotel room.

"Don't worry," he says, "it won't be long. Just sit down and try to relax," he continues in a reassuring tone as the cell door slams behind him.

I have always hated the slamming of doors. I sometimes wonder how people who consistently slam doors manage to open them, as they seem to have no understanding of the full function of the handle. This has been hard to process up until this exact moment. This particular slamming door is the worst slam ever, and as it rattles closed with a metallic clang, I very suddenly appreciate the enormity of my situation. A situation that is, of course, self-inflicted.

Alone in the confines of the miserable, featureless cell, reeking of bleach, I begin to ponder. How on earth was I able to inflict serious facial injuries on someone and leave them unconscious for four days? What exactly is meant by serious facial injuries, anyway? I question whether I could actually have caused such damage alone. Maybe someone else attacked him after me. Someone who had overheard the argument with Reese and the accusations he made, and who continued to attack him once we had left the scene. That must be it. I couldn't have caused all that damage alone, I just couldn't. Could I? Yes, I'm big and strong, so if I did this alone, is this an awful example of someone not knowing his own strength?

I have lost track of time completely. Have I been in this cell for ten minutes or an hour? I really don't know. Will they even let me out this evening? My thoughts are interrupted by someone approaching. It is the same officer.

"Time to go back to the interview room and talk to the solicitor," he informs me almost cheerfully.

"Okay, sure," I reply, relieved to be getting out of the cell and also out of my head—although at least when I was in the cell, the whole thing was on hold and maybe it would go away. Now I am moving slowly through the system and closer to facing up to—and being made responsible for—what I have done. I am led out of the cell and back to the interview room where the solicitor is waiting.

"Hello, I'm Mike Fletcher, and I'll be representing you today."

"Okay, hello," I answer a little less cheerfully than his introduction.

He shuffles through a small pile of papers while eyeing me quizzically over the top of his glasses between glances at his paperwork. "I have looked at the details and the incident you describe matches the one in the paper."

"Yes."

"So, do you know the extent of the victim's injuries?" he asks while looking me square in the eye, again over the top of his glasses.

"No, I don't," I say.

"Okay, well, he is still in hospital recovering from surgery to repair a broken nose, broken jaw, two broken cheekbones, and a broken orbit bone around the right eye."

I am stunned and can only manage a croaky, "Oh."

"There is some good news though; he regained consciousness today."

"That's something I guess," I reply, hoping that it really is something positive.

The solicitor then excuses himself and leaves to collect the arresting officer so we can begin the formal interview.

Things are very real now, and the interview covers every minute detail of the events leading up to the offense as well as the offense itself. The officer asks which hand I used in the assault and then examines my right hand for cuts and grazes, but there are none. My hand does not have a mark on it, which comes as a surprise to him. This is something I had not even thought about. It is hard to relive the events of the previous Saturday night with the extra knowledge of what I have done, but I have no choice, and I answer all questions truthfully. After almost two hours, the interview is finally brought to a close, and I am returned once again to the custody cell where I must now wait to hear the details of the charges I will face.

Once again the cell door closes behind me, and the metallic clang of the door as it rattles closed rings through my head like a tolling bell. I'm disgusted with myself. Why on earth did I behave like this? Such behaviour can only be described as thuggish, but I'm not a thug. Am I now, and am I to be branded as such? I sit in the stale, bleak cell with my mind in a fog. Eventually, the officer returns and leads me back to the interview room.

"You will be charged with grievous bodily harm with intent. This is a very serious charge, Mark," says the solicitor. "You have been charged as such due to the severity of the injuries."

"I see, but what does it mean?"

"First of all, it means it will be very difficult for me to get you bail, Mark."

"What? I might not be going home this evening?" I ask, as my heart sinks.

"That's right. Look, due to the severity of the injuries, it is considered you must have intended to cause serious harm," he explains.

"But I didn't, I really didn't," I say, frustrated at not being believed. I might be many things, but one thing I am not is a liar.

"I'll leave you here now while I make the case for bail," he says. "Try not to worry; I'll do the best I can for you."

I sit in a cold sweat while the case is made, and now I begin to fear the worst. After around ten minutes, the door opens and the solicitor appears. I stare into his face looking for clues as to my fate this evening, but his expression gives absolutely nothing away as he sits down beside me.

"Okay, Mark, you're going home this evening," he says very formally, but with just a hint of a smile.

"Thank you so much," I say, as a wave of relief passes over me.

"You will appear in court next week in Exmouth, to officially hear the charges and conditions of bail. You did yourself a huge favour by coming here voluntarily; it would be very different if you hadn't. You have also conducted yourself very well throughout."

Again, all I can manage is, "Okay."

So if Reese and his father had reported to the police without first consulting me, I would probably not have been granted bail. So have they actually done me a favour? But hang on, all Reese needed to do was say nothing, and no one would ever have known it was me. The interviewing officer said as much; they had no idea who was responsible. This is all so confusing!

I leave the station at eleven o clock, jump straight into my car and drive to Jo's house. She is waiting up for me and is relieved to hear the knock on the door. I struggle to tell her the details and she equally struggles to hear them.

Three

The Trial, 1997

T he following week passes in a haze, and at the first court appearance I
find out the conditions of my bail. I am to go to and from work at the
university only, and must be home between the hours of five p.m. and seven
a.m. I am not permitted to visit a licensed premise of any kind, including any
supermarket or local corner shop. A separate court appearance is needed to
request permission to use Tesco supermarket for food shopping and to
continue working part-time at the Cavern nightclub, where I've been
employed as a doorman for the past couple of years.

A few more hazy weeks later, my plea hearing is very short. I plead not guilty
to the charge of grievous bodily harm with intent, but guilty to a lesser charge
of grievous bodily harm. While I freely admit to causing the harm, I know I
did not intend to cause those terrible injuries. After a lengthy discussion with
my solicitor and gaining an understanding of the law in respect to intent, I
insist on pleading not guilty to intent, albeit against all advice. As a result, the
slightly lesser charge has now been added.

A week later Jo and I meet with my barrister in his chambers to discuss
preparations for trial.

"Hello, Mark, hello, Jo, nice to meet you both," he says sincerely.

"Nice to meet you too, thank you for agreeing to see us both," I reply.

Jo adds a polite, "Good morning," but without her usual smile.

"Okay, let's get right down to it. Mark, you are pleading not guilty to a
very serious charge. You understand that, yes?" he asks while lowering his

head and eyeing me under brows raised so high they almost meet his hairline.

"I do, I understand," I reply while holding his serious gaze.

"Look, you can still change your mind. There is plenty of time for that, and to be honest, it's what I must advise."

"I won't do it," I reply instantly, as I take a tentative look to my left and to Jo, prompting the barrister to look toward her also.

"I'm sure this is a very stressful time for you both, and I hope you have thought long and hard about this," he says as he shifts his gaze back to me.

"I have, we have, and I won't do it," I say with conviction. "I absolutely cannot and will not betray myself any further than I already have. I won't plead guilty to something I'm not guilty of. Yes, I caused unforgivable damage, I have admitted that, but I did not intend to and refuse to say that I did."

"Okay, Mark, so you're sure, I can see that," says the barrister with a resigned sigh. "If you are sure this is how you want to proceed, then rest assured I will do my level best when representing you in court."

My refusal is not stubbornness, nor is it borne out of ignorance or defiance of any kind. It is after much analysis of self and necessary understanding of the law. It is simply the truth.

"Yes, I'm sure and thank you," I say.

"But Mark, I must warn you," he says, and pauses deliberately for emphasis.

"Go on," I say.

"In any event, guilty or not guilty of intent, you will be sentenced for grievous bodily harm, a serious charge on its own. Due to the extent of the injuries you have caused, you must understand there is a very high chance you'll receive a custodial sentence."

I have no answer and simply momentarily rest my head in my hands. How on earth is a person supposed to prepare for that?

Then he continues, "If at trial you are indeed found guilty of intent, a prison sentence is certain. Of that there can be *no* doubt," he adds. "The maximum sentence if found guilty of the intent charge is life imprisonment, and you will get a harsher sentence for pleading not guilty. You could receive less prison time if you plead guilty now."

"Yes, I understand, but if I plead guilty now to something I believe I am not guilty of, I will definitely go to prison anyway, won't I?"

"Yes you will, and admittedly in that regard, it is somewhat of a gamble," he confirms.

"I won't plead guilty to it," I reiterate, "I won't."

Jo is in tears now, and when he looks at her, I know he feels terrible for her.

"Look, sentences quite this severe are never handed down," he adds in an attempt to mitigate what he has just told us. "I tell you only to demonstrate the seriousness of the decision you are making and the scope available to the judge."

Well, he has made his point extremely well, particularly to Jo. Despite the expert advice and opinion, I still cannot believe that I will be found guilty of the intent charge, and in the intervening weeks, I refuse to accept that I may be facing prison.

I have five long months before facing trial at Exeter's city centre Crown Court. I turn off the High Street at nine thirty, and the early morning hustle and bustle of the busy shopping street and the noisy, diesel-belching buses quickly melt away. It is just a thirty-second walk to the bottom of the hill leading to the city centre's highest point, still known as Exeter Castle, and now the site of the Crown Court.

I am met by my barrister at the three arches that mark the entrance to the courtrooms. As he approaches, he extends a hand and says, "Morning, good job on the baggy suit. It makes you look smaller and less imposing. Can't be a bad thing either," he adds.

"Morning," I reply, somewhat puzzled. This is the same suit I wore at my first court appearance some five months ago. It fit well.

"Is it baggy?" I enquire.

"Yes," he answers with a slight chuckle, "it is." Have I lost weight, and so much as to be obvious to someone who barely knows me? How could I not notice, and why has no one said anything? True, I have not been to the gym because I've had to be home by curfew, but I have been working out at home and I thought I was still eating well.

"Let's go through, Mark, and take a seat," he says as he gestures for me to go ahead. "We should be in court around ten o'clock. In the meantime, just sit and try and relax."

Once we pass through the arches and into the entrance hall, there is an eerie hush, and it is somehow colder inside than out. Shortly after ten we are called into court and the usher guides me to the dock where I am searched by the dock officer. It is never nice being the centre of attention, and especially under these circumstances. The courtroom is smaller than I had imagined, about thirty feet square but with very lofty ceilings, fulfilling the stereotypical mental image of a courtroom. The wood-paneled walls are stained a deep brown, and the baize, green-topped tables in the centre of the room should, perhaps, with their reflections of nature, give it a calming and hopeful feel. The dark bark-coloured walls hint at strength and resilience and the green at growth and hope. Is this in fact why theatres have green rooms? Are they actually green? Unfortunately, the colours offer me no comfort. I feel completely isolated, as if in a dark, scary forest, and unlike the trees and plants around me, I am shrinking rather than growing. I may, however, be green with envy for any position in the room other than mine. Nothing can detract from the stomach-churning portent the room offers.

As is normal, the prosecution opens the trial and states its case to the jury by outlining the charges I face and stating the case against me. I, in turn, stand and try to remain composed while I listen to the terrible picture being painted. A witness statement is read out from a person who lives in a flat overlooking the alleyway where the offense took place. This recounts the scene almost exactly as I remember it and doesn't paint a very good picture at all.

Reese takes the stand as a prosecution witness. He too paints a very dim picture of me indeed and relates that he has been stressed and reliving the scene. Cross-examination by my barrister reveals that Reese was indeed the instigator of the whole event and that I, perhaps because of our friendship and my intoxication, allowed myself to be influenced by him, and perhaps that was what he wanted. Reese attempts to refute this, but struggles to remain composed and ultimately leaves the witness box as a not overly credible witness.

My police interview transcript is also read to the jury, while I stand and listen and relive that day five months earlier. I have no idea if this damns me or helps in some way. The day draws to a close around three o'clock, and the trial will recommence at ten the next morning. I really have no idea how the day went, but my barrister assures me that things are okay, and so far the prosecution has not been able to prove beyond reasonable doubt that I acted with intent.

After a restless night, I make my way to the court in what I now realise is a rather ill-fitting suit. I weighed myself and discovered I weigh 175 pounds; I have lost forty-five pounds in five months. While commendable for one on a diet, I had been completely unaware of it, and I now observe that, for the most part, I have lost muscle. No time to dwell on it now, but perhaps I have been much more stressed than I realised.

Before I take the stand, Andy and Dave Goodchild, the owner of the Cavern nightclub, both appear as defense witnesses. Despite being nervous at first, Andy soon relaxes and does a good and honest job of representing me. Dave is next and does an absolutely sterling job. At times it is hard to work security in a nightclub, and Dave of course is aware of this. Despite sometimes difficult circumstances, I have never given him cause for concern. He makes it clear that I never bullied or behaved in an inappropriate manner towards anyone.

Finally it is my turn to be questioned, and the circumstances leading up to the incident—the dispute between Reese and the victim—are soon made clear. The court is informed, minus the details, that the claims made against the victim are true; he is indeed a convicted paedophile.

I was already aware this would be brought up, and while I have no sympathy for those who commit crimes against children, it was not for me to be judge, jury, and executioner. But did this knowledge, albeit unconfirmed at the time, form part of the reason why I attacked him? Standing here on trial, I am still not sure, and fortunately I am not asked. I know I was influenced by Reese's way of thinking, buying into his sentiment and carrying on his fight, so to speak. I know I was under the influence of alcohol, which of course obscures one's judgment. That's not to say I believe alcohol is an excuse for inappropriate behaviour, and I am not attempting to hide behind it. I know, too, that I succumbed to the petty, childish goading of the victim and reacted to his challenge. But I am unsure if I viewed it as a kind of defiance of his own moral standing, and I'm also unsure whether I accepted his challenge in the belief that he was deserving of some form of retribution.

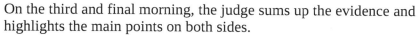

On the third and final morning, the judge sums up the evidence and highlights the main points on both sides.

Before retiring to allow the jury to deliberate, he says, "If you have any doubt as to Mr. Wilson's guilt in respect to the charge of intent, you must find him not guilty."

The jury retires, and I leave the courtroom to await the verdict. After less than half an hour, we are called back in, and I take the stand to hear the verdict.

The judge addresses the jury and asks, "Have you made your decision?"

"Yes, Your Honor, we have," the foreman replies.

"How do you find the accused?"

Time has slowed to almost a complete stop, and part of me wants to stay there in limbo. I don't want to hear it, but the wait is killing me. My heart is pounding, my mouth is Sahara-dry, and I'm burning up and sweating.

"Not guilty, Your Honor."

The relief is indescribable. I stand composed, while inside I am doing back flips. The judge turns toward me for a brief but significant moment before addressing the jury: "Thank you, and I'm sure the defendant would like to thank you for your decision."

I turn toward the jury, sweat running down my back, and deliver the most sincere thank you ever.

The judge sets sentencing for the lesser charge for December 15th, allowing time for me to meet with a probation officer to discuss mitigation and for presentence reports to be prepared. Also the prosecution team will gather relevant evidence from their side that may help the judge make his decision.

I leave the dock and am greeted by my barrister, whom I shake warmly by the hand and thank for all his work. I walk outside into the cold November air. As cold as it is, it still comforts me. I want to run around the car park to let off steam and release the tension that has been building for the past six months, and especially the past three days. I still have to face sentencing for the lesser charge, and it is a very serious one, so I can't afford to get too excited. But I am like a shaken champagne bottle that has just been uncorked and am brimming over, not with bubbles but with relief.

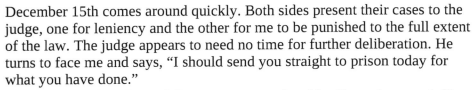

December 15th comes around quickly. Both sides present their cases to the judge, one for leniency and the other for me to be punished to the full extent of the law. The judge appears to need no time for further deliberation. He turns to face me and says, "I should send you straight to prison today for what you have done."

A long painful silence follows. An uncomfortable silence in court is like no other.

While I am still analyzing his statement, he adds, "But I will deal with you another way."

I'm not going to prison? Is that what this means? Oh my goodness, I'm not going to prison!

"You will pay a fine by way of compensation to the victim of six thousand pounds and will complete two hundred and fifty hours of community service."

I heave a huge sigh. Despite never really accepting the prospect of a custodial sentence, I feel tremendous relief that this is all over. I have no idea if it's appropriate, but I direct a subtle nod to the judge and mouth a silent thank you.

I leave the court and go straight to the university to visit Reese. As usual, I find his ofice door open. He looks up to see me approaching when I am a few paces away from the door. His eyes are wide and he appears frozen to the spot, like a deer in the headlights.

"All right," I say, "I've just been sentenced." Now I am shocked to realise that he is actually terrified. What's more, I am sure he wasn't expecting to see me but was certain I would have received a custodial sentence.

"Yeah, I knew it was today," he croaks. He is visibly shaking. I try to ignore his condition and say, "I was very close to getting a prison sentence, but the judge fined me six thousand pounds, and I have two hundred and fifty hours of community service to do."

"Oh, that's better than prison." He sounds shaken.

"Yes Reese, it certainly is," I say, "but what the hell's the matter with you?"

"I saw you and thought you were coming to beat me up," he says, still shaking and struggling with his words.

"You thought what? Are you crazy? Do you think I am an idiot?" I don't really expect an answer, and I don't get one. I have no interest in beating him up, and I'm offended that he thinks I would leave court and do such a thing. I guess his behaviour means he thinks I *am* an idiot. Or maybe it's something else.

Up until the day he told me his dad was coming to talk to me, Reese and I were good friends. Now I realise that will never be true again.

At some time in our lives we all make mistakes, some large and some small, some with consequence and some without. Many would say I got off lightly after this mistake. Perhaps I did. Time will tell.

Four

Scuba Diving, 1998

A fter thirteen years at the university, I recently applied for voluntary redundancy and am waiting to hear if my proposal has been accepted. Redundancies are being offered in many departments within the university, though not actually in mine. Still, I write a detailed proposal explaining how and why it is a viable for the university to offer me the redundancy package. After thirteen years, and all very suddenly, the prospect of staying another thirteen years frightens me. I have no idea what I will do if it is granted. I just know I must leave.

After a month's wait, I receive a letter confirming that my redundancy has been granted. The twelve-week notice period passes quickly, and I am soon a university employee no more. I have mixed feelings about this. The university has been a good employer, and I have done well enough and enjoyed my time here. But it is time to leave for a metaphorical destination unknown. One huge relief is knowing I will not see Reese anymore. As we work in such close proximity, we see each other regularly, and it is always a little awkward. I am not sure about his point of view, but I have absolutely nothing to say to him. Right or wrong, I feel he betrayed me for his own selfish motives and not out of any moral responsibility. I know his morals are not that high.

As Jo and I are spending a warm July evening in her flat listening to music a week after leaving the university, she makes an observation followed by a suggestion.

"You are always talking about sharks. Why don't you take up scuba and head off diving somewhere?"

She is, of course, right that I am always going on about sharks, but, apart from that one afternoon two summers earlier, I have been simply an armchair enthusiast for all things nautical, and particularly for sharks. She's right about another thing, too: I should learn to dive. I dash straight down the stairs to the dark entranceway where the house phone resides, grab the yellow pages, run back up the stairs with it, and start looking for a dive school. We soon find one, Teign Dive Centre, about fifteen miles away. The following morning I call and make enquiries. I need no further convincing, and I hang up the phone having booked the PADI Open Water and Advanced Open Water courses, which I will take back-to-back over a series of weekends.

Teignmouth, on the South Devon coast, is popular with the daytrip tourist, not least of all for its 695-foot Grand Pier which opened in 1867. Tourism aside, Teignmouth also remains true to its roots with an active harbour and fishing industry. Surrounded by rolling Devon hills, Teignmouth is nestled on the northern bank of the mouth of the Teign estuary, and the surrounding local waters provide many opportunities for the novice and experienced diver alike.

I turn up at Teign Dive Centre's indoor pool for the first of the confined water skills sessions a week after placing that first call. First of all we are introduced to the equipment and practice assembling everything together into the complete scuba unit. We enter the pool at the shallow end and then don our equipment. We remain standing, put our faces in the water, and take our first underwater breaths. At first it is a strange sensation, and my breathing is a little erratic. It doesn't take long to settle down, and soon we are assembled under water on our knees in a tight semicircle facing our instructor, Jamie. He expertly demonstrates regulator and mask skills, and we in turn copy him. We must get to know our equipment, become comfortable with it, and trust it completely. The session is almost over, and we all surface, remove our equipment, and leave the pool.

After debriefing us on our progress so far, Jamie says, "Okay, everyone back in the pool for the swim test."

I would gladly get back into the pool to escape the steamy, sweaty, uncomfortable sauna-like poolside, but for a swim test? No way!

"Swim test?" I exclaim. "No one mentioned anything about swimming. Why do I need to swim when I wear a wetsuit and a buoyancy jacket?"

"Yes, you will be wearing a wetsuit and a BCD"—a Buoyancy Compensator Device—"but it is a good idea to be able to swim and to be comfortable and confident in the water, don't you think?"

"I guess so," I say with a shrug. "How far do we need to swim?"

"Only two hundred metres," he answers casually, as if it were nothing.

"Two hundred metres?" I exclaim. "I can't do it."

"Well you have to, to pass the course, so jump in and give it a go."

The others are already in the water and ready to go. Now I feel like a proper fool, and know I will soon feel even more so. I get underway with a ridiculous bastardization of the breaststroke and front crawl. I manage one length, turn, and start the second, but halfway back I grab the edge of the pool, exhausted and humiliated, while the rest of the group carry on, as far as I'm concerned, like Olympic athletes.

"You have some work to do, don't you," Jamie says with a smile.

I leave somewhat dejected, but I do have a few weeks to prepare, and I know I must practice, practice, practice. A couple of weeks later, after lots of hard work, plenty of help, and many mouthfuls of chlorinated water, I can just about manage the required two hundred metres. The rest of the course goes more smoothly, and I am soon a certified PADI Advanced Open Water diver.

After perusing dive magazines and watching videos, I decide to go to South Africa for three weeks. World famous for its shark diving, especially cage diving with white sharks—sometimes referred to as great whites—this should be an epic first dive holiday.

A week after finishing the dive courses in mid-September I leave on a night flight from Heathrow heading to Cape Town on South African Airways.

I am not usually fond of cities, but Cape Town, with Table Mountain as its backdrop, does well to impress me, and no one could deny the drama it lends to the city. Perhaps even better is the view over the city from the mountaintop, and looking along the mountain toward Cape Point the view is also stunning. The city is great, but I am keen to leave it behind and get underwater.

My first port of call is Gansbaai for cage diving with white sharks. I book to dive for three days with South Coast Seafaris and am picked up at five in the morning from Cape Town in a minivan. We then make the two-hour drive to Gansbaai as the South African scenery rolls by and is slowly illuminated by my first African sunrise. Cape Town was fun, but this is why I came, and I can't wait to get there.

Gansbaai is a tiny town still in development and looks almost like something from the American Old West. If one side of the main street were viewed from afar, it would look like a huge mouth with more gaps than teeth. It is charming nevertheless, a fishing village that has only in very recent years begun to invite and embrace tourism, with a focus on white sharks and southern right whales.

After our bags are dropped off at the guest house, we are taken to the harbour to meet the boat. We all board and, before setting off, are given a thorough briefing on boat and cage safety. We soon cast off and make our way out of the harbour toward Danger Point—so named for the many ships lost in the surrounding waters—and beyond toward Shark Alley, the shallow channel between Dyer Island and Geyser Rock that I have seen many times on TV. Once we pass Danger Point, the seas begin to pick up, and we are pitching and rolling around enough to ensure that everyone remains, as instructed, in their seats and holding on.

After about an hour, we arrive in Shark Alley. I can't believe I am actually here, in this world-famous white shark site. The water is calm in the channel, the sky is blue, and water is so clear that I can see the bottom perhaps fifteen or twenty feet down. White sharks frequent this channel to hunt the noisy cape fur seals that are barking loudly in the background. As we watch them, they appear to be watching us just as intently as they turn their heads to look quizzically in our direction and bob them from side to side. While their barks are in the background, their smell overloads the olfactory senses. It is this odour that leads the sharks to the alley as the constant flow of waste seeps into the Atlantic and alerts them to the seals' presence. But we have something hopefully more inviting: chum, which is released into the water a cup or two at a time. Chum is a mixture of waste fish, fish blood, and guts all mashed into a pungent, oily, shark-attracting mixture. Its telltale slick is soon visible drifting down current while its smell stays with us as it wafts from the bucket. All being well, it won't be long before Mr. White puts in an appearance, and unlike others on the boat, I am on high alert and remain on constant lookout. Full of anticipation, I am looking directly down into the clear water and also further afield, hoping to see a dorsal fin cutting its way through the water. It is not long before my vigilance is rewarded, and I explode into life much like a white shark exploding through the surface of the water.

"Shark!" I shriek. "I just saw a shark, it swam under the boat," I exclaim even louder while bounding across the small deck to greet it as it reappears on the other side. "Here it is, here it is."

"Relax," says one of the crew with annoying calm, as if he has seen this a thousand times. I guess he might have too, so it's perhaps no wonder he seems unmoved.

I, on the other hand, am more excited than I have ever been in my life.

"There's plenty of time," he adds with a rather deadpan delivery.

"How long do the sharks normally stay around the boat?" I ask with fevered anticipation.

"There's plenty of *time*," he repeats. "Everyone will get to see the shark." Now his face slowly cracks into a broad smile in acknowledgment of my excitement and my inability to contain myself.

I scramble around the boat toward the stern to follow the shark's underwater path and squat down and lean over the side for a closer look. As I do, my nose gets close enough to the chum bucket that it's almost nauseating. I guess I really should be grateful for the smell that invades my nostrils. After all, it has attracted the shark and is also masking the smell of the cape fur seals. But it's no good, and I have to cover my nose and mouth before I rise to my feet as the shark moves out of sight. Much to my relief, the shark appears once again on the other side of the boat, and I bound across to greet it.

Seeing the shark from the boat is incredible enough, but my excitement continues to mount as I prepare for my turn in the cage. The water temperature around Dyer Island is around sixty degrees, not dissimilar to the temperature at home, so preparation for a turn in the cage involves wrestling into a damp, stiff, thick wetsuit, and is even harder when you're in a hurry to speed your turn in the cage. I try it sitting, I try it standing, I ask for help—any way, it's a struggle. If only I could dislocate a shoulder, it would be much easier. After sweating and heaving for three or four minutes, I'm in. Looking around at the other people on the boat, it is difficult to discern how many of them feel about the occasion. My new Italian friend is an experienced diver, and while he's not jumping up and down and shrieking like me, he is equally excited. Others are not forcing themselves into wetsuits, so I assume they are happy enough with topside viewing of the sharks. Now that I'm in my wetsuit, I try to remain patient as I wait for my turn to see a white shark underwater for the first time. The building anticipation is almost too much, as is the now tantalising viewing of the shark from the boat. It is clearly visible as it circles the boat and the small, rather flimsy-looking cage.

The cage is made primarily from wire fencing material. It floats with the top about two feet above the surface with the aid of boat fenders secured all the way around, and the majority of the cage sits five feet below the surface, so it's about seven feet high. Just below the water line is a small window in the cage about ten inches wide affording an unobscured view of the sharks. No dive equipment is used in the cages, only the wetsuit, mask, and snorkel. If you want a better underwater view, you simply drop down into the cage and hold your breath.

After what seems like an eternity—perhaps half an hour—it is my turn in the cage. I swing my leg over the boat rail, perch on top of the cage as it sways and bumps into the boat on its tether, slip my mask over my face, and lower myself into the cage.

Here I am, in the water with a white shark, albeit of course with the protection of the cage. It does, of course, offer protection, but apparently this does nothing to reassure many patrons on these trips who enter the water in a rush of adrenaline.

This is not the case for me. Although I'm very excited, as soon as I see the shark I become incredibly relaxed in its presence and am simply overcome with a feeling of awe coupled with respect. I experience no fear, apprehension, or adrenaline rush. To see that huge, powerful animal swimming languidly past and under me, with no regard for either me or the cage, is incredible. It must be at least fourteen feet long. White sharks can be much larger, but this is still a huge shark by any standard, and it is the most beautiful thing I have ever seen. As it swims past less than three feet away, I gaze into its large black eye. Some refer to such an eye as soulless, but I see a huge, beautiful black pearl. I am lost in that eye, and as I hold my breath underwater and time stops, I feel calmer than ever before. Nothing else matters, only me and nature's finest and perhaps most powerful animal. As it regards me with that gleaming black gem, I believe it understands me.

Considering where we are, a seal ought not to be unexpected, but all the same it is. There is also a shark around, and the seal swims with expert agility all around and under the cage. It is using the cage as protection from its mortal enemy, and occasionally it leaves the cover of the cage and swims directly on the tail of the circling shark. As quickly as it appears, it disappears, seemingly making its escape back to the safety of the island, for today at least.

One shark lured ever closer to the cage by the bait swims so close that its pectoral fin comes inside the window in the cage and rubs along my chest. It touched me, and while it is against all the rules, I am desperate to touch it in return. I could easily run my hand along almost its entire length, but I resist. But it touched me, accident or not; it still connected with me, and I'm elated. Mere minutes later it comes back and, heading straight for the cage, it opens its mouth right in front of me and stays there, mouth agape with its teeth touching the bars. This time I make no attempt to resist. I am not going to pass up on this opportunity. I break all the rules, reach through the narrow window and with both hands rub the shark on the snout, in the way you might rub a dog's head.

Seeing the shark from the boat is fantastic, seeing it underwater is incredible, but touching it, even for a few seconds, gives me a rush of sheer pleasure. I can almost see the sensory information race to my brain and light it up like never before. If I didn't already, I now feel deeply connected with the shark and, in turn, with the ocean. As silly as it might seem, I feel calm, relaxed, welcome, at home. I trust the shark and, unlike with people, I give myself over to it easily, freely, and completely.

I will never forget seeing a white shark underwater for the first time and feeling connected, but after three incredible days in Shark Alley, it is time to move on. I secure a ticket on the Baz Bus that will take me to Umkomass to dive on Aliwal Shoal with ragged tooth sharks, affectionately known here as raggies.

The shoal gets its name from a vessel, the *Aliwal*, which had a near miss with the shallow shoal in 1850 and subsequently warned other seafarers of its existence. It was too late though for the *Nebo*, which sank on her maiden voyage in 1844 while carrying the Amanzimtoti railway bridge. The official report says the Nebo struck an unchartered pinnacle, but there is uncertainty surrounding this report, and some experts believe she sank after being struck by a large wave. The *Produce*, however, had her hull torn open on the shoal in 1974; she was lost, but all her crew were rescued. Both ships are now popular dive sites at Aliwal.

En route to Umkomass, and along what is known as the Garden Route, I make a stop at Tsitsikamma to jump from the Bloukrans Road Bridge, the highest bungee jump in the world. Standing on the bridge with the bungee rope secured around my ankles, the view through the Bloukrans River valley and down to the river 708 feet below is a sight only the jumper gets to appreciate fully.

"Three, two, one, bungee!" yells the jump crew in perfect unison, and I leap without hesitation into the void.

I let out an involuntary scream until the bungee rope is pulled tight, and I am catapulted not only back up toward the bridge but back fifteen years.

I am fourteen years old and standing on the motorway bridge that spans Topsham Road just a mile from my house. I've clambered up the grassy embankment, climbed onto the bridge, and walked out on a narrow ledge until I'm above the middle of the road. I've climbed out with the intention of jumping into oncoming traffic on the road. Yet I'm hesitating and pondering if timing the jump to also hit a car is better, or if a car might break my fall.

Of course, I don't jump. I weep tears of frustration for not having the nerve to step from that narrow ledge, and tears of anguish for having to return to what I came to step away from once and for all. I eventually leave the ledge feeling even weaker than before.

I have been weak ever since, I think as I dangle on my tether beneath Bloukrans Bridge. But the bungee jump was at least easy and needed no thought. While initially it might feel like a jump into the void, it really isn't. There is a thick elastic rope wound around the ankles that brings all jumpers slowly to a halt, and after a bounce or two leaves you dangling over the river valley with entirely too much time to think until you're winched back up to the bridge. While I'm dangling, I consider how hard life seems to be, and what any of us are doing here and why. It feels like a copout that I've taken the bungee jump as a pathetic substitute for being the master of my own destiny.

Umkomass is a small lazy seaside and riverside town on the bank of the Mkomanzi on the South Coast of Kwazulu Natal. Its Zulu name, Umkomanzi, was given by King Shaka himself and translates as "watering place of the whales."

The fun starts for divers in South Africa long before they enter the water. Before we can dive, the boat must be launched from the beach, and everyone gets involved. At the dive centre, all the equipment is assembled and secured in the specially designed rack in the centre of the RIB (Rigid Inflatable Boat) and then hooked up to an open-back Toyota truck. I throw my gear bag into the truck where it lands with a satisfying *whump*, and I jump in for the short ride down to the beach.

At the launch site, the RIB, still on its trailer, is reversed at high speed into the water. As soon as the water covers the wheels of the trailer, the driver slams on the brakes and the boat shoots into the shallow water. With everyone's help, the boat is soon turned to face the waves. Then working together, and with some good timing, we heave and strain to drag the boat into waist-deep water. Now the captain jumps aboard as we slowly move into slightly deeper water while ensuring the boat is held facing directly out to sea. As soon as the captain has control of the boat he first shouts, "Ladies up," then, "All aboard." Everyone quickly takes their places on the sides of the boat, places their feet in the foot straps, and firmly grips the ropes slung around the boat.

Now we are prepared for the bumpy ride through the incoming surf. After an exciting few minutes racing along parallel to the beach, looking for the best spot and jumping over the waves, we are soon *out back*, beyond the surf zone. The water calms, and I am on my way to my first dive in Africa.

Fifteen minutes later we are at the first dive site, Raggies Cave. To avoid any mishaps it is essential that everyone rolls off the boat at the same time. Because both the boat and the water are in constant motion, it would be easy for someone to get a nasty whack from a tank if they do not roll off exactly on the *three, two, one, go*. So we roll off together and are soon on the bottom at Raggies Cave. It is really not much of a cave but that's not why we are here. We are here for the raggies, and they do not disappoint. They swim in and out of visibility, sometimes two or three at a time. They do look a little ferocious with their mouths agape, revealing their long pointed teeth of the kind Dracula would prize; but they are in fact extremely docile in nature. So much so that while I'm swimming directly toward one, we come almost face to face until at the last moment it alters its buoyancy and moves slightly below me. I can still feel its dorsal fin now as it makes contact with my chest, runs down over my stomach and halfway down my thigh before the shark turns away.

After two wonderful dives with the raggies, the return boat ride is just as exciting. As before, we place our feet firmly in the tight foot straps and wear the hull of the boat like a huge pair of flip flops, hands gripping the rope. Unlike the foot straps, the rope yields to the motion of the boat as your fists bounce repeatedly up and down on the inflatable tubes like a drum. Like a driver looking for a break in traffic, the skipper must find a suitable gap in the waves and then make his rapid advance toward the beach. Only when we are mere feet from the beach does the skipper kill the engines and allow momentum to bring the boat right up high and dry on the beach. We are certainly grateful for the ropes and foot straps, for without them we would all be in a heap in the bow. I enjoy two amazing dives a day for the next week and see many raggies as well as large potato cods, sting rays, and lots of reef fish. I enjoy every minute of my time in South Africa, diving and non-diving activities alike. I have a new interest in life and want more.

Five
———

A Revelation

I n late summer of 1999, Jo and I have a minor fall out, and after three or four days of not seeing or hearing from her, I realise it is my turn to make the first move and call or visit her. It was a silly falling out, the type that, in this day and age, would be easily resolved with a text message and smiley face. But I am stubborn beyond belief and think it is best to leave things as they are and let us go our separate ways. I have always known that I will never have a longstanding relationship; I just don't know how to do it, so this may as well be the end. When Jo tells me how she feels about me, I clam up and say nothing. I honestly don't know what she means, and don't want to find out.

However, after about a week, I find myself confused and really want to see her. So I make plans to "accidentally" bump into her. I sit on the wall of the Cathedral Green in Exeter city centre, knowing she will soon walk by on her lunch break. After a short while I see her round the cathedral. She sees me and approaches with a cute shy smile. As usual, she is dressed in trousers and shirt that are one size too big. All eyes are drawn to her and she's perfect. I remain seated while she stands in front of me in partial silhouette. The lunchtime sun is directly behind her, and as she shuffles slightly from one foot to the other, the sunlight flickers through her shoulder-length blond hair, lending her a shifting halo that perfectly frames her perfect, angelic, glowing face. She is a vision emanating beauty, positivity, and warmth. Unlike the beacon of light from a lighthouse warning you to keep your distance, the light from Jo is a welcoming, reassuring, guiding light that I should be following all the way to her heart. She *is* my light, and I'm crazy about her. But I don't quite know it yet. I should scoop her up in my arms and run all the way home with her. But I don't.

"Hi, how are you," Jo says, speaking first.

"Hi, not bad, thanks, you?" I ask.

"Okay, I suppose," she answers softly. "What have you been up to?"

"Oh, nothing," I say.

"Shall we go see a movie one day?" she asks after a few minutes and with a smile that, despite my squinting against the bright sun, is as clear and bright as ever.

Yes, great idea, that's what I want isn't it, reconciliation? Why else am I sitting on the wall waiting to see her?

But despite the fact that a yes is bursting to get out I say, "No."

Tears begin to well up in her eyes. We look at each other momentarily in silence until she walks away. I let her go. I am so confused, but I am convinced I must be strong as it is for the best. If not now, then later, so it might as well be now. Better not to have loved and lost. That's my logic, but why?

Jo and I don't see or speak to each other for at least four or five months after that "chance" encounter on the Cathedral Green. Slowly but surely over the course of months, I come to realise love is many things to many people, and it manifests itself and is demonstrated in a myriad of ways. More importantly, I began to realise what love is to me: what it means, and how I had unwittingly demonstrated it in the past, and, more to the point, that I actually feel it and don't like not having it. It is when I recall two seemingly incidental scenes from our recent past that I realise I love Jo.

Her flat is nice enough but the large communal entrance that leads to the staircase and the flats is dark, uninviting, and slightly musty. She told me she didn't like it, mainly because of the dark walk through the entrance toward the stairs before she reaches the poorly placed timer light switch on the far side of the entrance. Fine for leaving the house, but useless when entering. So I bought her a small but powerful torch that can easily be carried on a key ring. She can now happily light her way to the light switch and onto the stairs that lead to her flat.

Jo likes to speak to her mum in the evenings but doesn't as regularly as she would like because she doesn't have a phone in her flat. This is 1998, remember, and mobile phones were far from the norm. There is a phone in the building, but it is situated in the dark, uninviting, musty entranceway that she doesn't like. The phone and the timer light switch are also on opposite sides of the entrance, so she is regularly plunged into darkness, something not conducive to long talks with Mum seventy miles away up the M5 near Bristol. So I buy her a mobile phone as a gift, with the contract and bill in my name—not for a birthday or Christmas, but simply because she needs it. She can now talk to her mum from within the comfort of her own flat at her leisure. I realise now I was buying flashlights and mobile phones for Jo because I love her. I just didn't understand, acknowledge, or accept it, and until now, I have been terribly afraid of it—whatever *it* is.

Perhaps a couple of weeks after this realisation and while working at the Cavern, my mind is in turmoil. I have to talk to Jo. Now. I excuse myself and go to her flat. I am at bursting point. Will she even be at home? If she is, will she be happy to see me? Will she let me in? Just press the buzzer, you idiot. I do and instantly my heart begins to race. A few seconds later I hear footsteps on the stairs; she's home. Then the door opens.

"Oh, hello, what brings you here?" she asks, sounding very surprised but standing aside as if perhaps to invite me in. I hesitate until she adds, "Come in then."

I walk in, close the door behind me, and ask how she is as I follow her up the stairs.

"I'm fine, thanks, how are you?"

"I'm okay, I guess," I say, not completely truthfully as the tension builds inside me.

"Would you like a drink?"

"Yes, please, water's fine," I say, getting more and more nervous.

She returns with the water, and we sit down idly chatting for a while and without saying really very much of anything at all. My heart is galloping now and, unlike the last time at the Cathedral Green, I must not be an idiot and must say what I have come to say.

Jo gives me an opening when she asks, "Why have you come around to see me now? We've not seen each other for months."

This is it, an absolutely huge moment for me. I take a breath and blurt out, "I love you; I miss you like crazy."

She looks at me with almost no expression and with a coldness and nonchalance I've never seen before. "It's too late," she says. "I've done my crying; now you can do yours."

I do. A lot. I have just realised that I have a heart, and it feels as if it has been torn out and hurled against a wall. It's too late, and I had it coming. I listen to Pearl Jam's "Black" over and over.

As in the lyrics to the song, Jo will have a beautiful life, and she is as bright as any star, just not my star, not in my sky, illuminating my life. Unlike the song however, I know exactly why.

Some months pass before I realise quite how badly I am taking losing Jo. I wake up as usual one morning, get out of bed, but almost immediately lie back down and simply stay there staring at the ceiling. The next thing I know it is dark. I have lain there all day and barely moved. My younger brother Ian lives with me now at Newport Lodge, and it is around this time that he comments on how much weight I have lost, and how little I seem to be eating. I reluctantly use the bathroom scales and now weigh in at one hundred and sixty pounds. If I eat anything it is something like Drumstick Lollies or Jelly Tots—any kind of children's sweets including my favourite, Haribo Starmix. I acknowledge something is wrong and reluctantly agree to visit the doctor. It is difficult, but I have to open up about how I feel and talk about the previous six or seven months. As well as talking about Jo, the doctor also somehow gets onto the topic of growing up and asks about my experience and relationship with my parents.

Dad left the family when I was eight years old, and Mom rebuffed all his attempts at getting the family back together. While my birth certificate may record March 28, 1969, as my date of birth, I was truly born and life as I know it began on the day Dad left home.

Shortly after Dad left, Mother became an angry, dissatisfied person who probably needed an outlet for her frustrations. I could be a pain at times, of that I'm certain, but I also know I was very far from being out of control. Physical punishment for being five minutes late for a meal seems excessive, and as time went on, excuses for lashing out became ever more petty.

The original slipper soon proved inadequate, and a bamboo cane, ordinarily used for supporting one of her large plots of runner beans, became her favoured instrument. I made a big mistake one day in respect to that cane. While I was curled on the stairs receiving blows from said cane, I became bored, extended a hand, and intercepted the cane. I snatched it away and proceeded to snap it into pieces before throwing it back in her direction, gaining immense albeit momentary satisfaction from my uncharacteristic little demonstration of defiant strength. Despite there being plenty of canes in the garden, it was the end of that particular punishment. Snapping it was a mistake, though, because the next time she lashed out it was with the tip section of a fibreglass fishing rod, which left a large welt on the top of my leg. I showed her the following day, and she apologised and said she hadn't meant it. However, she would use the fishing rod again and again. Like the first time, the rod stung, but eventually I learned to fight it and respond to the blows with contempt, and despite the marks across my back, the only thing that hurt was the fact that she was doing it. The fishing rod lived at the top of the stairs, and the very top portion of it was always visible whenever I climbed the stairs or left my bedroom. Poking up behind a blue floral print laundry basket, it served as a constant reminder of her anger toward me.

After far too long at the surgery discussing things I really would rather not reveal, and delaying others' appointments in the process, I am prescribed a course of Prozac. After taking the Prozac for three or four weeks, I wake up one day feeling different. I feel slightly excited, as if a big day out or an event were planned. Two or three days later, I realise what I am feeling is some form of normality.

We all have our sad moments and, at times, our crosses to bear. This was my time. Over the course of the next six months, the huge weight I had been carrying like a rucksack full of lead slowly began to shrink. Much later it became a small piece that fits neatly into that tiny useless pocket on the hip of your jeans. That small weight has been there ever since. From time to time, I acknowledge it and touch it; it even makes me feel better knowing it is there.

Six

Baja California 2001

L ike me, Julia was a part of the rock and heavy metal crowd that
frequented the Timepiece and the Crown and Sceptre throughout the
1990s. We have recently come into regular contact at the gym we both
frequent. It is not until I'm told by a third party that I have any idea she is
interested in me. I am not terribly astute when it comes to girls, nor am I
attuned to their too subtle—to me at least—clues as to their intentions.
Besides, having another girlfriend, or any kind of relationship other than a
platonic one, has not even crossed my mind since Jo. Now that I am aware of
Julia, I am not at all interested in going on a date with her. That's not to say
she is unpleasant or unattractive—she is very much the opposite. I am simply
not ready.

Julia has a fair complexion and a face that would be spoiled by the
addition of makeup. Her eyes and smile have a slightly cheeky, mischievous
look, and her demeanor is confident and carefree. Her very short, spiky, dark
brown hair reveals ears pierced with stainless steel hoops and further serves
to show off her flawless face. She drives a bright red 1969 modified
Volkswagen Beetle which certainly stands out with its huge whale tail spoiler
and Porsche body kit, and owing to its souped-up engine and exhaust, it is
also a very loud car. Julia's outward appearance is the polar opposite of her
flashy car; normally casually attired in jeans, T-shirt, and skate shoes, and
without makeup, Julia needs no augmentation to look good or stand out.
Nevertheless, I am far from over losing Jo and not sure another girlfriend is a
good idea, either now or later.

After a further six months or so pass, I decide that going on a date can't do
any harm and might actually be a good thing. We get on well on our first date
and continue dating, and soon we are a couple. Perhaps moving on, as people

often put it, is a good idea, and maybe I have learned something. If all goes well, I might be a better boyfriend this time.

It has been three years since South Africa, and prior to getting together with Julia, I had already planned a diving holiday in Baja California, Mexico, in the exotic-sounding Sea of Cortez. Formed by the gap between mainland Mexico to the east and the Baja Peninsula to the west, this location was recommended to me by an Italian companion on the South African trip in 1998. Jacques Cousteau refers to the Sea of Cortez as the aquarium of the world. If that isn't tempting enough, reading John Steinbeck's *The Log from the Sea of Cortez* further adds to the allure. Published in 1951, it is a nonfiction work that chronicles a six-week marine specimen collecting expedition carried out in 1940 aboard the *Western Flyer* with Steinbeck's marine biologist friend, Ed Rickets.

When Julia hears of this trip, she expresses an interest in joining me. I am more than happy to go alone, but the idea of company suits me too. We book our flights and soon head off to Mexico together. Exactly like her father, Julia is a news addict and cannot get enough, and on an excursion into Exeter city centre to collect our tourist dollars, she leaves me at the travel agent's door to watch the TV news through the window of a neighboring electrical store.

Julia has a good relationship with both her parents, something I cannot relate to. Since moving out of the house five years earlier in 1996, I have barely had any contact with my mother, particularly in the past two years, and it is around this time that it deteriorates further.

Nan calls me one day to say she is upset because Mother spoke sternly to her, so I go to see her to find out why she distressed my grandmother. I tell Mother she needs to do better and be more patient with her. She can't help being on her own since Granddad passed away in 1997; she can't help being old and having the beginnings of dementia.

"What about me?" Mother asks.

"It's not about you; Nan needs help and patience now."

"Who will look after me when I'm old?" she replies, still not getting it.

"It's not about you," I say, confused by her answer.

"You don't have anything to do with me," she complains, looking hurt.

"I know, you never wanted anything to do with me, and I've accepted that," I reply by means of an explanation.

"What do you mean?" she complains.

"You never wanted me, and you treated me terribly." I am frustrated at the sudden topic change.

"What do you mean? I don't know what you're talking about."

"You don't know what I'm talking about? You don't remember how badly you treated me?"

"No."

"Well, try." I find it impossible to believe she can't remember, and now I'm annoyed the conversation has very quickly become all about her.

"I don't know what you mean," she repeats.

"Well, I have nothing to say to you until you do." I leave and don't go back to that house for many years. In the ensuing years, I would barely see or speak to her, and a year would easily pass without contact. She never wanted me or came to my aid when I needed her, and now I don't need her. I have been weak before, but I refuse to give in now.

She stopped lashing out physically when I was around sixteen years old but was still cruel in other ways.

On my sixteenth birthday she screamed at me, "I don't get any family allowance money anymore because of you, because of you." All I could do was apologize for turning sixteen. More than anything, those years weakened me. Paul, eighteen months my junior, who suffered none of the violence I did, moved out of her house when he was eighteen. I should have done the same, but I couldn't. I was too weak. The violence had stopped, but the tension and unpleasant atmosphere remained. When I was sixteen or seventeen, I learned that her boyfriend had left her and moved out of the house. This was great news. I had no idea why, nor did I care.

But apparently, according to Mother, it was my fault, and she bellowed, "You ruined my life, and I'm going to ruin yours."

Once again I am astonished; this is nonsense. In my mid-teens, I was powerless to do or say anything to influence him in any way, let alone force him out of the house. Unlike Dad, he returned shortly after.

Being beaten with canes and rods can hurt us and leave scars. But words hurt much more, and mental scars can run deep and be much longer lasting.

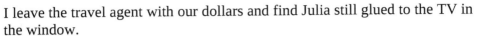

I leave the travel agent with our dollars and find Julia still glued to the TV in the window.

"I have the dollars, let's go," I say, while making no effort to see what has transfixed her.

"Hang on," she replies without turning her head. To this I only shake my head in disbelief. To me, watching TV through a shop window is ridiculous. I stand a few feet away from her with my back to the window, shifting impatiently from one foot to the other.

"Come on, then," I urge, growing ever more impatient.

"Hang on, hang on, something crazy has happened somewhere," she insists. "Look."

Reluctantly I join her in gazing through the store window along with an ever increasing crowd.

"What is so interesting?" I ask as I focus my attention on the TV.

"I don't know, but it's something bad," she says.

I remember tall buildings, chaos, and smoke, that's all.

"Well let's get back to your place," I suggest, "and you can watch it there in peace."

Julia lives in the city centre not five minutes walk away. Julia takes off in a hurry, and I can barely keep up with her as she marches through crowds.

Back at her flat, she immediately turns on the TV. There is indeed something crazy happening; two planes have just been flown into the Twin Towers in New York City. We sit and watch the frightening scenes unfold. A few days, later we are on our way to Mexico.

Originally founded by Hernán Cortés in 1535, La Paz is a growing city with a population of around 160,000. It gives the impression of almost seamlessly blending the embrace of tourism with traditional Mexican life, where tourists and tourist shops blur together with locals and local businesses. On the beach front promenade or *malecon,* you will find Mexicans and foreign tourists enjoying a seaside stroll in the sun or resting on a bench to watch the many fishing boats that come and go in and out of the bay.

We spend an afternoon walking around La Paz in search of a dive centre and stumble across an office that represents Club Cantamar dive resort. It has been owned and operated since 1983 by the Aguilar family, one of whom is the representative in the office. I am soon convinced that these are the people I want to dive with. The prices are so reasonable that we book a package for a seven-night stay at the resort with six days diving for me. Julia, who does not dive, will have six days of boat rides and snorkeling if I can convince her. For a very keen and undoubtedly very strong swimmer, Julia is not overly enthusiastic about swimming in the ocean.

A large part of my reason for taking this trip at this time is to encounter whale sharks. Unfortunately, I seem to have been misinformed, and we have timed our arrival just before the official start of the whale shark season. So while the resort has a spotter plane, it will not be flying this week, and there will be no dedicated whale shark excursions. However, with a bit of luck, perhaps we will still rendezvous with the elusive whale shark.

The following morning we are under way a little before eight and at the first dive site in a little over an hour. This gives all those aboard plenty of time to relax and take in the splendor of the Sea of Cortez from the comfort of our large vessel. The sun is already hot when we depart the Club Cantamar marina, and I need no persuasion when Julia suggests we head up to the sun deck. Once out of the confines of the natural harbour, we can fully appreciate the beauty of the Sea of Cortez and the surrounding landscape where the desert meets the sea. The sea itself is deep and blue and inviting and, as we know from Jacques Cousteau's description, full of life. The surrounding landscape is brown and mountainous and appears almost lifeless with few trees. In certain areas there are tall cactus plants and tough shrubs clinging to the ground with the same fervor with which they must cling to life in the harsh desert conditions.

Writing in *The Log from the Sea of Cortez*, Steinbeck perhaps summed up this landscape best when he wrote, "If it were lush and rich, one could understand the pull, but it is fierce and hostile and sullen. The stone mountains pile up to the sky, and there is little fresh water. But we know we must go back."

No one can argue with Steinbeck when it comes to description, least of all me. In any case, he sums it up perfectly. Despite the outward hostility, the area has a beauty and an allure that you must see with your own eyes, and like Steinbeck, I have felt its pull and have since returned, and will again.

When the boat stops at our first dive site, a look over the side of the boat through the gin-clear water reveals the bottom perhaps thirty feet below. All is calm and still, but not quiet. There is one familiar sound that I have not heard for a while. We are at an island dive site known as Los Islotes, which is noted for its resident sea lion colony. The last time I heard a similar sound it was from seals at Dyer Island in South Africa.

Here the sea lions bob their heads from side to side as they bark, as if excited about our arrival or perhaps in greeting. In the water they twist and turn, appear and disappear at the surface with effortless style and grace, like underwater ballerinas. Everyone aboard is smiling, something the crew must delight in every time they take new divers to Los Islotes. Some aboard cannot resist attempting to communicate and do their best to imitate the barking of our newfound friends. When an answering bark returns from the colony, the imitator is convinced he or she has made a connection, and the broad grin broadens even further.

The dive does not disappoint, and watching the females and particularly the young ones frolic in our midst is spellbinding. Their twists and turns and spirals, their speed and agility all highlight how clumsy and slow we are in the water with the burden of our scuba equipment. It is a necessary evil without which we could not stay under water for more than a minute or two.

It takes some persuasion on my part and that of the crew, but eventually, with fins, mask, and snorkel attached, Julia does venture into the water armed with a waterproof camera. She takes several great photographs, including one of a Dutch diver as a playful juvenile sea lion tugs on her fin, and another close-up of a large male that left his station on the rocks to check her out. At one point during the dive, our guide collects a stone from the bottom and throws it a short distance, and a pup immediately retrieves it. It doesn't quite drop it at our feet, but the display is a delight to everyone all the same. The sea lions' activity distracts you from the wealth of life at this site, and you must make an effort to enjoy everything else it has to offer. Schooling barracuda, all the usual reef fish, a fascinating jaw fish, and even a Spanish dancer wow everyone.

La Reina is a cleaning station for manta rays. It is another shallow site where we can see the bottom as soon as the boat comes to a halt, and the first manta is clearly visible from the dive deck within minutes as it glides effortlessly through the perfectly clear water. Diving with mantas for the first time is something I will never forget. Despite seeing mantas many times over the years, experiencing them will never become ordinary. Yet this first time will always remain extra special. They are majestic, graceful, and move effortlessly through the water. They are so perfect that you are entranced, and seeing a manta for the first time is beyond compare. Often referred to as gentle giants, mantas will sometimes come tantalisingly close. This has you almost holding your breath in anticipation of a really close encounter, only to have it silently and effortlessly bank away with wings outstretched as if looking for an embrace, or turn upwards in a steep curve while showing you the white of its belly, allowing you to fully appreciate its size. At other times it will keep coming, closer and closer, until you can look directly into its eye only a few feet away. They are the most graceful and calming of all fish, and being accepted into their midst is a gift. At times they seem to be as inquisitive about you as you are about them, and when you do get a chance to look into their eyes, the smile on your face makes it hard to hold onto your regulator, and the great sense of privilege will not leave you for days. Like the white shark, its eye is one in which you get lost, and though you only get to gaze into it for a second or two, you cannot help but wonder if the ray is feeling the same connection that you believe you are feeling with it.

Reaching the dive site known as El Bajo involves a slightly longer boat ride and more time to enjoy the scenery, though sometimes we lounge in the sun with our eyes closed. This group of three sea mounts is famed for its hammerhead sightings. Visibility here is less than we have been used to, and there is also a current which forces us to swim, not against it like salmon swimming upstream, but across it, as if trying to stay on course when confronted with a cross wind while driving. This is a dive you have to work for, and on a good day the rewards can be substantial. Sadly, there are no hammerheads at El Bajo for me, but it is a great dive nevertheless, with lots of moray eels and schooling barracuda. It's true I am extremely keen to see hammerheads, but the fact that I don't does not overly disappoint me in this early stage of my ongoing scuba adventure. I don't want to dive and see hammerheads simply to tick them off my bucket list, nor do I mind if someone sees something exciting on a dive that I don't. I want to see them just to know they are out there and that they have a chance, despite the huge threat they and others of their kind are under.

The diving in the Sea of Cortez has been amazing. From the Spanish dancer to the sea lions and manta rays, this lesser-explored part of Mexico is unforgettable and inspirational, and I can't help but shed a tear when it is time to leave. As great as holidays are, I now know for sure holidays alone are not going to be enough to quench my building thirst for the ocean. I love the ocean. I love travel. I want to live it. The ocean is becoming a passion, something we should all have in some form in our lives. Diving and exploring the world's oceans and peoples and cultures is what excites me. But how can I achieve it? The obvious answer is to pursue becoming a scuba instructor or, just one rung on the ladder below an instructor, a divemaster. Rather than teach new divers, divemasters assist instructors with certain aspects of dive courses, lead dives for certified divers, and crew on dive boats.

While I have almost made enough dives to qualify starting out on a divemaster internship, I do not yet have the confidence in myself to take on such a role. Some people ooze confidence, but I do not. It takes me much longer to become confident in my abilities. In fact I underestimate myself, a trait I am rather proud of. To me there is nothing worse than someone who does not know his own limitations or depth of understanding, or who exaggerates his experience and capabilities. This can be dangerous, especially in an alien environment like the ocean. As frustrating as it might be, this route will have to wait until I have much more personal experience.

Seven

Cruise Ships 2002

S ince returning from Baja California, my frustration with living in the UK is increasing almost daily. I do not want to be here. I want to be out in the world, exploring, learning, discovering, and scuba diving in all the exotic places I read longingly about in the dive magazines. Holidays are not enough and serve only to frustrate me further. Frustration can get us down, but we can also use it as motivation to achieve what we want, whatever it may be. I want a lifestyle that allows me to immerse myself in diving and travel; I want to explore the world.

In autumn of 2002, I hit upon an idea of how to combine an existing interest in fitness with my newfound loves of diving and travel. I apply for a job as a fitness instructor aboard cruise ships. While I have no desire to upset Julia, this is something I have to do, and getting out into the world is more important than any relationship. I have an interview in London with a company called Steiner that provides fitness and spa staff to cruise lines. The interview is a two-stage process, involving first a formal interview and then an exam covering various aspects of diet and exercise. These people don't mess around, and I am offered a position the same day. Wow, I'm excited, very excited. But the first thing I have to do is tell Julia that I will be heading off to meet a cruise ship in Florida very soon, and I'm not looking forward it.

"How was the interview?" Julia asks tentatively. I can see in her eyes she is sincere and hopes it went well for me, but she is also torn and doesn't want to hear that it went truly well. Julia's flat is already cold at this time of year, and the electric fan heater whirrs in the background as it blows warm air into the room. I wish it would blow me out the door so I wouldn't have to answer the question.

"It went well, thanks," I say slightly cheerfully. Right, don't mess around, I think, and I shift uncomfortably in the sofa as I quickly add, "I was offered a job on the spot."

"Oh wow, well done, congratulations," she says sincerely, but clearly shocked.

"I wasn't expecting it."

"No, I bet you weren't," she says, still somewhat cheerfully.

Already there is an elephant in the room. What does this mean for us and our relationship? Coward that I am, I attempt to avoid the issue and add, "I also have to teach step aerobic classes."

"Ha, I can't imagine you doing that." She grins.

"No, I don't know how well I'll do," I say, "but I guess I'll have to figure something out." With this, I unwittingly move the conversation into the inevitable uncomfortable territory.

"So you accepted already then?" she asks, looking rather hurt.

Julia has an interesting collection of pets: a cat, two cockatiels, and a California kingsnake. The cat is absent, the snake is quiet, but the birds are not, and they begin to scream in unison.

"Umm, yes I did," I concede over the din.

"You didn't want to talk about it first?" she asks as the screeching chorus continues.

I hate this and feel so uncomfortable; I want to just get up and run out of the flat to avoid the conversation. I like Julia a lot, everyone does. I know, I know I am supposed to like her in a different way, but the truth is I haven't allowed myself to. Although I now understand what love is, right now I don't want it. I won't go down that path, not with Julia or anyone. Not because of her but because of me. I guess Julia was right when she once said I had a shriveled heart.

"I guess not," I say a bit too coldly. I just want this conversation to be over as soon as possible. I have stopped shifting in my seat; I have shrunk into the corner of it. Maybe we should simply scream at each other like the cockatiels, and then I can just go.

"Oh, so that's that then, you are just going to up and leave without a thought or a care?" she says, becoming noticeably upset now.

"No, it's not like that," I say in an attempt to make the situation and my behaviour sound less hurtful than it clearly is.

"What is it *like* then?" she says.

"Look, I'm sorry," I say, and I mean it. I am sorry, sorry for inflicting myself upon someone like Julia; she deserves better than me and my shriveled heart and uncaring words and actions. I don't do any of it deliberately, I really don't, but right now I think we never should have gone on that first date.

"If you were sorry, you wouldn't do it, now would you?" she says with a growing anger.

"I am sorry; don't believe me if you don't want to, but I am. I'm not enjoying this you know."

"Oh, *you're* not, you'll soon be swanning off around the world, and you'll be enjoying *that*."

"Yes I will, it's what I want to do, and I can't help what I want to do. I have to do it, I just have to." I just about manage not to say "I'm sorry" again.

"When are you going anyway?" she asks, sounding much calmer all of a sudden.

"It should be in around six weeks. Before I go, I have to take an exercise-to-music course in London, get a C1D visa, and attend a boot camp," I reply almost apologetically. I do feel bad about leaving Julia and doing this to her. But the truth is that I want to go away more than I want not to hurt her. I'm sure she'll soon forget about me anyway.

Julia simply says, "Right, I see," with resignation.

I have no experience of step aerobic classes, little confidence in the area, and perhaps even less of the required coordination. Nevertheless, I still have the job, and the interviewer was not in the least bit concerned, suggesting I would soon get the hang of this aspect of the role. So before returning to London for the exercise-to-music course, I decide it will be a good idea to take step classes myself. Luckily, I know someone who gives step classes: Debbie, the same person who gave me the crash course in swimming back in 1998.

Walking through the door of the fitness studio for the first time will be hard. This is really not my thing. Before doing so, I linger at a door in the leisure centre foyer. Looking through the porthole window, I can see the girls in their aerobic wear gathered in the corridor outside the studio. I decide it will be better to wait until most are in the studio and walk straight in at the last minute. But damn, I don't see Debbie either, so she must already be in the studio. I was hoping to say hello beforehand; that would relax me at least a little bit. I am beginning to feel stupid in the foyer, peering through the porthole window at all the girls in their spray-on Lycra outfits. I dread to think what someone might be thinking. It's now or never, I must walk through the swinging door into that corridor and into the studio to join the class. As I navigate the short distance down the corridor, the few girls remaining outside turn to see the latecomer. I give a sheepish half smile, walk past them with head slightly bowed, and enter the studio. A quick glance around the room reveals that there is another male in the room, and there is an unoccupied space next to him, so I scurry over and say a quick hello. I'm no longer sure if I am hoping to catch Debbie's eye now or avoid it.

However, she sees me and exclaims, "What the hell are you doing here?"

"I'll tell you after," I reply, feeling a spotlight fall upon me.

In true Debbie style she seizes an opportunity instantly and says with glee, "You're either gay or a pervert."

I can only shake my head, and hope she gets on with the class soon.

She continues picking on me throughout the sessions, and on one occasion, with a smile of pure pleasure, she shouts, "Mark, stop staring at her ass."

I have no time for staring at asses during class, although I do stand behind the same girl each time. I am transfixed, not by her behind but by her feet as I struggle to keep time and in sync with the steps. I find this easier than trying to follow Debbie at the front. Debbie knows this, of course, but that doesn't matter. I feel terribly awkward in class, awkward in my ability and in simply being here. But Debbie's approach and the way she makes reference to my presence actually makes it easier. Better than being hidden away in a corner with the whole class wondering who I am and why I'm here. I am determined to do well in the classes, and the fact is I need to. Debbie's teasing is actually making it easier for me to achieve my goal and to get through something that, given a choice, I would really rather not do.

I return to London a couple weeks later to take the week-long exercise-to-music course. With a lot of effort, the course goes well, and I'm really glad I took the time to join the classes beforehand. I'm also glad to see I am not the only one to which this skill does not come naturally. I am far from the best, but along with everyone else at the end of the week, I pass the course. It will be a while before I am as good as I would like to be, but I am confident I can run the required two classes a day without too much trouble.

I have already given Graeme, my friend and landlord at Newport Lodge, notice on my room, and when I return to Exeter, I begin packing up my things and storing them in the garage. My excitement in anticipation of my new adventure mounts while I wait to receive the C1D visa. After about a week, the mail I have been waiting for arrives and I can't believe what I see.

Inside is a letter stating that my application for the C1D visa has been declined on the grounds that I have committed an act of moral turpitude. I am in shock, in a haze; my excitement evaporates, and, like being rudely awakened from an exciting dream, all that's left is disbelief. After taking some time to gather myself, I call the exorbitantly expensive premium-rate number provided on the refusal letter and make arrangements for an appeal.

I decide to wait until after the appeal before calling Steiner. The letter has come through to me reasonably promptly, and I'm sure there is still plenty of time before the Steiner team will be expecting the call informing them that I have the visa. I have an appointment for an appeal interview at the American Embassy in Grosvenor Square in London in five days' time.

I turn up at the American Embassy armed with all the required paperwork, including character references from people who know me well, one from Graeme and another from a teacher. When my name is called, I jump to my feet and approach the bank teller–style window, where I expect to be ushered into an environment more conducive to an appeal interview.

"Why are you here?" the clerk asks rather dismissively.

This strikes me as odd. I'm not really here by choice, and surely he should be aware of my case, since he called my name. "I am here to appeal the decision to not grant me a C1D visa," I say.

So it looks like the "interview" is taking place here and now. He turns to his computer screen somewhat reluctantly, as if I am making his life difficult just by being here, and proceeds to tap away at the keys.

Then all of a sudden he says, "No."

I am a little taken aback by how curt he is and actually a little confused as to what the no refers to. "Excuse me?" I say, bemused.

"No," he repeats while looking slightly smug and regarding me as if I am stupid.

"I'm sorry, but I thought I was here for an interview," I say. "I've come to discuss my case in person."

This seems to annoy him and he almost angrily repeats, "I have said no."

"But I have come here to discuss it, that's why I'm here isn't it?"

Again, and while stabbing a finger toward me, he now very angrily says, "I told you no."

I believed this was a chance for someone to look at my case individually and in more detail and for me to demonstrate that the mistake I made was uncharacteristic and does not really say anything about me.

This is not the case and I'm gobsmacked. I stand motionless for a second or two before asking, "Really? Is that it? Do I not get to discuss it with anyone?"

"I've made my decision, that's it, the answer is no," is all I get.

I have no choice but to reluctantly turn from the window and leave the embassy utterly dejected.

On the train journey back to Exeter, all I can do is stare out the window at the green and pleasant countryside and cry. During the course of the two-and-a-half-hour train ride, I go from sad to angry to sad again and back to angry. This is where I remain until I realise something. I really don't like bullies. Bullying can take many forms, and the officer at the embassy definitely used his position to bully me. He took pleasure in turning me down, of that I'm certain, and he knew I was powerless to defend myself. I was powerless while I was growing up, and feeling that way again really hurts.

I also realise not liking bullies has played a large part in why I have done well as a doorman. Yes, I am diplomatic and can resolve tense, stressful situations calmly and efficiently, but often being a diplomat is not enough. Some situations escalate beyond reason, and often these situations involve a bully. When someone is bullying a member of staff or a customer, I take offense, my mood changes quickly, and I ratchet up a gear or two either physically or mentally. I deal with these situations accordingly and remove such people rather more unceremoniously than they might have liked. I have never felt out of control in these situations, and I can say with confidence that I never bullied anyone. Those I have unceremoniously removed have deserved it.

I realise something else too, and it comes as a real revelation. This is the missing factor in understanding why I attacked the guy that night in Exmouth back in 1997. I reacted to the fact that he was a bully, that he sexually abused a child. He took advantage of someone weaker than himself, someone vulnerable, which made him the worst possible kind of bully. This is what I subconsciously reacted to. At the same time though I'm extremely bothered by something. When I began work at the university it was not long before the culture of high jinx in the workplace became apparent. Being ordered into the back of the van for very bumpy, bone jarring rides along a dirt track, play fights and being punched in the groin when not paying attention were sometimes unpleasant; but they became the norm and I didn't question them. Later, I carried on the traditions and between us my colleagues and I came up with new and ever more inventive ones. Being soaked in freezing cold water and sitting in the huge freezer with stopwatch running was a fun challenge to me, Andy and to others. One colleague would constantly instigate wrestling matches and revelled in seeing me hit the ground with more than one perfectly placed surprise groin shot. Another on the other hand was really not so keen on any activities or challenges. At the time the significance of his reluctance to participate and making him do so were ignored. It was all just fun, but I realise this forced fun was often not fun to him at all. Have I too acted as a bully? I fear I have. I'm shocked and disgusted with myself.

What makes not getting the C1D visa all the more difficult to swallow is that five years have now passed, and my conviction is considered spent under the Rehabilitation of Offenders Act. So why does it still appear on my police record? Surely if a conviction is spent, it should be removed from my record. But this is not the case; it remains on my record for all to see, as a spent conviction. So it would appear I am still branded a thug. Does this mean I am? As well as feeling upset, I still feel angry—and not just at myself but, rightly or wrongly, also at Reese. Not only that, but I feel something truly awful: I hate him.

In the eyes of the law, my offense is behind me now and I am no longer bound by it, yet it continues to hold me back. That one snap decision five years ago still follows me around like a bad smell and refuses to leave my side. I know I did wrong, but I still blame Reese for sharing it with his father, knowing full well what this would mean for me.

It is hard enough for some of us to even find a path to follow, never mind to get to tread it. So to do so, only to have it swiftly and cruelly snatched away as I'm just about to take my first steps, is heartbreaking.

Despite knowing what I did was wrong, I have trouble accepting that I am still being punished. If we have served our time and paid in some way for a mistake, surely it is not right for us to continue to pay after the fact. Is it? Will the consequences of this foolhardy outburst ever leave me?

I call and speak to the same lady at Steiner who conducted my interview, and she is a little surprised at the news. She already knows I have a criminal record, for I disclosed it in the interview. She kindly says she will enquire with her superiors if arrangements can be made for me to be posted on ships that will not venture into waters requiring the C1D visa. No promises, but she will enquire.

She calls me a few days later to explain that, unfortunately, this is not possible. I will not be working and exploring the world on a cruise ship.

Telling Julia I will no longer be going away is awkward, to say the least. We don't split up, and we still spend some time together, but we are not exactly on the best of terms either. She is understandably hurt by my decision. Spending nine months apart at a time did not necessarily mean we would have to split, but this is how she sees it.

Then I learn from Graeme that my room has already been promised to someone else, and I will still have to move out of the Lodge. He will kindly move me into another of his properties. Nevertheless, moving out of the Lodge under these circumstances is hard; it has been my home for six years. A flat close to the city centre has become available, as the previous tenant has recently died. It is devoid of furniture and appliances of any kind, and in addition, it is devoid of the character and homeliness of the Lodge. I have far too much time to think while I am here, and I dwell a lot on not getting the C1D visa and on the choices I made that brought me to this place. My brother Ian helps me understand why moving out is so hard. The Lodge is the only home I've known, and I recall very well the circumstances of how I first came to move there. It all happened very suddenly.

I had returned to the house after the gym one day and was met by Ian on the driveway. He was in a highly agitated state as the result of a confrontation with our mother's boyfriend. There had been a minor squabble involving the telephone. Ian had raised his voice and the fuss was over, but when Ian turned to leave the room, *he* rose rapidly from his chair and uncharacteristically rushed the few paces across the living room toward Ian who quickly turned to confront him.

Ian immediately saw the intent in those steely eyes and chose to react quickly, demanding, "What are you going to do?"

This unexpected small but significant show of strength and defiance slowed *him* down considerably and removed some of his vigour.

"There's no need to speak to anyone like that," he protested.

"What are you going to do? There's no need to fly out of your chair to say that either, is there? What are you going to do?" Ian repeated in a way as to goad the excuse of a man into some kind of action.

"Oh, no need for that," he almost stuttered in a considerably softer tone.

"No need for that?" Ian repeated *his* words in a questioning and angry manner. "You're nothing but a bully, but you're bullying no one today," said Ian as he stepped and bent to grab *his* little used shoes sitting beside his oil-stained, threadbare, and disgusting reclining armchair, a chair so horrid someone living on the street would reject it.

Ian remained crouched at his feet while attempting to put *his* shoes on his feet for him while saying, "Come on, let's go outside into the garden, I am going to beat you, then drag you around the streets and tell everyone exactly what you are."

Numerous attempts and offers from Ian were all declined and dismissed as ridiculous until Ian himself left and went outside to calm down. It was a few short minutes later when I met him in the driveway.

Ian's incident brings memories of past violence at *his* hands back to the fore, and right then I knew getting out of that miserable house was long overdue and I had to leave immediately.

I don't know exactly how and when it started, but as far as I remember, I was eleven or twelve years old, after he had been a part of the household for perhaps a year. What I do know for sure was he seemed to relish punching a defenseless young boy in the face. It didn't take long though for the attacks from him to not really hurt or bother me too much anymore. Somehow taking his violence and not reacting was a way of being defiant to it; I would rinse my bloody mouth, dry my bloody dripping nose, and forget it.

Around this time, what might now be called obsessive behaviour began. I would stand staring out a window and a tune would begin to play in my head. I had to end the tune correctly on the right note, or there would be consequences. The tune was almost impossible to end, and at times would play in my head for a half hour or more before I could end it correctly. Then I could relax until it began again. The tune left me, I think in my late teens, but was replaced until this day by counting. I add up the numbers on car number plates in different sequences and the number of letters in a sentence— sometimes my own words, sometimes those of someone with whom I'm talking, or sometimes while reading or watching a movie.

One day after being prompted by a friend who was shocked at my condition, I approach Mother for help. Why, I don't know, but I nervously begin to explain what happened while tripping over my words.

"Look what he did to me," I say as I stand before her with two black eyes.

"What?" she moans. As I suspected, besides the sour nauseating smell and taste of hairspray and cigarette smoke filling the kitchen and my nostrils, her mood is sour as well.

"Look at my face, he beat me up again." I am almost pleading as I look into her eyes, hoping beyond hope for a glimmer of compassion.

"No he didn't," comes the harsh reply, as she turns back to the mirror on the small medicine cabinet that hangs on the wall next to the work surface.

I don't accept the clear dismissal of my news immediately, and for a second I stand tall and exclaim with some disbelief, "Yes he did. Look at my face."

"He told me you were playing around and you bumped your head."

Playing around, bumped my head, this is ridiculous. We have never *played around*. Ever. We have never even thrown or kicked a ball, never mind engaged in any form of play fighting. The suggestion is absurd and outrageous, and she knows it.

"What are you talking about? We weren't playing around; he beat me up again."

"Just go outside and stop trying to stir things up."

"What are you talking about? Stir things up?" Actually this is why I am tripping over my words somewhat—I know by speaking up I am indeed stirring things up. But it's too late now.

"Go outside and leave me alone."

I leave the kitchen and go back outside. Mother's not giving a damn and her coming to his defense hurts more than any of the times she hit me, even with the fishing rod—perhaps more than all those times combined. It was perhaps surprising that her lack of concern hurt, because she was mistreating me as well. So why did I even seek her help? I guess we all seek help and protection from those who should want to give it the most.

I moved into Newport Lodge three days after meeting Ian on the driveway in February 1996, shortly before Jo and I started dating. No rooms were actually available in the house proper, but there was an old caravan in the garden, so I moved into that. The instant I moved in, despite not being far away, I might as well have been on the moon. I felt massively removed from everything I had known up until that point. I was out of that miserable house at last.

The following week, Ian left to live with Dad. Six months later, he came to live with me.

It was nice having my youngest brother around at the Lodge, and it gave me a chance to be a brother to him. I should have stood up for him more when he needed it in the past, but I was very young and afraid back then and didn't quite know how. Ian is seven years my junior, and when we were growing up, he was the funniest, most entertaining little brother anyone could want. But this wasn't always how Mother felt about her youngest son, and at times she didn't want him at all.

When she didn't, she would lock him in his room and leave him there for hours at a time. She used the rope from her dressing gown to tie around his door handle and the banister. He would pull on the door from the other side and attempt to grab and loosen the rope enough to afford his escape; at times, if we thought it safe, Paul and I would help loosen the rope, allowing him to sneak through the gap, if only for a few minutes. At other times he would sing a one-line song over and over again, begging to be released from his cell. I am crying enough now and cannot bear to even type the words of that awful mantra.

Having to move out of the Lodge, especially under these circumstances, is very hard to say the least. It is my home, and one I shared with my little brother. It took having to leave, with nowhere to go to, that made me realise perhaps what home means. Home is a place of safety and comfort, where healthy strong relationships thrive, where people care and share and listen, are honest, and look out for one another.

I try to stay out of the new city-centre flat as much as I can. One way I do this is to continue with the step aerobic classes three evenings a week. I have come to enjoy them, even with Debbie's teasing. I'm also spending a lot of time at the tattoo parlor, working on what will eventually be full sleeves on both my arms. Slowly, over the course of a few weeks, Julia and I become better friends again, too, so I'm spending some time at her flat. Bit by bit, we put the whole affair behind us.

Spending time with Julia is always good, but I really thought I was going off to collect new experiences. Unfortunately, my criminal record put a stop to my dreams of adventure. I have lost my home and a dream job, and have come close to losing another girlfriend. In every quiet moment, I dwell on what might have been, what should be, if it were not for my criminal record.

After being back together for about five or six weeks and discussing my disappointment at losing the job, Julia and I decide we will take a yearlong holiday and explore the world together. Looking at a map of the world, treating WH Smith like a library, and sifting through *Lonely Planet* guide books is all terribly exciting. Slowly we piece together where we will go and which route we will take. Mostly we would both like to visit the same places. I always want diving and Julia wants some snorkeling and beaches and the like, but more hikes, jungle treks—sometimes on horseback—mountains, and ancient ruins, all of which suit me too.

After a couple of months in the new flat, I admit to Graeme how miserable I have been there, and we hit upon a solution. I will move back to the Lodge but under slightly different circumstances. I will have the use of the house as before, but because the house is full, my bedroom will be another caravan parked outside on the ample driveway. It is a 1969 Sprite Alpine, the one in which I spent the best days of my life. Nan and Granddad took my brothers and me to Cornwall for two weeks in June and—in the earlier years—also one week in September every year in this caravan since before I can remember and up until I was eighteen years old. Forget Mother Teresa or Gandhi, my grandparents were the two most amazing people ever to have graced this planet. I like sleeping in the caravan again. I feel safe. I feel as if I am on holiday from all the nonsense in the world and in my head. After Granddad passed away in 1997, Jo and I took Nan away on holiday in 1998 and 1999 to the same place my brothers and I went when we were growing up, and Nan and I went without Jo in 2000. It felt good to give even a little bit back and to spend quality time with the two powerful lights in my life, Nan and Jo, even though I may have taken Jo's goodness for granted. But what I know now, and what being in the caravan has made me realise, is I still miss Jo terribly.

After being back at the Lodge for about a month, I find myself in the Australasian-themed Walkabout pub in the Exeter city centre. A fairly new addition to the city, the venue is always busy and lively on the weekends, and this evening is no different.

Suddenly I am approached by someone unknown to me. "Hello, mate, I'm Mark," says the stranger with a subtle smile.

I feel a little awkward, as I have no idea who he is, but because of how he introduced himself, I feel as if I should at least have some idea, since he seems to know me. I think my puzzled expression gives me away, as he quickly follows up and says, "Mark, Jo's husband."

How I don't know, but I am aware Jo is married to someone named Mark. Like me, he is tattooed and bald, but unlike me, he seems to have a face that smiles easily.

"Oh, yes, okay. Hello, mate," I say, as the penny drops. "Nice to meet you."

"You too." He smiles as he extends his hand and adds, "How are you?"

"Not bad, thank you, how about you?"

"Very good, thanks," he says.

"How about Jo, is she okay?" I ask.

"She's very good too, thanks," he replies warmly.

"How are the two of you, all good?" This might seem like a probing question or a bit too personal, though it wasn't meant to be.

"We are both well and very happy, thanks," he answers with another smile.

As soon as I hear these words, I feel comfort and a broad smile stretches across my normally taciturn face as I say, "Good, good, very glad to hear it, I really am."

Mark beams back at me in response and says, "Well I just wanted to say hello, and I'll leave you to your evening."

"Okay, mate, thanks for saying hello, and say hi to Jo for me please."

"I will."

As far as I remember, that was as far as the conversation went and we parted company with another handshake. A little later, I see him leave the pub, and I hurry through the crowd to catch up with him.

"Mark," I call as he walks up the street.

He turns immediately, stops, and walks back toward me.

"Yes, mate," he says, as I extend another hand in his direction. As he takes it, and wholly out of character, I impulsively lean forward and hug him and just say, "Thanks, mate."

I don't know his motivation for introducing himself or even how he knew who I was, and it matters not. But my reason for thanking him was for making Jo happy and for letting me know that she was.

I appreciate not everyone would react in this way when meeting a lost love's new partner. But I would never want anything but the best for Jo in all avenues of life. In fact, on the day I went to visit her and told her I loved her, I also said if she was ever in trouble or needed help, I would always be there for her. I meant it. If I am not the one to make her happy, then I am glad she has found someone who can. I don't feel upset; I don't feel anything but peace. I go home and sleep better than I ever have in my life in the warm embrace of the caravan where, as a child—if only for two or three weeks out of every year—happiness reigned. Even as I sleep, I actually understand again what it is to feel happy.

Eight

World Tour April 2004–April 2005

Exmouth, Australia

J ulia and I land in Perth, Western Australia, on Anzac Weekend, and two
 days later we hire a small car and embark on the eight-hundred-mile drive
north to Exmouth. This is a small but, to many like me, a powerful isolated
magnet of a town. It is one of the best and most reliable places in the world to
snorkel with the largest fish in the sea, the magnificent whale shark that
eluded us in Baja California. Tourists flock here between March and
September every year for a chance to see one, and divers come for a chance
to dive on Ningaloo Reef. I'm not ordinarily a fan of driving, but setting off
for Exmouth at six this morning is different. This is a road trip, changing the
driving experience entirely, and I quickly become a fan. A road trip doesn't
need to be long, but the longer and the less known, the better. It will probably
lead you somewhere, but it doesn't have to. The point of a road trip is the
road trip. We set off on the black, often dead straight tarred surface and are
propelled along toward Exmouth, one revolution of the wheels at a time.
Once we leave the suburbs of Perth behind and take in the stunning coastal
views, it doesn't take long to begin to appreciate how much space there is in
Australia.

My last road trip was in 2000, with Andy, a fantastic trip that spanned the
entire breadth of the United States. We left New York City with no plan other
than to eventually reach Los Angeles. Andy, though he missed her, learned
just how much he loves his wife, Lorraine; and I, with Andy's help, learned
to laugh.

The black, single-lane highway and its steaming tarmac is fringed on both sides by deep Australian red sand and peppered with towering termite mounds that rise proudly from the soil like steeples. The first time you see a road train—a sort of articulated lorry on steroids—and feel its turbulence as it buffets you around your lane like a pinball bouncing between two bumpers, you wish you had rented a larger, heavier, and perhaps more stable truck. We drive on through the day, one road train at a time, until our destination is tantalisingly close as dusk approaches. We are not going to make it to Exmouth before sundown, and consequently the final hour is in the dark. With every passing minute, the roadside slowly comes more alive with glowing eyes that appear to hang suspended in the darkness at varying heights. We creep along at ten miles an hour, and when the angle of the light is just right, the bodies belonging to the taunting eyes that force us to slow down are themselves revealed to us. Kangaroos, cows, sheep, emus, and—if I remember correctly—horses too at times crowd the roadside with the posture of Olympic athletes in the starting blocks. They seem to be daring themselves to cross ahead of us, which is disconcerting to say the least, but after thirteen hours and a very slow last hour, we make it without incident to Exmouth.

We soon find Pete's Backpackers, pitch our tent, climb in, and fall asleep. Our dream of seeing a whale shark should become a reality the next day. We are awakened at six in the morning by something outside our tent that turns out to be a kangaroo sniffing around. There is no question that we really are in Australia!

Even though Exmouth was on our itinerary all along, and the town name comes as no surprise to me, now that I am here, I cannot help casting my mind back to 1997 and that other Exmouth in the UK. Some incidents in life appear monumental, and right now I can't help but think that my actions in 1997 led me down a very different path, and perhaps without it I would not be here right now about to swim with a whale shark. So does being glad to be here now mean I should be grateful to Reese for involving me with the police? Would I choose not to have behaved as I did and take life without it, or would I choose it and still be here? I don't think I have an answer. But I would like to think that without it, Jo would still have suggested I take up diving and led me down a similar path.

We walk to the dive centre and are greeted warmly by two of the boat crew, quickly complete all relevant paperwork, and leave for Tantabiddi port where we meet our boat. During the drive to Tantabiddi, we are given our briefing on the protocols for swimming with the whale sharks. There are very strict rules for both boats and swimmers when interacting with whale sharks in Australian waters. The Department of Parks and Wildlife is responsible for the protection and management of whale sharks here, and commercial operators must obtain a license before being permitted to conduct activities involving them.

The license and strict interaction rules serve two purposes: first and foremost to protect the sharks, and second to protect the valuable tourist income. For boats there is an exclusive contact zone, a 250-meter radius around the whale shark or sharks. Only one boat at a time may conduct whale shark swimming activities within this zone and must observe a maximum speed of eight knots or less. The first boat to enter the 250-meter zone is the boat in contact with the shark, and any other operators must be four hundred metres from the shark. When dropping swimmers into the water, the boat must approach from ahead of the shark's direction of travel and must not approach closer than thirty metres from the shark. When swimmers are in the water, the boat must display its whale shark and dive flags.

For swimmers there are also strict rules of contact. The contact zone while swimming is three metres from the head and body and four metres from the tail. No one must attempt to touch or ride a whale shark or in any way restrict its normal movement or behaviour. Flash photography and motorised swimming aids are prohibited, and no more than ten people are allowed in the water at any time.

As soon as we set off from Tantabiddi, the excitement begins to mount, and we have about half an hour before the spotter plane takes off. Once it does, it should not be long before the radio crackles into life and the pilot informs our captain he has spotted a shark. When the plane is in the air, we are instructed to put on our full-length wetsuits, compulsory to guard against stinging jellies. Now we sit patiently waiting with wetsuits on and with masks, snorkels, and fins in hand. The crew are all on high alert and looking to spot a shark from the boat. Suddenly the boat slows and we are invited to move to the large marlin board at the back of the boat in our two pre-assigned groups of five. This is it; a shark has been spotted, and we will soon be in the water with it. The onboard spotter communicates with the captain, and once he sees the shark, he does not take his eyes off it but continues to point at it the whole time. When we are around a hundred feet from the shark, the in-water spotter enters the water and, once he is in contact with the shark, he signals by raising one arm into the air. The boat repositions, putting us directly in the shark's path, and when the time is right the onboard spotter shouts, "Go, go, go!" We all enter the water and split into our two groups. A quick glance to the onboard spotter confirms where we should be looking, so I put my face in the clear blue water and wait. In a few seconds, I see the spotter and the shark at the same time, passing between the two groups of swimmers. As soon as the shark is alongside I begin swimming.

Seeing a whale shark for the first time really is a dream come true, ever since, at eight years of age, I first saw a photograph of a whale shark in a Ladybird book. Now I am here on Ningaloo Reef in Australia with my first whale shark. I am so excited there is no room in my head for any other thoughts; I even have to remind myself to breathe, in, out, in, out. Breathing through a tube underwater, I am aware of vision as my only sense, and I am completely alone with the shark. I could swim with it all day and never get bored. Maybe it will accept me as a larger-than-life remora, and I can live forever at its side or under its broad flat chin. The fantasy is eventually interrupted as one of my other senses is fully awakened. Something is touching my back. I look up and slightly behind me and see a rope. Now another sense is awakened, sound: the rope is attached to a man in a small tender just off to one side of me, and he is talking and seems agitated, but I don't know why or what he is saying.

I look down into the water to see only the shark's tail, and then back to the man in the boat who is a little closer now and who yells, "Get in, that's not your group."

I am puzzled. "What do you mean? Of course it is," I protest.

How could I have changed groups? Or sharks, for that matter? I have been with the same shark the whole time, I know I have. I climb into the boat still confused when the man explains that I have been swimming with two different groups from two different boats, and he has been trying to get my attention for ages. He is not at all happy with me and goes on to explain I have caused two other operators to be in breach of the regulations, something everyone involved takes very seriously here. I was so completely engaged with the shark I forgot one crucial point from the briefing: after about two minutes, our spotter would be joined by a spotter from another boat. At this time he would lower his arm, shout, "Stop," and put his hands out in front of him with open palms in a stop signal. Easy for those on his side, not so for those on the other side, but all must pay attention. But I was completely immersed in the experience with the shark and did not pay attention. Swimming with the largest fish in the ocean was hypnotic and beautiful. Time not only stood still, but it ceased to exist. It was just me and the shark, nothing else. This felt real to me; it felt like home, it felt like everything I could ever want.

Back on the boat, I am immediately called to the front and given a stern telling off. I apologize sincerely and explain that it was not deliberate. I was simply lost and excited beyond compare. Fortunately my accuser believes me and seems to truly understand. He is not too annoyed with me but reminds me to pay closer attention for the rest of the day and indeed for the next two days as well. I rejoin the rest of the group on the marlin board, and it is soon our turn to reenter the water. I pay close attention to everything this time, not only the shark.

On the last swim of the third day, the spotter and I swim alone with a shark for at least ten minutes. The other boats have gone, and the rest of our group is tired. This shark is swimming a little faster, though still effortlessly. Its tail still seems to be barely moving, yet we are kicking our legs as hard as we can and breathing heavily to keep up. Having to work to swim with the shark makes it all the better, and it is the perfect end to a perfect three days snorkeling and diving on Ningaloo Reef.

The last activity of the day is a snorkel over a shallow spot on the reef. Much to the crew's surprise, I opt out of this and sit alone on the boat to reflect on the past three days while watching the others have a good time. It is a very strange feeling to fulfill a childhood dream. I have wanted to see a whale shark for at least twenty-five years. Now I have, and it has been wonderful, but what next? We have a whole year still ahead of us and many more great experiences to come, both in and out of the water, but already I know I never want this to end. It is hard to accept this simply as a holiday experience, or what some refer to as ticking things off a bucket list. If we were talking about a girl, you would say I was smitten. But there is more to it than that; everything is different when I am in the water. It is as if the world goes away, and there is only the ocean. Arthur C. Clarke got it right when he said, "How inappropriate to call this planet earth when it is quite clearly ocean." Fulfilling the dream is one thing, but now I want to live it.

It's September now, and since Australia there have been many great experiences both in and out of the water, in Malaysia, Thailand, and—my favourite of the three countries visited in Southeast Asia—Cambodia.

But we are now in Gansbaai, South Africa, staying in the same place I stayed in six years ago when I came here on my own in 1998, and we are poised to venture out on another white shark cage-diving trip.

Since April it has become very clear that Julia gets terribly seasick, and she has vowed never to get on a boat again. I do understand, as after being seasick just the once back in Australia, I certainly have no interest in a repeat performance. But I can't accept that she won't see a white shark. I truly want her to see one, more than I want to see one myself. I have pestered her to the point of despair and have somehow managed to convince her to join me on board. She was seasick on the whale shark trip back in Australia but still managed to swim and see a whale shark. Since then she has snorkeled with black tip reef sharks and with gray reef sharks, both times from the beach. So she is becoming quite comfortable in the company of sharks now, but still has a remnant of apprehension, particularly perhaps for the shark of all sharks, the white shark. The majesty and grace of a white shark is unparalleled among sharks, and I am confident that when she sees one, the last remaining fear will disappear like a ship into the fog and be replaced with wonder, awe, and admiration. I am desperate for her to see one.

We arrive in Shark Alley at nine in the morning, the bait is set, and the chum is slowly being carried off on the current. Everyone including me is busy selecting wet suits. Julia, however, is sitting at the front of the boat staring diligently at the horizon, as the boat slowly lurches from one side to the other in a slight but hopefully not significant chop. I find her a wetsuit and hope she can stave off the sickness.

"Here's a suit that should fit you," I say as I offer it to her.

All I get in response is a dismissive wave of her hand. We have been here barely ten minutes, and already she is struggling.

"Just keep looking at the horizon and ..."

"I know," she barks, interrupting me. "I am, and it makes no difference."

"Have you been sick?"

"No, but I will, I feel awful," she groans.

"Watching the horizon will make a difference. If you give in it will get worse," I urge, trying to be helpful. "Here's your suit, try and put it on as soon as you feel better." But remembering how much of a struggle it is to get into a wet suit, attempting it now is not a good idea. With bowed head she just slaps a hand beside her on the boat, to suggest I leave it there.

"Don't look toward the centre of the boat, that will make it worse for sure," I say.

"I'm going to be sick," she says as she pulls herself up to the rail and leans over to evacuate her stomach. I hope actually being sick will help her feel better; it certainly did with me that one and only time. But experience has proven different for Julia, and it seems once it starts there is little relief.

"Go and wait your turn, leave me here," she says.

"Do you want some water?" I ask.

"Please."

"I can wait here, it doesn't make any difference where I wait, there's no shark around yet anyway," I say.

"I'm fine here on my own," she says with her head hanging over the side. "Just bring me some water."

"Well, I'm going to head back there then and stand on the platform to look out for sharks."

"Okay," she groans. I wish there is something I could do, particularly as I convinced her to come on the trip against her better judgment.

A shark does turn up soon enough, but no amount of encouragement from me or the crew will get Julia into her wetsuit. I take my turn in the cage, and afterward the shark remains swimming around the boat. Try as I might I am unable to even encourage her to stand and view it from the boat. Between dives I check on her, as do the crew, but she is in no mood for conversation and spends the morning draped at the bow of the boat while occasionally leaning over the side. Unable to move, she sees nothing but the trails of her own breakfast drifting away on the current.

Graeme is flying into Cape Town tomorrow and will be joining us here in the evening. All three of us are booked to go out to Shark Alley again the following morning. I now have forty-eight hours to convince Julia to try again. I really want everyone to see sharks. I hate seeing Julia tortured by seasickness, but I hate more that she will miss out. I hope it is not selfish to want someone to experience something you are convinced will enhance their life, in spite of their initial discomfort.

When Graeme arrives the following evening, Hilda, who works at the guest house, suggests that taking sea sickness tablets the evening before a boat trip can be better than taking them in the morning. Reluctantly Julia vows to take the trip and swallows the pills. So in the morning the three of us set off into white shark territory together. Once we round Danger Point, the sea is much calmer than two days ago, so all being well, the boat will be moving a little less today and help Julia to stave off the sickness.

A shark turns up very soon, and Julia, Graeme, and I sit and relax and let the others get into the cage first. In the few times I have done this, I have learned that sharks seem to hang around the boat for longer as the morning progresses. After about an hour and no sea sickness, the three of us get into the cage together, and a shark swims all around, offering us an unrestricted 360-degree view. Later in the morning Julia even gets in the cage on her own and later writes in her diary: *Saw white sharks today and I was not at all nervous, it was the greatest thing I have ever done, thanks Mark.* Knowing this gives me great satisfaction. My love for the ocean is growing every day on this trip, but being able to share and experience it with others makes it even more special.

We ride the Baz Bus around the coast to Margate about sixty miles South of Umkomass where I dove on Aliwal Shoal in 1998. We have come here so that I can dive on Protea Banks. Well known within the diving community, Protea Banks is famed as a shark diving destination with the opportunity to see black tips, duskies, guitar sharks, raggies, hammerheads, bull sharks—known locally as Zambezis—and, for the very fortunate, occasionally a tiger shark.

Protea Banks is a fossilized sandbank ridge that rises from the bottom at two hundred feet up to 125 feet at its deepest and around eighty feet at the shallowest. Diving on Protea Banks is relatively new and was pioneered in the early 1990s by a few locals including Trevor Krull, a former spear fisherman with whom I will dive. Protea is four miles offshore straight out of Shelly Beach and comprises two dive sites, the Northern and Southern Pinnacles. There will normally be a current on the dive, sometimes mild and sometimes not so mild, and the surface current is very likely to be different from the bottom current, so it is imperative the group stay together. Once below the surface, the boat captain traces the group under water by following a large orange buoy trailed by the dive leader.

The dives on Protea are without question serious dives and very different from many other popular dive destinations around the world. They are deep offshore drift dives and are not for the novice or the nervous diver. This is not because of the presence of sharks but for the combination of being offshore, the depth, the current, the need for excellent buoyancy control, and the importance of staying together as a group. Also to avoid missing the dive site due to surface currents and having to make much quicker descents than are perhaps normal. There may well also be a thermocline, which can see the warm seventy-five-degree surface temperature abruptly give way to sixty-degree water.

I didn't come here in 1998, as I was newly certified at that time and did not feel ready. I am certainly still a novice but I have been diving enough in the past few months that I feel ready for a challenge. Trevor's dive briefings are heavily focused on all aspects of safety. He has a way of configuring divers under water, and when he turns he expects to see you where he has told you to be. We drift together as a group, and we must work if necessary, perhaps across a current, to maintain our assigned positions.

Unlike on Aliwal Shoal, you cannot get away with hot tubbing here. It was somewhat frowned upon at Aliwal but it did happen. Hot tubbing is the somewhat derogatory term given by South Africans to the usual procedure prior to descending on a dive. Ordinarily divers enter the water with plenty of air in their BCD's thus ensuring they float when they jump or roll in, and everyone assembles as a group at the surface, like sitting around in a hot tub. The dive leader will check that everyone is okay and then give the signal to descend; everyone deflates their BCDs and begins a normal controlled descent. On Protea, however, the entries are negative, meaning all the air must be removed from the BCD before rolling from the boat, and upon hitting the water you remain in a head-down position and kick hard straight down. The group meets at around fifteen feet, checks that all is okay and then descends the rest of the way down as quickly as possible.

As soon as you roll off the RIB and start to descend, the anticipation of seeing big sharks is there. This, combined with not knowing exactly what you might see, makes every dive on Protea unique and exciting. Dropping from the RIB to be greeted by two circling Zambezis is a great start to any dive. As their curiosity builds, they swim in ever decreasing circles in a slow, almost lazy, calm, and relaxed manner until both sharks are within a mere six feet of us. They stay and check us out for a while before moving off with their curiosity perhaps satisfied. Each encounter on Protea with the Zambezis is different; sometimes we see only one or two but often groups of five or six. At the end of one particular dive, a fellow diver is excitedly talking about my close encounter. Apparently I missed a Zambezi that swam right over my head only three feet away. I insist it must have been another diver, but everyone witnessed it except me. How I missed it I don't know. But perhaps I could be forgiven just because we were on Protea and I was distracted by the resting sand sharks and schooling hammerheads swimming below.

Speaking of hammerheads, during his briefings Trevor always insists that dives are never over until we are back on the boat, and even on the safety stop we should keep looking down and all around, as you never know what might show up. This proves to be very true for me while I am on a safety stop. As usual, I am primarily looking down when I glance up to see Trevor pointing at me, or in reality behind me. I turn to my right and am instantly greeted by a large black eye only inches away. It takes a second for me to realise that the eye belongs to a hammerhead. I could have easily touched it but resist this time and watch with a grin as it slowly swims past. After the dive Trevor is certain that, had I not turned when I did, causing the shark to turn as well, it would have casually bumped me in the back of the head.

I have had many memorable encounters on Protea over the years, and although each was different, they all have one thing in common. Not once have I felt threatened by the sharks; each encounter on Protea served only to reinforce my love and respect for these fantastic animals and for the ocean. Diving on Protea Banks has been my most memorable and rewarding diving. The unpredictability combined with the reward of seeing apex predators in their natural element makes diving on Protea with Trevor and African Odyssea one of the best dive experiences on the planet.

Graeme is still with us as the three of us hire a car and set off on a 550-mile road trip from Pretoria, South Africa, over the border to Tofo in Mozambique, where we will once again swim with whale sharks.

We eventually make it to Tofo in the early hours of the morning and the next day get to see the beauty of Mozambique for the first time. I read somewhere once that Mozambique has the accolade of being the most stunning country in the world when viewed from the air. This is not hard to believe because when you see it for yourself, it is stunning enough at sea level. In places the palm-fringed, endless, pure white sand beaches stretch away to the distance and sometimes with not another soul in sight.

Whale shark trips here in Tofo are very different from those in Australia. To begin with, the trips are taken in a RIB that is launched from the beach in exactly the same manner as they are in South Africa. No amazing lunch or room to spread out, just some pineapple, some water, and your own space on the comfortable, bouncy side of the boat. No spotter planes either, just a keen-eyed crew and hopefully alert passengers, the more eyes the better. After just half an hour, a shark is spotted and we enter the water. The shark is obliging and swims at a leisurely pace. It is well in excess of twenty feet, considerably larger than the ones we saw in Australia.

Ningaloo Reef in Australia is known primarily for its abundance of juvenile males, and most are around fifteen or sixteen feet, a big fish by any standards, but this one is huge. Here, as in Australia, we have numerous swims as the afternoon progresses and people slowly opt out, and soon just Graeme and I end up swimming alone for easily five minutes with a shark over a sandy bottom in water so shallow that, if the shark were standing on its tail, half of it would be out of the water. This gives a new and different perspective and a further appreciation of size.

"Fancy a swim?" Graeme asks later as we relax on the balcony of the Bamboozi Lodge bar with drinks.

"Yes, definitely," I say, already on my feet, finishing my Sprite, and setting the empty can down on the sun-drenched table.

"Great, let's go then." He smiles as he removes his T-shirt and drapes it over his chair.

I remove my sunglasses, leave them on the table, and off we go. Reaching the beach from the lodge bar involves walking down a sturdy but very rickety-looking set of wooden steps. As the waves thunder and crash on the shore, I wouldn't want to be anywhere else. No sooner are we in up to our waists when the first breaker picks up just in front of us. Graeme ducks under it while I let it hit me and knock me over. I pick myself up and duck under the next wave and join Graeme breaststroking over the top of the following wave. Despite being rough, the water is warm, clear, and inviting, and all the better for being a little challenging.

Eventually, with stinging eyes and nostrils, we get out of the water and are walking back up the beach when Graeme says, "That really was a buzz today swimming with the sharks."

"I know, isn't it just amazing?" I reply as the day's images flood back to the front of my mind.

"Just you and I swimming alone over the sand was the best," says Graeme, beaming.

"Yep, there is nothing like it, nothing."

"Nothing?" he enquires.

"Nope," I answer with a subtle cock of the head.

"It must compare to some other buzz?"

"It is a buzz and I get so excited every time, but really it's more a feeling of connection, of peace and awe and wonder."

Graeme just smiles and says, "Hippy."

I immediately burst out laughing as does he.

"Let's stick with calling it a buzz," Graeme says, looking over his shoulder to face me with a smirk, while we climb back up the staircase.

"Yeah, sure," I agree. "Why?"

"Well how about comparing it to sex?" Graeme suggests.

"*Pft*, there's no comparison," I say with no need to think about it.

"No? They are both a great buzz that you want to experience again and again," Graeme explains.

"Ahh, okay, I get you, put it like that and swimming with sharks still wins, no contest."

"Really? But they are comparable?"

"No, not really," I say.

"So swimming with sharks is better than sex for you, is that what you're saying?" Even though I can only see the left side of his face as he half turns on the steps, I can tell his face is contorted in disbelief.

"No contest. I would give up sex in an instant if I had to choose," I say without hesitation. "There's no way I could give up swimming with sharks."

"Does Julia know?"

"Ha, I don't think she'll mind," I say, grinning broadly.

Graeme looks at me and grins just as broadly. Then he shakes his head and says, "Another Sprite?"

"Please."

The tiny island of Utila is one of the Bay Islands of Honduras on the backpacker route of Central America. A popular year-round hot spot for those wanting to swim with whale sharks, it is also very popular for those wanting to learn to dive, due to its reputation as the cheapest place on the planet to do so.

For the already certified diver, Utila offers year-round coral reef diving on warm, calm, clear, relatively shallow reefs. For those wanting to move forward in their dive journey, Utila is well known for its PADI Career Development Centres where you can be trained up to instructor level and beyond. The island is around eight miles long by three miles wide, and its highest point, Pumpkin Hill, rises to 240 feet at its summit. Not initially an overly impressive statistic, but once at the top, the view over the entire island certainly is impressive. The island is lush and green, two-thirds of it covered in dense and largely impassable mangrove. These are vital to the island and to the coral reef, providing shelter from storms and a nursery for juvenile reef fish. The mangroves are also important to land animals, not least of which is the endemic iguana known as the swamper, an endangered reptile in good hands due to the efforts of the dedicated team at the iguana station.

Looking to the rugged north coast from Pumpkin Hill, you will see waves rolling to shore, unlike the sheltered south side that for the most part remains relatively flat and calm. You will also see the dive boats en route to the much anticipated north side dive sites, knowing that all on board will be on the look out for whale sharks. The sharks are seen all around the island but more reliably on the north side, and interestingly they are found in a very different way here than anywhere else. When looking for whale sharks around Utila, you don't actually initially look for a whale shark, you look for a boil. A boil forms when small panicked bait fish are chased to the surface by larger fish, often tuna. The small fish become trapped at the surface by their would-be predators, giving the surface the appearance of a pan of boiling water. On a good day, all this commotion attracts a whale shark to the scene where it will often enter the boil and suction feed on the bait fish right at the surface. The whale shark will hang down vertically in the water with its head at the surface and open and close its huge mouth, creating a bellows effect to draw in large amounts of water and small fish to be filtered through its gills, and the fish drawn down into its narrow throat.

Another clue, and sometimes the first to all this activity, is circling seabirds that dive on the boil and take their share of the bounty just below the surface. The island is so green and dense that almost the entire human population of Utila inhabits a tiny area around the curved bay and natural harbour on the south side, around which you will find many restaurants, bars, and of course dive centres. The town is certainly a charming one, with one main unpaved road, and only very occasionally will you have to move aside for a passing golf buggy or a small truck delivering desalinated water to the townsfolk.

I, of course, can't wait to get out onto the water and hopefully see another whale shark. Julia has had enough of boats just coming across from the mainland on the ferry, and she elects to stay on shore this time. Absolutely no amount of cajoling will tempt her away from the beach or CNN.

The morning after our arrival, I grab my mask, snorkel, and fins and head out the door, leaving Julia in our small rented apartment. It is a short walk to the premises of Johnny's water and desalination plant on the corner. Numerous small blue trucks that deliver the water are parked outside in various states of repair, and I can see Johnny inside filling out his tickets. Many hummingbirds hover at the nectar feeders over the door, their wings a blur, much to everyone's delight. It is only seven o'clock, yet already the day is warming up, and during the short walk to the dive centre, my anticipation of seeing another whale shark builds. I can't wait to get into the water.

Three minutes later, I am at the dive centre and boarding the boat while we wait for the last remaining guests to arrive. We cast off from the wooden dock and slowly make our way out across the natural harbour. Even at this early hour the breeze, once we are under way, is welcome. Past the lighthouse we turn left and are on our way to the north side. Soon we are passing the old airport, and Pumpkin Hill looms as large as it can to our left. It is not long before it is behind us, signaling we are in whale shark territory, and the search for boils and circling birds begins in earnest.

After searching for about an hour, someone onboard spots our first boil. Our captain races toward the boil and slows to a crawl as we approach its perimeter. The water does indeed look like it's boiling, and the activity is frantic as the tuna herd and then consume the hapless bait fish trapped at the surface. Cruising around the outside of the boil and following it as it moves proves fruitless this first time, and we do not find a whale shark, so reluctantly we move off to continue our search.

We continue looking further offshore of the northeast corner of the island and regularly see other boats in the vicinity that are out here for the same reason. Perhaps an additional hour passes, and many aboard appear to have lost interest and are sitting under the ample shade in small groups casually chatting, their voices raised to be heard over the drone of the diesel engine below decks.

I, however, am standing on the edge of the boat holding onto the top of the shade with my eyes scanning for boils and birds along with the captain and crew. Suddenly the boat takes an uncharacteristic turn to the right and speeds up at the same time. This could be a good sign, so I scurry along the port side of the boat toward the bow while firmly gripping the top of the shade. I bend into the window when I reach the cabin, and as I do the captain points to a boil ahead with telltale birds circling above.

I hurry back toward the stern, jump down onto the deck, grab my mask, snorkel and fins, and I'm ready to go. Others see me, take the hint, and busy themselves looking for their gear. We have not been briefed, so I wonder exactly how things are run here. I soon find out. As before, the captain slows as he approaches the boil, and we scan the water for the telltale dorsal fin of a whale shark. It may also be hanging down vertically in the water if the shark is suction feeding on the bait fish. The boat stops, and the divemaster points to the shark that is indeed feeding in the boil.

"Okay, who's ready?" she shouts enthusiastically.

I am very ready, my mask is on, and all I need to is slip on my fins and slide into the water. Four of us are ready, so we get into the water together and swim toward the shark amid clouds of bait fish as tuna rise from below to pick them off. The sun's rays penetrate the perfectly clear, warm water and dance over the backs of the tuna and deep into the blue. It is only a matter of seconds before the whale shark is visible hanging straight down in the water with its mouth just at the surface. It opens and closes its mouth like a huge bellows, forcing water and the hapless bait fish to pour in. As much as I have enjoyed the swimming effort in the past, viewing a whale shark in this way is certainly a welcome change. It also offers a new perspective and way to appreciate its size and strength as it is hangs vertically and steadily in position at the surface.

The peaceful scene is interrupted when a splashing, thrashing group of snorkelers swims between us and the shark, some perhaps within a few feet or so. Almost immediately, the shark sinks down into a horizontal position and starts to swim. I swim after it with the group, but it dives quickly. I climb back onto the boat, annoyed that our experience was interrupted, and wondering whether its quick dive was connected to the arrival of other snorkelers. I can see there are three boats here now full of people hoping to see a whale shark.

Later another cry of "Whale shark!" comes from the captain, and all aboard busy themselves looking for their equipment. I am scanning the surrounding water for a boil or a shark but see nothing until someone aboard points and shouts, "Here, here it is!"

The shark is right next to the boat, no more than twelve feet away. I am dumbstruck while others aboard leap from the boat all around the shark; I just cannot believe what I am seeing. This is no way to interact with nature. It's a terrible practice, and suffice to say, I stay on the boat.

After witnessing the smooth operation—my terrible faux pas aside—and organization of the trips in Australia and Mozambique, and appreciating how well such trips can work and how unobtrusive the interactions can be for the shark, I find this very disheartening, and I can't help but feel we are wrong for being here. It bothers me that I continue to see boats driven dangerously close to sharks. This must be stressful for the sharks, and coupled with the close proximity of snorkelers may explain the brief encounters. There was not a hint of this in Australia or Mozambique.

On the third day after seeing numerous sharks mostly from the boat, I can't help but speak to the divemaster about it.

"It's a shame the sharks don't stick around for longer so we can all get a decent swim with them," I point out.

"Yeah, they pretty much always swim away when we get into the water," she replies casually.

"Do you think there might be a reason for that?" I'm not trying to be sarcastic but to prompt her to think about it, if she hasn't already.

"Don't think so," she answers somewhat quizzically. "They just always do."

"There must be a reason," I suggest.

"Don't think so."

"I have recently seen whale sharks in Australia and Mozambique and had some really long swims there," I say. "Everything was so well organized. I think you could easily do the same here."

"Yeah, but they always swim away," she repeats.

I am trying to be somewhat subtle, as it could be argued I am not in a position to behave as if I am an authority on the matter, but I believe I have seen enough to comment, so I continue. "In other places just one boat at time approaches the shark at a safe distance, and one group of ten snorkelers enters the water at any one time. Everyone rotates turns in the water, and everyone gets to see the shark."

"Maybe that works elsewhere," she answers, sounding a little fed up now.

"How about when two or three boats all turn up very close to a shark at the same time and it turns into a free-for-all. Do you think that's right?"

"Everyone wants to see the shark, so you have to hurry to get a look before it swims away," she says by way of explanation.

I am dumbstruck and can't believe she can't see it. I am unsure if she is unwilling to accept that they are doing something wrong here or if she just doesn't understand.

Cooperation does not appear to be an option here. I have no doubt that marine tourism is a good thing, but any activity needs to be conducted mindfully, and first and foremost with the animals' interests at heart.

The year comes to an end all too quickly. I've been home only two days and, while cycling through familiar Exeter streets, I suddenly feel lost all over again and have to stop before I have an accident. It's hard for me to see through my tears. Feeling lost in your home town is strange, but lost I am. More lost than on a dive at Aliwal in 1998 when I was low on air, ascended early up the buoy line, and could find no boat in sight. More lost than when Julia and I somehow strayed completely off the trail while hiking in the Blue Mountains of Australia, and more lost than when Andy and I had no idea where we were driving across America. I truly am glad I spent the past year with Julia and wouldn't want to have spent it with anyone else. It was an amazing year, and one that I don't think could ever be surpassed. But Julia and I need to part; I have known this for some while now, and being home solidifies it. I don't want to settle down to a house and a family—what some might call a normal life. I want to carry on where we left off just two days ago and continue exploring the world and the ocean. I want to get straight back on a plane and get back into the water. So a girlfriend wasn't a good idea after all, and I won't be doing that again.

The ocean has given me so much this past year, but I want more of it, I need more. Simply being near the ocean is calming and reassuring, and being on it is even more so. But once I'm immersed in its magnificence and beauty, pain and torment begin to evaporate until, when I'm below the surface, almost instantly everything is okay in the world. This is living the dream. As soon as my head sinks below the surface and the ocean envelops me completely and to my very core, I am free. It wraps me in its complete embrace, and the ocean is the whole world; there is nothing else, nothing. But equally important as the feeling the ocean gives me is a strong desire to give something back. After seeing all I have seen this past year, I know what I must do. When we find our passion, we must pursue it with all our strength. I have found mine. I will study marine biology, and once qualified, I will work with whale sharks and combine conservation and tourism together, educating people on sharks, and helping people understand how important sharks are to the oceans and, in turn, how important the oceans are to us.

Nine

Education 2005–2011

Exeter College

W alking over the threshold of Exeter College for the first time fills me with apprehension and some degree of dread. I have absolutely no idea what I am getting myself into or if I have any chance of passing the Access to Higher Education course I am about to begin. During 1983–1985, my last two years of school, I can honestly say I did nothing at all except waste time. I did not even take a pen to school. I went to class most days, but spent my time fooling around and frequently being a minor pain in the backside. During history class with Mrs. Tapper, for instance, you would often find me removed to the small storeroom at the back of the class or outside in the corridor.

On one such occasion in the corridor, Mrs. Davies, my geography teacher, is walking toward me. Wearing her usual smile, matching blue skirt and jacket, her hair pulled back in a graying bun, and her glasses resting against her chest on a chain, she approaches me with curiosity. I always liked Mrs. Davies, who was patient with a nurturing manner. I'm sure she was a good teacher, but she had the presence of a nurse.

"What are you doing out here?" she asks in her usual jovial manner and without judgment.

"Mrs. Tapper sent me out here," I say dryly.

"Why, Mark?" she asks with a hint of concern in her voice.

"For being a nuisance I guess," I say, with a hint of sarcasm, as if it must be obvious.

"What were you doing that made you such a nuisance?"

"Every time she looked away, I lifted up my desk just enough to drop it and make a loud bang," I say with a stifled grin.

"Why would you do that Mark?"

"No reason, Miss," I say with a shrug of nonchalance.

"There must be a reason; would you rather be out here than in the classroom?"

"I don't really care where I am."

"I see. Do you not like school anymore?" she asks, crouching down on the floor beside me.

"It's okay, I'm not bothered," I say dismissively.

Mrs. Davies enquires further, "How often do you come out here instead of being in the classroom?"

"Not *every* day," I say somewhat defensively. "But sometimes I do go into the cupboard," I add, "and *sometimes* I stay in the class."

"Cupboard?" she exclaims.

"Yeah, the storeroom, at the back of the class, it's called the cupboard," I say as if she should know already.

"How long do you stay in the cupboard?" she asks with some concern.

"For the rest of the lesson," I say with a shrug as if that were obvious too.

"What do you do in the cupboard, Mark?"

"Read."

"So is it just history class where you misbehave, and get sent to the corridor or cupboard?"

"Umm, no … what about your class?" I say cheekily.

"What about it?" she asks, still kneeling beside me. "I never send you out of class."

"You tell me off for staring out the window and not listening to you."

"Of course I do, when you're not paying attention," she says kindly and almost reassuringly.

"Oh," I say.

She doesn't let it go and asks, "How about your other classes?"

"Physics, I suppose."

"Suppose?"

"Mr. Burt sends me to Mr. Reeder's class when I get on his nerves."

Mr. Reeder is the head science teacher, and along with Mr. Burt, I can't help but make fun of him. On the occasions when I would go to Mr. Reeder's class, I'd burst into the room and demand to see God. I referred to him as such as a way to ridicule Mr. Burt and the fact that he didn't know what to do with me, so he sent me to a higher power. But I'm sure only I found it funny.

"What do you do in Mr. Reeder's class when you're there?" she asks, sounding interested not only in my behaviour but also in what I really do with my school time.

"I don't always actually go," I say, anticipating trouble. Mrs. Davies just looks at me, waiting for me to continue. "Sometimes I do, but sometimes I just walk around the school."

"Oh, I see," she says as she looks me firmly but kindly in the eye. "Why, though, Mark?" she asks softly.

"Because I must have got on Mr. Burt's nerves," I say.

"No, Mark, why do you just walk around?"

"Oh, that. Well, it's nice and peaceful with no one else around, isn't it?"

"How are things outside of school?" she asks with genuine interest and, I'm sure, a certain degree of insight.

"What do you mean?" I ask without thinking.

"How are things at home, Mark?"

"Fine," I say mechanically.

I'm not sure if she believes me or not, but she doesn't push. This was a chance for me to open up and perhaps get some help, but I chose not to take it. Mrs. Davies was the only teacher who had any time or patience for me. In fact she was the only teacher who had anything good to say about me in school reports or at parents' evenings. I don't know whether I needed help, but I was definitely not happy, that I do know. Looking back now, I really don't know if my home life explained my disruptive behaviour and disinterest at school.

Suffice to say, apart from being able to read and write, I left school with nothing. Walking into Exeter College to sit an Access Course with the same standards as A levels, but taken over one year rather than the usual two, is daunting, and I am quietly petrified.

Our classroom is long and narrow, with room enough for two rows of ten two-seater tables and chairs and a small gap between them. We are twelve in the class and are fairly well spread out in the room. I am seated not at the front or by the window or out in the corridor, but in the middle. It doesn't really look and definitely doesn't smell like a classroom; it lacks the aroma of musty books and floor polish. If anything, it smells a bit like nasty spray deodorant, a slight improvement over floor polish. It is a bright, naturally lit room, but still somehow a dull room, and if it weren't for the two shelves at the back of the room, full of the brightly coloured math workbooks we have to get through this term, no one would suspect it was a classroom at all.

It is just a week into the course when we are given the title for our first essay: "The Important Factors that Led to the Discovery of the Structure of DNA." Now it is said there is no such thing as a stupid question, but I'm not sure how true that is. So, hesitant to ask such a question but with more fear of complete failure if I don't, I have to speak up.

"What exactly is an essay, and how do I go about writing one?" I nervously enquire, doing my best not to catch anyone's eye. I understand it is a body of writing, but I also understand that bodies of writing can take different forms, and I have no idea what form an essay should take.

Looking slightly stunned and perhaps barely managing not to roll his eyes, my tutor replies, "You've no idea what an essay is?"

"No, I don't," I say, feeling awkward and under a spotlight. I know he's thinking, What on earth is this fool doing in my class?

"Okay, I'll print you something that explains it," he says, his tone revealing a combination of annoyance and bewilderment.

"Thank you," I say with relief.

Two weeks later, after much research at both the college and the city libraries, it is with great trepidation that I hand in my first essay. I don't own or have access to a computer and have been granted special permission to hand in the only hand-written essay in class, perhaps in the entire college.

Three weeks later, first thing in the morning, our tutor walks into the brightly sunlit room carrying a bundle of papers.

"Morning all," he says breezily. "I have your marked essay papers."

Immediately I get a sinking feeling, and the room goes dark. I have done the best I could, of that I'm certain, but I really don't know if I have any chance of attaining a passing mark, let alone a good one. I have been dreading this. I can feel my heart pounding, anxiety consumes me, and I feel hot and clammy and very out of place. What am I thinking? I can't do this, I should probably go straight home and forget all about university and marine biology. I am just not cut out for study.

The tutor walks up the aisle, placing papers face down in front of my classmates and eventually he reaches me and does the same. I don't look at him. A blank page stares at me, and I stare back at it, almost in a trance. I really want to do well and progress to university, study hard, and follow my dream, but at this early stage I can feel it slipping away, ending before it has even begun. The sun shines through the window, and the light reflecting off the blank sheet burns into me. I have to get this over with, so I turn the small bundle of pages over.

I can't believe it, level one! I want to jump up and down and scream, but I sit in silence. Now a wave as powerful as the ones in Mozambique washes over me, but it doesn't knock me over. Instead, it gives its energy over to me. I can do this, I can really do this. It could be an essay, it could be getting a place on a team or baking a cake. Simple achievements where we thought we might fail will give us great satisfaction and a huge boost and drive to continue. I am elated, I know I have a chance—more than a chance—and somehow I am off to a flying start. I will approach the rest of the course with a renewed vigour, confidence, and determination.

In 2006, just before the Easter break, a good friend named Pat tells me she has been talking to Lee who in turn wants to talk to me about an opportunity that might interest me, so she has given him my number. Lee is a marine biologist and scuba diving instructor who currently lives and works in Sweden. Over the years, we have met and spoken very briefly a few times at the gym. He has been commissioned by the museum in Stockholm and on behalf of an NGO in El Salvador called FUNZEL to carry out a reef survey in El Salvador, and he needs some help. FUNZEL was formed in the late eighties with a mission to implement different programs that contribute to the conservation of wildlife in El Salvador. The goal of the survey is to form a protected area just offshore from a small fishing village called Los Cobanos.

Lee calls that same evening and will come and see me at the Lodge the following evening. Around six thirty the next day there is a knock on the door, and it's Lee.

"Hello, mate, come in," I say, pulling the kitchen door open wide.

"Hi, how you doing?" says Lee in a unique accent that I would later learn is a result of his being a Devonshire lad, raised in Spain, working in Mexico, and now resident in Sweden.

"Is the car okay there?" he says, pointing to a Transit van in the driveway.

"Fine, mate, come on in," I reassure him. "So you've been talking to Pat," I say as I offer him a chair at the kitchen table.

"Thanks," says Lee as he sits down. "Yeah, we were just chatting, and I mentioned what I am doing and that I need help, and she suggested you," he says, his gestures turning his words into a question.

"Sounds like an interesting project. What kind of help do you need, exactly?"

"More than anything, I need a good dive buddy," he says.

"There must be more to it than that, though."

"Yeah true, there is. You'd have to learn all the fish species in the area to help with the surveys, carry slates and tapes and other equipment under water, and be prepared to do at least three, maybe four dives a day and log data," Lee explains.

"Potentially hard work, but I'm sure I can do that," I say with a smile.

"Yeah, and it should be a really cool project and a great insight into marine biology."

"So Pat told you I have just started at college then?" I shift the focus slightly just for a minute.

"Yes, she did. I graduated seven years ago," he says, shaking his head. "I can't believe it."

"Time is the enemy," I agree, quoting my granddad. "Where have you worked, in respect to marine biology I mean?"

"I worked for a reef conservation project in Mexico until recently."

"I loved Mexico. I've been twice, and Cozumel was amazing, but Baja was even better," I say with a huge smile.

"Yeah, Mexico and the diving are great," he agrees.

"I don't know anything about El Salvador though. Do you?"

"No, nothing really," he says with a chuckle. "But I'm sure it's an interesting place, and the diving and the project will be great, and it's all expenses paid."

"Is it? Wow, can't be bad."

"It's not a holiday, but when is diving not fun?"

"Oh, yeah, definitely," I concur.

"So, do you wanna come, are you in?"

"I do, I am, this is great, thanks," I say trying not to get too excited. But excited I am. Here I am about to get a taste of marine biology, taking part in a project that will hopefully lead to a marine protected area, and I've not even finished the Access Course. What a great opportunity.

Two weeks later, we are on a plane to El Salvador. Making the trip means I will miss three weeks of college, but after speaking to my tutor, the college gives me its blessing, and I will use the data we collect for a college project. On the flight to El Salvador, I relish learning all the fish species we are likely to encounter on the surveys.

The small, beautiful, rocky, crescent-shaped bay where Los Cobanos sits consists of a narrow strip of nearly black sand beach, lined at the back with palm trees. In front of the trees are the tiny cabanas owned by the artisanal fisherman who have plied these waters for generations. It is these same fishermen who, after noticing a difference in their catch, approached FUNZEL and asked them to investigate their fishing grounds, come up with a management strategy, and create a no-take zone and protected area.

Ropes attached to the cabanas trail down and crisscross the entire beach, securing the many small wooden fishing boats that rock gently in the shallow surf. Unless the tide has retreated, leaving the boats temporarily high and dry, the ropes move gently up and down, offering a knee-high hurdle to the unsuspecting beach walker. When the tide is high, the beach is so small that the water approaches the steps of the cabanas, behind which tall palms gently sway in the ever-present and cooling breeze.

Our captain and guide, Mario Campos, has over thirty years' experience fishing in these waters. We have it on good authority that he knows the area and all the local fishing and dive sites better than anyone and was also instrumental in setting up the project. The different sites are formed by rocky reefs of varying sizes in an area that is otherwise predominantly sand. The rocks vary in size from large stones to huge towering boulders the size of houses. The sites have very picturesque names: Panpanera, La Pichelara, Zavaneta, Quinoguerita, Ja Ja Ja, and Rajadura, to mention but a few.

As usual we are up and loading the boat before sunrise and consequently get to watch the day come alive every morning. Weary night fishermen return as day fishermen head out. They exchange stories in the growing light and share details of their catch as the rising sun casts long shadows across the dark sand.

This morning we are headed to La Pichelara, a site with house-sized boulders and home to huge schools of jacks. We have been here for almost a week, conducting our initial rover surveys, and the transect dives and survey proper start today. From what we have seen already, Los Cobanos is certainly a rich area. If local fishermen are now finding it harder to sustain their catches, I can only imagine how it must have been thirty years ago.

We head out in the boat, and Mario displays his unique skill at finding sites. Not uncommonly he uses landmarks as a guide, but he combines this with listening to the rocks. Periodically during boat journeys, he lies down in the bottom of the boat, puts his ear to the wooden boards, and listens. This struck both Lee and me as odd at first, as we had no idea what he was doing. We could only eye him with suspicion. However, through this technique, Mario can describe almost perfectly the underwater topography he has never seen.

Descending onto La Pichelara, the first thing you notice is the abundant soft coral growth which turns this rocky reef site into a colourful, diverse, vibrant, and complex marine habitat. There are almost more reef fish here than you see on some coral reefs. Territorial damsels swim frantically around their chosen patch of rock and defend it with vigour from all intruders. Butterfly fish swim in small schools close to the bottom, and if you look closely you will see a Moorish idol accepted among them. Surgeons swim often in mid-water just a short distance from the cover of the rocky reef, as large schools of snapper circle in tight unison.

During our first survey dive, we have to work hard not to become too distracted. Throughout the dive we are accompanied by the song of a male humpback whale. We have seen them at the surface already this week, but to see one underwater would be an incredible experience. We can't help looking all around and hoping, but we must nevertheless focus on the job at hand.

On the return journey, out of nowhere, Mario gives us a clue to how close to and how passionate he really is about this project and the future of his little part of the ocean.

"I had a dream we built a wall, kept everyone out, and protected all the fish," he says almost woefully.

Lee and I look at each other and smile. Then Lee says, "We will make a plan to protect this area and make sure it stays as rich as you remember it."

Mario replies most sincerely, "Thank you for coming here and helping us with this project and saving our fish. When I was a boy catching fish was easy, but now it is hard, and sometimes we only catch small fish. This is very bad."

I can't help being drawn in by Mario's passion, and his words resonate with me. It would be amazing to be able to protect all life in the ocean, though perhaps not with a wall, but the sentiment remains. Mario's passion, insight, and drive to do something positive for the marine environment and for his community for generations to come is most inspiring.

With Mario's help the survey goes very well. Six months after its completion and Lee's submission of the recommendations, the protected area and no-take zone are indeed implemented and remain a great success to this day.

My time at Los Cobanos has been an exciting and inspirational learning experience, and the success of the project solidifies my passion and motivation to study hard.

September soon comes around, and it is time to walk over yet another frightening threshold, this time at Plymouth University. Just an hour away from Exeter, Plymouth has a rich history in seafaring and ship building. Plymouth is also home to the Marine Biological Association and the Plymouth Marine Laboratory, and between them they conduct research in all areas of the marine sciences. So without a doubt, Plymouth is the ideal place for a budding marine biologist to study.

After doing so much better than I'd expected on the Access Course, I am really focused on the my dream now. All my energy will go into this. I will get this degree, I will become a scuba instructor, and I will work in marine conservation and be in, on, under, or near the ocean every day.

I meet lots of new and interesting people in the first weeks at Plymouth, and meeting new people is great, but I find that young people like to hug a lot these days. This is new and difficult for me. It seems to me hugging has replaced handshaking and smiling as the modern way to greet friends. It's not something I grew up with, and perhaps that's why I find it uncomfortable, but maybe I'll get used to it.

After one term of study, I realise I need to make a subtle but significant change in direction and switch from marine biology to marine ecology. Marine biology is the scientific study of all life in the oceans, from the enigmatic whales and dolphins down to the lesser-known but equally fascinating planktonic life. Very often marine biologists will concentrate on a particular species or family of species and, using the scientific method, will ask questions like, What do pilot whales eat?

Marine ecology, on the other hand, is the scientific study of marine life, populations of species, their habitat, and how they might interact with the living and nonliving factors in their environment. Marine ecology considers what is known about the biology of a species and other plants and animals in the environment, allowing marine ecologists to ask questions like, Does a decline in parrot fish numbers and diversity affect live coral cover on a reef?

To fully understand and appreciate the biology of a species, we sometimes have to consider it at the cellular level. It is during a series of chemistry lectures that I realise I am not interested in understanding exactly how species work, but in how species interact with others of their own kind, with their environment, and with other species. I am interested in the big picture—in other words, ecology. This is where my interest lies, so I change course and join the ranks of the marine ecologists.

Before I know it, my first year at Plymouth is complete, and I can look forward to a long summer. But then, just before term ends, I hear from Lee via email. Currently he is working as a dive instructor and resident marine biologist at Guludo Beach Lodge in northern Mozambique. His role includes taking guests on dive and snorkel trips, guiding certified divers, teaching new divers, and in season conducting humpback whale–watching trips. As well as the trips, he will be giving educational presentations to the guests, recording data, and taking photos of the whales for the International Whaling Commission.

Lee spells it all out in the email. The busy season, humpback whale season, is fast approaching and he needs another member of staff for four months. This could be a long summer like no other; I love Mozambique and would love to have a look further north. I need no convincing and email Lee straight away to accept the offer.

Soon after that email from Lee, I head to Mozambique for a PADI divemaster internship where I will learn everything about diving and dive training. As part of the course, I will drive the RIB, assist on PADI courses, lead certified divers on guided dives, and conduct whale-watching trips.

Guludo Beach Lodge is situated on a perfectly white and often deserted seven-mile stretch of unspoiled beach. Lined with palm trees gently swaying in the cooling breeze and lapped by the perfectly blue Indian Ocean that covers pristine coral reefs just offshore, Guludo Beach really is an idyllic and unspoiled paradise. The local people are humble, charming, friendly, and engaging. They have next to nothing, but at the same time they have everything. I have never met such happy, contented people. They live close to the edge, and are concerned only with what really matters, such as food, water, shelter, and relationships. While they may not have all of these in abundance, they do have them, and they strive every day to make sure they have enough to get by. Their lives are real.

I have more than once asked myself, "What is the meaning of life? What is the point?" After spending time at Guludo, I realise this is a First World question. The trappings of living in the modern Western world make us lose sight of the essentials. I feel certain this way of thinking is not relevant in the developing or Third World, and I doubt people living in northern

Mozambique ask such questions. I don't believe they have many distractions or unimportant elements in their lives. Everything they have to deal with is real.

Everyone here is wonderful, but for some reason I quickly form a special bond with one of the kitchen staff, Moringue, a smiling, happy, funny, charming character. Quite how we become so close while communicating in only broken Portuguese and rudimentary English I don't know, but perhaps that says something about relationships. One day he asks me more about mine.

"*Boa tarde*," I say to all as I enter the outdoor open-plan kitchen. "Any bread rolls left over today?" I regularly call into the kitchen at this time in the afternoon, looking for delicious leftovers.

"Boa tarde," is the chorused reply.

"No, sorry, nothing," answers Mimadi.

"I'm hungry," I say cheekily.

Mimadi says, "You are always hungry."

"That's because you make nice food," I say with a broad grin, and he soaks up the flattery by grinning broadly back at me before turning back to his work.

"Mimadi," I say getting his attention again, "pumpkin curry again tonight?"

"Maybe, maybe," he answers.

Then Anna, one of the waitresses, walks in from the adjoining restaurant and bar. She is a lot of fun, and she is great to wind up.

"Anna, why do you not have any bread for me," I say in mock disgust.

"You have to wait; bread is for the guests, not you."

"What? You people need to look after me better. I work hard all day," I protest while doing my best to stifle a laugh.

"You are swimming and driving around the water in *Calypso* all day. That's it, you don't work," she exclaims.

Perfect, I thought that would hit the spot.

"What do you do?" I say baiting her further. "You hang around here hiding in the kitchen eating my bread rolls when you should be out there in the restaurant looking after the guests." I duck as she takes a swipe at my head.

I turn to Moringue smiling with glee, while he does his best not to smile back. Despite not exactly understanding the exchange between Anna and me, he knows me well enough now to know I have been winding her up.

"Monkey, you have wife in England?" he asks.

"No," I say, "I don't have a wife," not yet realising the significance of the question.

"No wife, Monkey?" He sounds surprised.

"No wife," I repeat. "I'm too young for a wife."

"No, Monkey, no problem," he says reassuringly. "You have wife, no problem."

Now I feel bad for joking, as it was lost in translation. He is being very sincere and believes it is a problem that I am not married.

"I don't want to be married," I say sincerely. "I don't have anyone to get married to anyway."

He looks at me puzzled until I say, "I don't have a girlfriend."

"In England, no girlfriendy?" he asks, sounding more surprised now.

"No girlfriend," I confirm.

"Ooh, problem," he says. "Why not have girlfriendy?"

"I don't want a girlfriend," I tell him.

"No girlfriendy, no children?" he asks again.

"That's right, none," I say.

"Why, Monkey, why?" he asks with an almost pained expression and a look of utter disbelief.

I can only shrug and say, "No reason, I just don't."

He can't quite believe it and beckons two other kitchen staff, who are squatting on the floor shelling crabs, to stop what they're doing and enter into the conversation. They leave their task and join us at the kitchen counter. As they do, Moringue says something I don't understand in Portuguese, and they both eye me with puzzled expressions.

"That's right," I say, defensively now working out what he said, "I don't have a wife, or girlfriend, or children."

"Crazy," one of them says.

"No, it's not crazy," I say, "Having a wife is crazy." I open and close my thumb and four fingers in jest and say, "Blah, blah, blah" to illustrate the nagging wife cliché. I also hope it will shift the direction of a conversation that is becoming too serious and making me uncomfortable.

"No, no, no," one of the newcomers says, sensing my jest, "why do you not have?"

I can only repeat again, "It's no big deal, I don't want one." I demonstrate a nagging wife once more, excuse myself, and leave them laughing.

I didn't find out until it was time to leave Guludo that there had been a misunderstanding on the day I arrived. Someone thought my name was Monk, which soon turned to Monkey, and it stuck. These wonderful people and their concern about my single state got me to thinking about something I had not considered for a long time. Not necessarily why I don't have a wife, but why I behaved badly, was self-destructive, and why I said no to Jo when I wanted to say yes to a movie. It was because I believed I didn't deserve her, and behaving badly was a subconscious way of keeping my distance. More than that, I know why I believed this. It was because I believed I had no value. I'd had none growing up, and it is perhaps that more than anything that has left a mark on me.

When the wildlife turns up, you really know you're in Africa. We see snakes and hear leopards occasionally at night. Much to his shock and discomfort, one of the kitchen staff even sights a leopard on his way to work.

One afternoon at the changeover from the day to evening shift, Anna runs excitedly into the dive centre and screams, "I've just seen elephants at Mapondie."

Mapondie is just half a mile away on the sand road between here and Guludo village.

"I'll run and grab the keys," exclaims Lee.

"We'll meet you at the Land Rover in one minute," I say.

Anna and I trot behind Lee on our way to the Jeep as he disappears running down the sand path past the restaurant and toward the office. He quickly returns with the keys and camera. The three of us jump into the Land Rover and drive as fast as we dare on the sand the short distance to Mapondie.

"Here," shouts Anna. "Stop!"

We pull off the road slightly, climb onto the roof, look into the bush, and there they are. Perhaps two hundred feet away stand four elephants. They are on the edge of a patch of tall grass, and like the still air this afternoon, they seem to be barely moving a muscle.

"Wanna go take a closer look?" I ask, as my eyes dart between Lee and Anna.

Anna says nothing and climbs down from the roof.

Lee says, "We won't get a chance like this again. Let's see if we can get a little closer."

Lee leans into the cab to grab the camera, and the three of us take off into the bush. The wildlife of Mozambique paid a heavy price during the civil war between 1977 and 1992 and is still in a state of recovery. Seeing elephants here is incredibly exciting and a once-in-a-lifetime opportunity that I am not about to miss. Half a minute into the bush, it becomes too thick to take a direct route, so we meander our way slowly toward where we think the elephants are. We dip down into a small hollow where there is not a sound and we are surrounded on all sides by small trees.

"Which way now?" asks Anna.

"I *think* straight on," says Lee.

"I'm not sure, dude. They might be over here a little to the left," I say as I trip and stub a toe on a fallen branch.

Just a hundred and fifty feet from the road, I find that flip flops are no longer appropriate. In addition to my throbbing toe, my arms are itching from some irritating plant that I've brushed against.

"Okay, you go that way, we'll go ahead," whispers Lee.

"They can't be far now, whichever direction it is," I acknowledge, as I move away from them.

I truly feel alive, out in the bush, if only a hundred and fifty feet from the sand road. This is an in-the-moment adventure. An opportunity presented itself to us, and we seized it.

In the years that follow, whenever I relay this story, people say it was stupid to seek out elephants in the wild. But at the time, it feels like the right thing to do, to embrace a once-in-a-lifetime encounter with one of nature's finest and most majestic beasts. To feel close to nature, to feel connected and be at one on the same terms. Actually the elephants have the upper hand; the encounter will be on their terms.

I continue on for about a minute, edging my way through the bush to where I'm certain the elephants are. The vegetation thins, a gap in the trees appears, and the bush opens up to reveal a patch of tall grass. I keep walking until suddenly there they are: two elephants. Both stand tall and proud, perhaps fifty feet away on the other side of the clearing, snapping branches and munching on thick green leaves and twigs. I reach behind, grab a small branch, and bend it until it breaks with a crack. Both elephants look up from their grazing and look in my direction for a second or two. Whether they truly see me I don't know, but it seems wise to alert them of my presence. Then, believing the elephants know I am there and don't care too much one way or the other, I walk clear of the tree line and out into the waist-high grass. Just a few strides in and I can see the others. All four of them are busy breaking young branches and grinding up their fibrous afternoon snack. I walk halfway across the clearing and stand alone, twenty-five feet away from four amazing elephants, and they pay me no attention whatsoever.

Life doesn't get much better than this, alone with nature on its own terms —how wonderful! I stand transfixed as the sun beams down, illuminating the scene perfectly. My toe has stopped throbbing, my arms have stopped itching, all is calm and still, and I'm smiling. I spend a minute or so like this until I begin to wonder where Lee and Anna have gotten to. I follow the snaking tree line a short distance to my right, and there they are. Lee is behind a tree with the long camera lens poking out, giving away his position.

"There you are, dude," he says. "Where have you been?"

"Just back that way a bit," I say with a gesture.

"What, out in the grass?"

"Yeah," I say, beaming.

"That's crazy."

"It didn't feel crazy, man."

Being close to magnificent creatures like elephants makes you realise how small and weak you are, but more than that, it makes you appreciate the wonder of nature. It is deeply saddening to think that we humans are doing so much to destroy it. It has been a moment in time, a snapshot of life that will never be forgotten.

Guludo is a place where you could easily drop out of modern life forever and never miss it. Like the village of Guludo, one mile inland, the Guludo Beach

Lodge has no power or running water. It takes merely a few days to realise you really don't need these conveniences. Water is drawn from the pump in the village or taken with buckets from the water hole on the Lodge property and then boiled for drinking, yet still retaining its unique taste that takes a little getting used to. Lighting is provided by gas lanterns which the dedicated staff distribute around the grounds at dusk every day, while solar lights illuminate the paths leading to the traditional African-style tented structures, or *bandas*. Life is simple and perfect at Guludo. I can feel Africa's rhythm like a heartbeat beneath my bare feet, and I am enraptured by it.

The diving at Guludo is incredible, and when I'm suspended in the endless blue beauty of the Indian Ocean, my mind is empty. As I glide through her, I'm certain I can feel the individual water molecules as they pass over my fingertips. I am at one with the ocean and want to melt into her, for my molecules to merge with hers and to remain forever in her warm embrace. Any thoughts I might have underwater are simply concerned with the wonders of the deep all around me, and the anticipation of any special treats that might be revealed to me.

Seeing huge schools of jacks and barracuda on almost every visit to the dive site known as Rushour is mesmerising, as the dappled sunlight bounces off their silvery sides and they move effortlessly as one body. I might see a shark or a ray or hear the distant song of a whale as in El Salvador. The vivid colours of the myriad reef fish and coral and the constant pops, clicks, and scratches heard coming from the reef combine to indicate a thriving, healthy population of fish and crustaceans and give a clue to the many more reclusive species not revealed to the eye. The ocean's calming, all encompassing embrace consumes me. There is nothing else when I'm underwater. The water is the world, and the world is the water. Often I don't shower at the end of the day, because doing so feels like a betrayal. The ocean cleanses me, and I need no other. I know even more than ever that I want to be in, on, under, or near her every day. From dawn till dusk, every day at Guludo is as perfect as any day could be.

Returning to Plymouth and to studying is a challenge after such a wonderful time in Mozambique. But at the same time, my focus has been further sharpened by the experience. The second year begins as well as the first had ended, and throughout the year I don't falter for even a minute. Like the first, the second year flies by, and before I know it I am in the third. My final year dissertation sees a return to the El Salvador data set and an examination of the relationship between fish and their habitat entitled "Life without Coral: The Abundance and Diversity of Reef-Associated Fish on Rocky Reefs in El Salvador." Ten weeks after our final classes, it is graduation day.

We are high on the perfectly manicured lawns of Plymouth Hoe. A rare brilliant September sunlight illuminates and dances on the surface of the perfectly calm waters of Plymouth Sound that stretch out in front and below us. Smeaton's Tower lighthouse stands proud, and the smell of freshly cut grass fills our nostrils, while my eyes hurt as the sun reflects off the large white marquees that will soon play host to our graduation ceremony. Plymouth Hoe is surely the perfect setting to mark and to celebrate the end of three years of study, and I almost can't believe I'm here.

"You better go and get your robe," Dad says with a beaming and slightly cheeky smile.

"What time is it?"

"Nearly midday," Uncle John replies.

"Okay, I'll see you after I've had my official photograph taken."

"We'll see you when you're all dressed up then," says Darron with a grin.

Claudia is also here today. We met on the first day at Plymouth and soon became good friends, spending a lot of time studying, and on occasion, partying as well.

Together we walk into the stifling heat of the smaller marquee that is the robing area and are greeted by the smiling faces of the hire company personnel and the smell of hot tarpaulin. Claudia and I collect our robes and snigger at each other as we try to figure out how to get them on. I, at least, am struggling.

"Do you need a hand?" asks one of the kindly assistants as she adjusts my hood and corrects my slightly disheveled appearance.

"Yes, please, I do," I say with some relief.

Eventually, decked in my robe and mortar board, I feel a bit silly and self-conscious. But I put a brave face on it and proceed to the official photography area. Once immortalized, digitally at least, Claudia and I walk together back out into the warm glow of The Hoe where Dad, John, and Darron are waiting

—Dad with his camera, John with a beaming smile, and Darron, like me, with a barely stifled "wow, look at you I can't believe it" chuckle.

A quick look around reveals almost everyone is now dressed in their black gown, mortar board, and blue-and-orange hood. Slowly I begin to relax and feel less self-conscious. If my teachers and schoolmates from Priory could see me now, they would never believe it! I couldn't blame them. I can't believe it myself. Suddenly I'm starting to enjoy everything about the day, and Dad is positively glowing. I'm sure he is still ever so slightly surprised at my achievement, but he is absolutely spilling over with pride nevertheless. I never sought his approval, nor did I need to, but I know he is absolutely overjoyed at my success.

During the course of my studies, and after my diving and snorkeling experiences of the past eleven years, I have developed a bond beyond compare with the ocean. I believe we should conserve the world's oceans for their own sake. Not everyone feels this way, of course, and many do not realise that, directly or indirectly, we all rely on healthy oceans for our own health. This has forged my ethos and approach to marine conservation, and I want to share it with as many people as possible. The oceans are a major source of protein and direct employment for millions. Like the rain forests that perhaps get more attention, the oceans provide us with oxygen and absorb carbon dioxide and heat. Governments backed with sound science have the power to affect great change in the way we use the oceans, and plenty of research is conducted in the name of marine conservation. But I believe this is not enough. Some research projects might be years in the making, and motivating governments to act upon their findings is seldom easy. So it's really up to members of the public, who can achieve great things when they are inspired to care. People are more likely to care about and protect things they understand. With this in mind, I believe the ocean is a vastly underused classroom.

Anyone who sees a coral reef, a humpback whale, a manta, or a shark will surely have a new appreciation for the ocean. Inspired people may become a voice for one species and, in turn, for the broader ocean. Every new ocean advocate can make a difference. This is my ethos in respect to marine conservation and where I will focus my job search.

Applying for jobs in the months after graduation bears no fruit, and all I hear is lots of talk about "ordinary" degrees. Ordinary? Four years of dedication and hard work dismissed as *ordinary*? I enjoyed studying immensely and cannot accept *ordinary*. In January of 2010, I apply once again to Plymouth, this time for a master's degree in marine biodiversity. I will continue to work too many hours at the garden centre where I have been employed for the past three months, and also begin a new divemaster internship, this one at Teign Dive Centre, where I did my first dive thirteen years earlier. It has been three years since the internship in Mozambique, and I have not worked as a divemaster since. Since I am slow to gain confidence in my own skills, I happily sign up to repeat the training. In my opinion, a willingness to own up to one's weak areas and a determination to do something about them is a true strength. In September I will return to study, to further improve myself, and to better this *ordinary* degree.

One year later, in October 2011, I have a master's degree, I am a PADI Open Water Scuba Instructor, and my qualifications are a little less *ordinary*. I am now like a sapling in a forest beside a newly fallen tree, and I will stretch toward the new path of light beaming in through the gap in the canopy.

Ten

———

Mozambique December 2012–July 2013

C ompetition is still fierce, and it is not until the winter of 2012 that I am offered a six-month contract working for All Out Africa starting in late December. This is a tour and conservation group that runs, among other things, a whale shark and marine conservation volunteer program in Tofo, Mozambique. Ecotourism with whale sharks has grown every year since the late nineties, as has scientific study in areas such as their distribution, populations, migrations, and foraging behaviour. There have also been behavioural studies into their reaction and response to tourism in respect to boats and to snorkelers in the water. Studies such as these are particularly important from a regulatory point of view as whale shark tourism continues to grow. I do believe the more people who enter the water the better, but I am well aware that it needs to be done mindfully and with the ocean's best interests at heart. Tourism and scientific study have been combined in numerous citizen science programs around the world, including the one in Tofo. Volunteers are first trained and then actively get to contribute and take part in scientific research.

Identification photographs play a large part in behavioural, population, and migration studies, and at Tofo volunteers are taught how to take good identification photographs of many different species including small-eyed sting rays, turtles, leopard sharks, and perhaps most exciting of all, the whale shark. Let's not forget the equally exciting two species of manta. It was research conducted at the Marine Mega Foundation in Tofo that uncovered that there are indeed two species, the giant manta (*Manta birostris*) and the reef manta (*Manta alfredi*).[1]

Despite being only a six-month contract to cover an extended leave, I am excited. This feels like the beginning of the end of a quest toward living the dream.

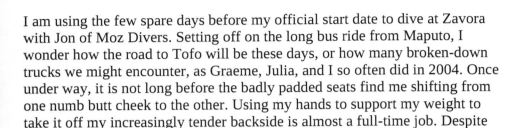

I am using the few spare days before my official start date to dive at Zavora with Jon of Moz Divers. Setting off on the long bus ride from Maputo, I wonder how the road to Tofo will be these days, or how many broken-down trucks we might encounter, as Graeme, Julia, and I so often did in 2004. Once under way, it is not long before the badly padded seats find me shifting from one numb butt cheek to the other. Using my hands to support my weight to take it off my increasingly tender backside is almost a full-time job. Despite the uncomfortable bus, I find the journey is much less bone-jarring than I expected, as the road has been vastly improved since I last took it.

Trade links between China and Mozambique are increasing, and the Chinese are mostly responsible for the improved roads here. Perhaps the most contentious issue concerning Chinese activity in Mozambique is in the forestry sector, after China banned logging in much of its own natural forests in 1998. But for many in Mozambique, fishing is the real bone of contention. The Chinese are accused of fishing illegally using long lines and gill nets. Both fishing methods indiscriminately catch sharks and turtles, among other species. They are also accused of poaching shrimp and lobster. All these affect the artisanal fisherman. Perhaps of most concern is the rise of illegal fishing for sharks to procure fins for Chinese buyers. Some say the government ignores this in exchange for the building of roads. For more on the rise of shark fining in Mozambique, look up the documentary *Shiver*.

On the ride to Zavora, I don't see or feel a single pothole, never mind the vehicle-sized ones we encountered the last time around. Despite the vastly improved road, it is still an uncomfortable six hours later before I am dropped off at the junction to the sand road to Zavora Beach Lodge. Right off the bus I manage to hitch a ride. I slap my bag into the back of the pickup and sit atop it as we bounce our way along the rutted sandy track.

The weather is hot and sunny at around ninety degrees. It is so hot that when I jump from the truck, I have to put on my flip-flops as protection from the scorching sand. As I'm checking into my room at reception, there is talk of an approaching storm, and sure enough, in the early evening the weather turns bad and the rain pours. It pours relentlessly through the night, so much so that it cascades in through a particular spot in the roof above my room, wakes me up, and forces me to move my bed away from the leak. It's not until I swing my legs out of bed in the morning into shin-deep water that I realise just how bad the rain has been. A look outside reveals the entire grounds are now under at least ten inches of water.

Despite the awful weather and poor visibility, we head out for a dive. The boat is launched into the gray surf that extends to the horizon and meets and melds together with the equally gray sky. Not an inspiring scene, but once beneath the gray water, the world will become clean and clear again. I am on board with just one other customer, an Italian whose name eludes me but who is otherwise a very memorable character.

While attempting to get into his dive gear, he somehow manages to fall overboard and struggles to clamber back aboard while looking very bemused. We all stifle laughter and look away to save him further embarrassment. Five minutes later my clumsy dive buddy and I sit next to each other on one side of the RIB, and our dive guide sits alone on the opposite side.

"Three, two, one, go!" commands our guide.

I roll off backwards into the water. A second later, as I am still sinking, I feel a thump on the head. Our clumsy friend has gone from being early to enter the water to late, despite just hearing the briefing reiterating the importance of rolling from the RIB in unison.

Fortunately, his clumsy landing delivers only a glancing blow from his tank. Had he timed it a second or two later, it could have been a very different outcome. He offers no apology, and I choose to stay silent. He must know he rolled off late and hit me, but maybe he is among the ranks of the blissfully unaware. I soon forget the bump on the head because after being underwater for only one minute, we see five eagle rays. It's my favourite fish, and a great welcome back to diving in Mozambique.

After the dive, my Italian friend's haplessness continues. He is unable to get back into the boat unaided. Despite removing all his gear, he needs to be pulled and pushed aboard until eventually he slumps rather unceremoniously onto the deck, mouth agape and looking rather like an exhausted, freshly hauled fish.

"Boa tarde," I say to the lodge barman at lunch time, taking the opportunity to exercise my limited Portuguese.

"Boa tarde," he replies with a smile. *"Todo bien?"*

"Bem, obrigado, e voce?" I ask.

"Bem," he replies, before adding in English, "What can I get you?"

"Could I order fries and a Sprite please?" I ask, not unhappy to have moved to the mother tongue, as my Portuguese is about exhausted.

"Sure," he says with a nod. "Glass and ice?"

"The can is fine, thanks."

It is still very gray and miserable outside, so it looks like I will be confined to the bar for a few hours. It is a nice bar with a nicer view, so I am happy to sit, eat fries, drink Sprite, and chat with the barman.

"Have you been working here long?" I ask as he rises from the low fridge, Sprite in hand.

"Maybe one year," he answers.

"Oh, not too long then?"

"No, not long. Excuse me, I need to take your food order to the kitchen," he says, apologising for breaking off our conversation.

"No problem."

"Is it a good job here?" I ask when he returns.

"Yes, very good, better than my old job."

"Oh, how come?" I ask, intrigued.

"I was a spear fisherman," he says quickly.

"Oh, yeah, that must be a hard way to earn a living," I acknowledge.

"Yes, but a shark bit me, then I could not continue."

"Really, shit, that sounds scary. Were you badly hurt?"

"Yes, on my arm. The shark was crazy and tried to kill me."

"How did it happen?" I ask, eager to hear the whole story now.

"Okay," he says as he quickly rolls up the sleeve of his shirt to reveal a line of inch-long scars along his arm.

"I had two fish already on my float and was coming up with a third one in my hand." He pauses but I just look at him waiting for him to continue.

"Just when I reached the surface, a shark attacked me, took the fish, and bit my arm," he says, looking shocked to be reliving the experience.

"Did you see it coming?"

"No!" he almost squeals, "I only knew it was there when it was biting me. I hit it one time, and it let go and swam away with the fish."

"Wow, that's scary, so you didn't go fishing after that?"

"Never. That shark was crazy, and it tried to kill me." He regards me as if I am mad for asking such a question.

"Very scary, but it wasn't trying to kill you," I chuckle.

"Yes, it was crazy."

"It wanted your fish and bit you by mistake," I say, trying to offer a little reassurance to the aftermath of a frightening ordeal.

"No, no, he tried to get me, but the fish was there, and then I hit him, and he swam off," he tells me by way of explanation.

"Don't you think the shark came after you shot the fish because it sensed it struggling?" I suggest, offering some reality and again hopefully reassurance that the shark was not out to get him.

"No, the shark was trying to get me, but I hit it," he reiterates.

We go back and forth like this for a while, but he remains adamant that the shark was after him and merely got the fish as a consolation prize. No amount of reasoning and explanation will convince him otherwise. Our conversation serves to reinforce my passion for passing on knowledge to as many people as possible and helping to undo the demonization of sharks.

Two days later, it is time to head up the coast to Tofo. There, I am met first of all by gray skies and warm drizzle in a town very different from the one I remember from 2004. It was and still is a fishing village, but it has grown, along with tourism. The centre of town, often simply referred to as the market, is loosely set out in an American grid pattern and has an instant charm. I would soon learn that everyone who visits is enthralled by it. Jon and I leave Tofo centre and head to the Albatross Restaurant to meet Amy and Ross. It's a great eatery where, I would later learn, due to the extremely slow service you get to enjoy fantastic views over the bay for long periods of time. I walk into the restaurant laden with heavy dive gear bags, and two people instantly rise from their seats.

"Mark?"

"Yes, that's right, you must be Amy," I say releasing a bag and extending a hand in her direction. Amy, who appears to be in her mid to late twenties, has a warm smile and long, blond sun-bleached hair.

"Welcome to Tofo," she says as we shake hands.

Almost simultaneously and before I can answer, Ross says, "Hi, Mark, I'm Ross, nice to meet you," and he too offers a hand.

"Nice to meet you both," I say as I move to shake Ross's hand, attached to an early twenties lad who simply looks very happy to be here.

"Thank you, it really is great to be back," I say with a smile.

"You've been here before?" Ross asks in surprise.

"I have, in 2004," I say, remembering it fondly and pondering how much it has changed.

"Oh, wow, it must be different now," says Amy.

"Definitely, I don't even recognise the centre; there was nothing really there before."

"We'll have a proper look around later," suggests Amy, "to reintroduce you."

"Great."

"Was the trip up on the bus okay?" asks Ross.

"Ha, well, numbing but okay," I say with a chuckle met by knowing smiles.

"Okay, well, to business shall we?" says Amy. "Are you happy to start shadowing Ross starting the day after tomorrow?"

"I certainly am, I can't wait. I'm itching to get to work and to get in the water."

"We'll work together for two weeks," adds Ross, "which should be more than enough time to introduce you to everything you need to know."

"I'm sure it will be," I say.

"We've discussed it over Skype, but just to confirm, we meet for work at seven, starting the day after tomorrow. You'll shadow Ross, as you know, for two weeks, so quiz him on as much as you need to. I'll fill you in on other aspects as we go along, and again ask me as many questions as you need to."

"Sure, it all sounds good to me," I reply.

While we talk about the role of All Out Africa, Amy continues to ooze an infectious energy and enthusiasm for the whole project. "There's not really much else we can do now. Do you have any questions?" she asks.

"Many, but nothing that can't wait, I'm sure," I say. Actually, I'm so excited that the many questions elude me.

"Sure?"

"Well, only my accommodation actually. Where will I find it?"

"I can take you there now; we'll drop off your gear at the dive centre first and then head over. Sound good?"

"Yep, perfect."

I feel almost instantly at home in Tofo and with everything about it, even though I've only been here for half an hour. The people of Tofo and the job are a perfect fit with my ethos. The extra year of study is paying dividends now, as the master's qualification played a role in securing the position. Work duties include training volunteers in identification techniques, leading research dives, and guiding the in-water activities with whale sharks. Photographing whale sharks, manta rays, leopard sharks, small-eyed sting rays, bowmouth guitar fish, and turtles is high on the daily to-do list as well.

Volunteers come from far and wide to take part in the All Out Africa marine conservation program here in Tofo, and most stay for one or two months. As well as the marine program, volunteers learn about the people and culture of Mozambique. Whether they are recording dolphin sightings, conducting a reef fish survey, or recording data on manta rays and whale sharks, the volunteers are involved and engaged every day. I have no doubt all those taking part will leave better for the experience. They will also leave with enough knowledge and motivation to do something to help the ocean and pass it on those in their circle. It feels right and fulfilling to be a part of it.

Days begin early in Mozambique, and Tofo is certainly no exception. Sunrise is around five in the morning, and unless you are a heavy sleeper, the first stirrings of life are heard shortly afterward. Those within earshot may get an early alarm call of hammering and sawing from a building site shortly after five. Or, if you are lucky, just a little later chattering children will wake you up as they pass on their long walk to school in the relative cool of the early hours. Meanwhile keen fisherman will be preparing their nets and their small traditional wooden boats and launching them together into the early morning surf.

The market begins to stir around seven when traders arrive and start setting out their stalls. Some peddle hand carvings or canvas paintings depicting traditional African scenes, while others sell flip-flops and sunglasses to locals and tourists alike. My favourites are the smiling faces of the ladies in the fruit and vegetable market who will soon recommence the daily friendly squabble for business. Anyone who approaches, whether looking for a week's worth of vegetables or just a banana, will be accosted by all the ladies and will have to somehow decide where to bestow their business.

As far as tourism in Tofo is concerned, it is all about scuba diving or snorkeling with whale sharks. However, some make the effort to come to Tofo for the surfing. It is fair to say that life in Tofo revolves around the ocean. It provides protein to the local people and memorable dive and snorkel experiences to the tourists, which in turn allow many locals to earn a living.

Life in Tofo is dictated by the rising and setting of the sun and the rhythm of the ocean. Everything happens on African time, and those wanting anything done must be prepared to wait. There isn't always power, there isn't always running water, and as much as we all tend to rely upon these things, after you've been here for a while, you realise they're not important. But if you can wait, they will eventually come.

Being back in Tofu in a professional capacity, even on a six-month contract, makes me feel like I have the dream in sight and all my previous hard work is starting to pay off. The waters of Tofo are very dynamic, and on any given day you never know what you might see. Known for its megafauna, the waters surrounding Tofo are certainly rich. But on some days, the enigmatic species just don't put in an appearance, and it is on these days that you can fully appreciate the wealth of life on offer. Moray eels, big potato cod, schooling jacks, all the wonderfully colourful reef fish, and some cryptic species such as frogfish, ghost pipe fish, leaffish, and the absolutely incredible weedy scorpion fish, to name but a few. Every dive is full of anticipation for what may or may not show up. Everyone wants to see a manta or a whale shark, and if they elude us for a day or two, we will normally see one or the other by the third day. The uncertainty and dynamic nature of the Indian Ocean makes every single dive day at Tofo seem new.

RIBs are launched here exactly as in South Africa, from the village centre close to Tofo Point. There, in the shadow of the rising dune, you will find the small fishing boats when not at sea. The beach here is popular for swimming and surfing, as the waves tend to be small and clean, great for those new to surfing. The swimming, it must be said, is often more about frolicking in the ever-present small but powerful waves than clocking laps. Once through the breakers, we round Tofo Point on our way to the aptly named Manta Reef. A look to the shore reveals the quieter beach of Tofinho. Tofinho Beach is around a quarter of a mile long and is much emptier than Tofo Beach, in part because it has no facilities. The larger waves and rocky bottom make Tofinho the reserve of the more serious and skilled surfer. Since it is often completely deserted, if you are lucky, you can have it to yourself. At the far end of the beach is the cliff known as Tofinho Point where a rather rustic monument stands in memory of those lost during the civil war that ended in 1992.

The highly anticipated Manta Reef is a manta cleaning station and is high on all volunteers' list of favourite dive sites. Certified divers come from all over the world to dive here, as it is renowned as a manta hot spot. At a maximum depth of around eighty feet, and with rock walls and pinnacle topography that is full of life, it would be well worth a dive, even without the opportunity to see mantas. The dazzling schools of fusiliers, shimmering schools of snappers, and lazy schools of red tooth triggerfish make it a great dive. Suddenly they part, and a manta is right there effortlessly gliding by. You can scan the water as vigilantly as you like, but often a manta will surprise you. It moves its huge triangular wings independently and displays some of the most wonderful shapes of any creature in nature. You can't take your eyes off it. One day I get another chance to look into its eye; now more than the connection, I feel as if it knows, it is intelligent, somehow it speaks. As it passes by or often over you, it is so perfectly streamlined that you feel nothing, no disturbance in the water. Not even when occasionally, with a beat of its powerful wings, it disappears into the blue.

At the cleaning station, there will often be more than one manta in attendance. Circling over the station like planes in a holding pattern above an airport, they glide in one by one as the cleaner wrasse and butterfly fish swim up as fast as they can to attend to their cleaning duty and get an easy meal in the process. They only follow the manta for so long, though, and dart back down to the safety of the reef as quickly as they left it to wait for the next pass. Each encounter with a manta is just one fin stroke away from being as thrilling as the first time. However satisfying and enriching your dive with mantas, you are always left wanting more. Back on the boat, as soon as the initial buzz of excited and lively chatter of the volunteers is over, everyone wants to get straight back in the water and do it all over again.

Today, on another perfect morning, we are on our way to Reggies dive site, so we turn left to follow the four-mile gentle crescent-shaped beach toward Barra Point. About a thirty minute boat ride from Tofo and with a maximum depth of around eighty feet, it is one of the more distant and deeper dive sites, suitable only for the more experienced diver. As we move offshore, the deep blue gets deeper both literally and in hue. We arrive at Reggies miles offshore. Here you can fully appreciate the calm, blue, still silence of the Indian Ocean. You want to stay at sea and never return to land, to be adrift forever in the perfect expanse of blue.

We gear up and roll from the boat in unison, and no sooner are we in the water when it is already a great dive. The water is warm and clear, and after five minutes we have found the resident lazy leopard shark and a wealth of reef fish, including butterfly fish, angelfish, large schools of banner fish, plenty of parrot fish, and numerous big potato cod. Suddenly I notice one of our group pointing almost directly up toward the surface. As is not uncommon, the visibility is at least eighty feet, yet when I look up, I can't see anything. We are at a depth of around forty-five feet, so if there were anything to see, I'm sure I would have seen it. I continue the dive along the reef. Perhaps thirty seconds later, I see the same diver who has now ascended a few feet above the group in the water column and is looking somewhat frantically between the group below and the surface, with one arm still extended in a rapid stabbing motion. Then I see it: a whale shark swimming just below the surface, and from this perspective it appears as a perfect silhouette as yet without form or texture.

I raise both hands in a double okay signal to the diver, then quickly change it to a stop and wait signal. I quickly alert the rest of the group and as slowly and calmly as we can, we swim up toward our waiting dive buddy and whale shark. As we rise in the water column, the shark takes on more form and complexity until we are alongside it and can see its patterns, its broad flat head, its huge fins and slowly fluttering gill slits as it undulates with the surface chop. We swim and interact with the most obliging whale shark I have ever seen. The shark circles around us and seems to frolic in our exhaled air bubbles, passing so close at times it would be mere inches from brushing one of us with its pectoral fins. We spend almost half an hour just below the surface at about fifteen feet until our tanks, low on air, force us to ascend. No one wants to leave the water or the shark, but we must.

This particular encounter was all the more special as it was a Swedish couple's last day with me, and they were the only two in the group who had not yet seen a whale shark. The fact that they did so on their last day, and on a dive rather than the usual snorkel, made my day as much as it did theirs. I know they will never forget their experience and will talk about it forever. This is why I love doing what I am doing. To be able to give people something that they will never forget is an enviable position indeed. I know I am doing the right thing for the ocean, and so will they.

My time in Mozambique comes to a close all too quickly, and I am soon on my way back to the UK. My passion for the ocean and for informing people about the threats and challenges that the ocean and its inhabitants face has been further enriched. I only wish I could introduce everyone to the ocean and to sharks.

Eleven

Utila: November 2014–May 2015

S o here I am back on Utila where ten years ago I did my rescue diver course, where Julia got attacked by sand flies, where I had many great reef dives, but also where I didn't interact with whale sharks nearly as much as I would have liked. This time I am here to work at the Whale Shark and Oceanic Research Centre (WSORC). The small town has changed greatly in ten years and, like Tofo and Gansbaai, tourism is largely responsible. The sand road through the main street is now paved and, along with the previously lone truck and golf buggy, numerous cars and small trucks are now prominent features. So too are the many squashed land crabs that litter the road after their ill-fated, mistimed sideways skittering attempts to cross the road.

WSORC shares a site and facilities with the Bay Islands College of Diving and Utila Lodge, all owned and operated by Kisty, an extremely hard-working, well-respected, and resilient lady. Much like All Out Africa in Tofo, WSORC has a volunteer program, but WSORC offers numerous options from the longer-term research assistant to the most popular one-month marine conservation internship. Volunteers of all ages take part and hail mostly from the US, though many also come from Europe and Central and South America to take part.

As in Tofo, the first thing those joining the marine conservation internship must do when they arrive is learn to scuba dive. This happens at the college, and the newly certified Advanced Open Water divers then join the WSORC program. There are many elements to the program including conducting coral health surveys, reef fish identification, and subsequently conducting reef fish surveys as part of an ongoing monitoring program. Once a week they conduct beach and in-water cleanups, usually while snorkeling. They will gain an understanding of ecotourism and conservation issues on a small Caribbean island, and those who are interested will be trained to participate in the lionfish removal program. I will personally add to the education program and deliver numerous presentations on aspects of coral reef and mangrove ecology, pollution, and much more. Finally, they will take part in a longstanding whale shark monitoring project designed to uncover answers to a number of questions. Why do whale sharks come to Utila? Where did they come from and where do they go? Is the number of whale sharks visiting Utila increasing or decreasing? I am excited to be working on another whale shark project, and the role blends with my ethos. I am thrilled to be in a position to educate, inspire, and motivate budding marine conservationists, both in and out of the classroom.

Like most dive operations on Utila, WSORC has a waterfront site with a long wooden dock that juts out into the natural harbour where, when they're not out diving, you will find three boats gently tugging at their moorings. Under the very end of the dock in ten or twelve feet of water are numerous discarded concrete blocks in an otherwise sandy area, placed there at the time the pier was built and subsequently developed into a small but charming artificial reef. I soon organize fish identification dive sessions under the dock, and it's perfect. Many of the species that we see on the fish surveys out on the reef can be encountered in a small area no more than 300 square feet. A modest but shining example of how valuable artificial reef systems can be.

One of the closest dive sites is a mere five-minute boat ride away from the dock. Lying just outside the harbour in ninety feet of water is the fascinating wreck of the *Halliburton*, purposely sunk in 1998. As soon as you leave the boat, the crystal clear water immediately reveals the wreck below. The very top of the wreck lies at about sixty feet, and there are always large schools of silversides waiting to greet you as you descend into the blue. When a group descends together down a line as we do here on the *Halliburton*, I always descend last. I like to watch and catch the exhaled bubbles from the divers below, feel them bounce off my skin and then waddle their way to the surface and disappear.

As you descend toward the wreck, snappers begin to circle, and as you get closer, you notice how time has allowed large areas of the *Halliburton* to become encrusted with vibrant coral and sponge. Colourful angel and butterfly fishes move effortlessly in and out of the cover of the wreck.

The remainder of the dives on the south side of the island are on shallow sloping fringing reefs, and like all the dives around the island, they have permanent buoys in place. No anchors are dropped in Utila. Much to everyone's delight, turtles and eagle rays are regularly spotted on the south side. But let's not forget the small, equally captivating squid and, high on almost everyone's favourites list, the spotted drum, particularly the flamboyant juveniles. The keen-eyed might even spot an occasional weird and wonderful seahorse.

But it is the rugged exposed north side that gets everyone aboard really excited. Here we can do wall dives. The even clearer, bluer, and deeper water of the north side is also where we have a greater chance of spotting a boil and hopefully a whale shark. On my first trip to the north side, two very fortunate volunteers, also in their first week, get to swim with a pod of over fifty spinner dolphins. This is what it's all about, and watching them interact with the dolphins for nearly half an hour gives me great satisfaction.

Diving along a wall and floating above hundreds of feet of water is always inspiring. As you look down, you can see the colour change from blue to deep blue to purple as you scan the depths, hoping for something new to rise up and greet you. If nothing does, you are not disappointed, for you can happily wait until next time. For now you are satisfied to be a welcome guest in the warm caress of the blue depths, and you feel very much alive.

The wall is adorned with gorgonians and sponges, and if we are lucky we will see the normally reclusive moray swim out of its refuge. The coral and many nooks and crannies hide lobster, crabs, and another of my favourites, the hawkfish. Everyone smiles when a huge barracuda swims almost right into the mask of one of the volunteers. She squeals through her regulator as, with near-perfect timing, she turns to see it inches from her face.

I encountered problems with whale shark tourism here last time around, and other regions of the world are sometimes no different. Often operators promise visitors that they will see whale sharks—something that is not done here on Utila—and then many boats race to a sighting to fulfill their promise, dumping large numbers of snorkelers into the water for a mere glimpse of a shark. In regions where whale shark tourism continues to grow and many parties have a vested interest in the whale sharks, responsible cooperation sometimes proves difficult, making regulation essential. I soon learn from Kisty that, despite complications at times, she and WSORC have done considerable work over the years to unite all interested parties when it comes to the whale sharks.

From its ongoing educational program and data collection and monitoring, to tagging programs and hosting different researchers, WSORC strives to fight for the whale sharks of Utila and beyond. There is still much to do here, though, and I am keen to rise to the challenge. I am determined to continue and expand upon WSORC's work.

After working with Kisty for ten weeks, a new manager turns up and sadly, after less than ten days, it is clear we will not get along. In short, he is a narcissistic fool and is slowly driving me crazy. Today after about two weeks, the current volunteers and I are enlisted to help in the rearranging of the WSORC office. It looks fine the way it is, but change is sometimes a good thing, and maybe the place could benefit.

After more than an hour of shifting furniture and computers with no direction or purpose, he is looking a little perplexed and at a loss for inspiration.

"If we knew why we were moving everything around it would be easier to decide what to do," I suggest. "What was the problem with the old layout?"

He looks dumbstruck for a second and then regards me with a scolding look, as if I have spoken out of turn. I realise then that there is no reason except he wants to mark his territory, and I find it pathetic.

Once a week the volunteers have an activity day. This week the volunteers and I are taking a kayak trip to the north side of the island. This involves paddling out of the harbour, up the coast to the entrance of the mangroves, then cutting through and across to the north side. There we take lunch on the beach, have a swim, and return the same way. As I recall, we set off a little after nine and return around two, and a fine time is had by all until we get back.

Before I am all the way through the door, I hear my colleague's dulcet tones. "Where have you *been*," he says, clearly upset.

"We've been to the north side, you know that," I reply, puzzled and irked by his tone.

He gives me a disapproving look. Now I know he's annoyed, and that makes me the same. What is wrong with this guy?

"It's two o'clock," he says, petulantly.

"Yes, so?"

"You've been gone five hours."

"Yes," I say sarcastically, "of course we have, it's a long paddle." I manage to refrain from adding parenthetically, "you idiot."

"You should have been back earlier," he protests.

"Why? What did you have planned that you failed to tell me about?" I try to sound less annoyed, though I know he had nothing at all planned.

"Nothing, you just should have been back before."

"How? Like I said, it's a long paddle." This answer is not acceptable to my narcissistic colleague, and he gets more upset.

"We should all be here so we can rotate for lunch," he whines.

"So the two of you couldn't have lunch separately just one time, or one of you collect two lunches and bring them back here to the office? Come on."

"That's not the point," he insists through gritted teeth.

"The point is, this is activity day—not hour or morning, *day*. The day is for the volunteers, not for you."

I can tell that he's biting his tongue while boiling inside. "I'm going to have to go home early, I'll see you in the morning," I say, as I gather my things to leave.

He gets the last word, admonishing, "This can't happen again."

Once again he has proven himself to be absolutely infuriating in his self-centreed complaining over nothing, simply because he can't stand a situation in which he is not in control. Once again he has behaved like a spoiled child.

In the ten weeks prior to the new manager's arrival, Kisty and I had been discussing new research projects. One, as you might expect, had to do with whale sharks, and another involved spotted eagle rays, which are regularly sighted on dives and also most evenings from the boat dock. The third idea was to expand upon the current reef fish and coral health monitoring program to attempt to better understand the condition of the local reefs in relation to local anthropogenic pressures and grazer abundance and diversity.

All three projects are dismissed by the new manager simply because they are not his ideas. I believe he said something like, "We can't just go ahead with a project that I am not aware of, can we?" I find this frustrating and shortsighted, as the whale shark and coral reef questions are highly relevant to the island, and in the time I have been here, I have already been working on them. He says something to the effect that "The work you did alone is appreciated, but I'm here now." He says "I" a great deal.

Instead, a preexisting removal program of the invasive lionfish is expanded upon in conjunction with a partner conservation group to include some research.

Throughout the Caribbean, much research has been conducted on the lionfish in an attempt to further understand a number of issues. These include trying to predict future population growth, their effect on the coral reef ecosystem, their reproductive capacity, and their survivability, which includes gut analysis to determine their primary diet, as well as sexing and aging the fish. All well and good, but it has been widely accepted for some time that lionfish are here and are sadly not going away. Furthermore, we know that they are thriving, and in places decimating juvenile reef fish populations. They are voracious invasive predators with stomachs that expand enormously, allowing them gorge themselves to the point of obesity. Because other fish fail to recognise them as predators, they can move around the reef relatively freely and eat their fill. When species like the algae-grazing parrot fish, already at times subject to fishing pressure, are reduced in number, the health of the entire reef can suffer. It is widely accepted that lionfish populations will continue to grow, and that eradication is impractical and would likely prove unsuccessful.

What is needed in the Caribbean is control. Much is known about their reproductive biology and rates, their trophic level in the ecosystem, and their natural predators, groupers. Where possible these predators should be protected, and lionfish removal programs should continue in earnest. There is certainly some value in continued dedicated lionfish research, but it is ridiculous to dismiss other research proposals here on Utila in such an unfounded manner, when we have the time, the facilities, and the need.

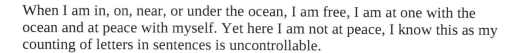

When I am in, on, near, or under the ocean, I am free, I am at one with the ocean and at peace with myself. Yet here I am not at peace, I know this as my counting of letters in sentences is uncontrollable.

The days roll into weeks and the weeks into months, and many volunteers come and go. All have a rewarding, educational and hands-on learning experience, but some do not see a whale shark. Other operators see many, but WSORC struggles at times. I have actually seen none. This doesn't bother me so much personally, but some volunteers are disheartened at not seeing a whale shark, which makes it hard to inspire them at times.

We are, of course, dealing with nature, and no one—least of all me—expects a waiting whale shark each day. It pains me to recall, but I cannot help but think about what I witnessed ten years ago. I would say there is anecdotal evidence to answer one of the research questions, and whale sharks around Utila are indeed decreasing. Some researchers suggest that whale sharks use memory to find annual aggregation sites. Well, if this is true, and whale sharks indeed remember being bothered by the snorkelers in the water while they were feeding, it might go some way toward explaining their current apparent scarcity.

I struggle for six months, and as much as I hate to admit it, I am no longer satisfied on Utila or at WSORC. I am feeling stifled and being driven somewhat mad by the petty politics of my manager. I realise too that, when I was interviewed by the previous director and asked which role I would prefer, I should have taken the managerial role over the hands-on position I chose. It is disheartening to be involved in a great project but unable to thrive.

"So what's up?" asks Kisty from across the table in Utila Lodge restaurant.

I have asked if we can speak in private, so we are tucked away at a little-used table in the corner next to the kitchen. I take a deep breath and say, "As much as I want them to be, things just aren't right."

"I knew you weren't happy, and I think I know why," she says.

"You do?"

"Well it's not hard to figure out."

"It's not?"

"No," she says with a look that says "I know you know I know."

"It's almost impossible to work with him," I say, shaking my head. "Things were great before, I really thought I was going to be here for a long time."

"It won't be forever, things will change soon enough," she says trying to reassure me.

"How do you mean?"

"He won't want to stay for the long term."

"He won't?"

"No."

"But you can't know that."

"I'm pretty sure," she says confidently.

"I'm slowly going slightly mad, and I'm not having fun anymore. I've really tried, and I've bitten my tongue a lot," I say.

"Is everything else okay, besides this? I know you would like to be teaching the volunteers to dive. Is your teaching bug satisfied with the WSORC and whale shark activities?"

"Well, that's another thing; we haven't seen so many whale sharks," I remind her.

"You've still seen none?"

"That's right, and more to the point, some volunteers haven't either."

"I'm starting to think you've already made up your mind," Kisty says.

"I've been thinking about this a lot for at least two weeks now," I confirm.

"So *have* you made up your mind?"

"Sadly, I have."

"I want to ask you to reconsider, but I'm not sure it will help."

"Well, actually it might, but to be honest, I don't want you to change my mind."

In every way except one, Utila has been amazing—the people, the diving, the project—but these things are not enough. I came here to work and to achieve. That is just not feeling possible now, and even with all the will in the world, I don't see it changing any time soon. It doesn't feel as if I am giving up, but I feel like I am being honest with myself and acknowledging when something is just not for me. I could stay for the sake of spending time in the ocean, but I came here for much more than that, and to remain would feel like too much of a compromise.

So it is with reluctance and sadness that I leave. I will miss the many amazing, friendly, warm, welcoming, upbeat people. I will miss WSORC, the volunteers, and the interaction I have with them. I thought this was going to be the culmination of all my previous years' work, but sadly it is not. I am confident that something good lies just around the corner, and because I love teaching people to dive, I am also starting to believe I can achieve just as much within a like-minded dive centre as with a dedicated conservation project.

Twelve

Finding Work or Not: June 2015–March 2017

I have a dive instructor position on the Greek island of Kos in the Aegean Sea; I leave Utila with a heavy heart and head home for a few days before proceeding to Greece.

The conditions and facilities at Kos and Kos Divers are perfect; this place has something to offer everyone, novice and expert alike. The dive centre is just a few steps away from an Olympic-sized swimming pool, wonderfully designed to resemble the site of an ancient Greek ruin and essential for those first breaths underwater. The beach dive site is a two minute walk away, and just a few steps from the water is Kos Divers' large bench, perfect to perch on, rest for a minute, and make those last-minute checks before entering the water.

Turkey is easily visible a short distance away, and every day ferry loads of tourists make the short crossing in each direction many times. A little way along the beach to the left is the wind and kite surfing centre, and the ever-present wind provides many hours of topside fun for the wind and water sports enthusiasts.

But for us divers, it is what lies beneath the waves and out of the wind that has brought us here. Immediately off the beach in just four feet of water, you will find a patch of sea grass full of life. Large schools of bream are always in attendance, as are the damsels and wrasse that swim in and out of your hands as you tap two stones together to attract their attention. This spot is perfect for children and for divers' first underwater experience outside the pool. A few feet away from the sea grass and still on the twenty-five-foot-wide sand shelf with a maximum depth of twelve feet is Toilet Reef, a small but interesting artificial reef of porcelain sinks, toilets, and rubber tires put together by Kos Divers. This shallow sand shelf is perfect for those first fin strokes in the ocean. There are easily fifteen species of fish in attendance here at any one time.

From Toilet Reef, a short swim down the sand slope takes you to a depth of around thirty-five feet. Here you will bump into another artificial structure, a shipwreck, also constructed by Kos Divers staff from scaffold poles and rope. Keep a sharp lookout here for nudibranch, scorpion fish, and triggerfish. Leaving the shipwreck behind and following the bottom of the sand slope, you can swim among many Greek statues. Here the keen-eyed will find octopus hiding in holes and tiny gobies tucked into the statues' texture. Swim a little farther and you can glide over fields of sea grass where even larger schools of bream will accompany you. If you are lucky, you will see a large butterfly ray partially buried in the sand or even an eagle ray gliding effortlessly by. The Mediterranean cousin of my favourite fish, the spotted eagle ray, the common eagle ray is also wonderful to see.

As usual it is a hot and sunny day at the dive centre, and we instructors are waiting for our first clients of the afternoon session. Mine will be a young girl of twelve years old joining me for a Discover Scuba Diving experience (DSD). DSDs are exactly that, a chance to discover what diving and the ocean are all about without the need for a full course and lots of training, study, and exams. All you need to do is read a few pages, answer some basic safety questions, and you are ready to take your first supervised breaths under water.

She sits on the side of the pool—let's call her Jane—in the shadow of the mock–ancient Greek architecture, and I help her into the equipment while her father sits nearby snapping photos. As she dangles her legs in the water, anticipation rising, I explain how the equipment works, show the hand signals we will use underwater, and demonstrate the few skills we will need, and she mimics me. Confident she understands everything, I help her into the pool, we put on our masks, put regulators in our mouths, put our faces in the water, and Jane takes her first bubble blowing breaths underwater. After perhaps a minute, I'm sure she is comfortable, so I give the sign to descend to the bottom. The pool session goes exceptionally well. Jane is comfortable and confident in the water, so we swim to the ladder on the far side of the pool, climb out, and take the short walk to the beach.

The wooden runway makes the walk on the fine gray stone beach a little easier to carry our heavy dive equipment. As we tramp along it, we receive many inquiring looks from the sun-seekers bronzing themselves in the Mediterranean heat, a heat that makes us uncomfortably warm in our wetsuits. We reach the Kos Divers bench, make our final checks, put our fins on, and we are ready to go. We look to all like clumsy, disorientated penguins as we reverse our way toward the inviting Aegean Sea, but we don't mind because we will soon be in the water. The small gray pebbles make a satisfying crunching sound under our fins that softens into more of a slosh with every cautious step as the beach yields to the water. A few more steps and we can hear the crunch no more, only the gentle tumbling of stones being pushed and pulled up and down the shore by the tiny ripple of the wave that laps the island's fringes. I keep one hand attached to my student at all times as we descend and then glide over the sea grass bed amid a school of more than a hundred bream. I give the okay sign and a confident okay comes right back. We kneel, and I pick up a pebble, hand it to Jane, and encourage her to tap it against another. Seconds after she does, an ornate wrasse appears and dances between her fingers. She quickly glances at me with a smile. You can just about recognise a smile when one is wearing scuba gear, but perhaps the smile is more in her eyes. We stay for a few minutes until I signal to swim, and I stay in constant contact and control her buoyancy as we swim a lap of the shelf.

We look like clumsy penguins no more but like divers, appearing and feeling weightless suspended in the water column. The bream accompany us in water that is as clean and clear as that of the pool, only here there are fish all around. We settle on our knees at Toilet Reef where at times we are unable to see each other clearly through the sheer numbers of fish that circle all around and between us. All too soon for Jane, I think, our time is up, and we head back to the bench and her waiting father.

"It was amazing!" she squeals with a full and brilliant smile this time. Before Dad can answer, Jane asks, "Can I do it again another day?"

Dad smiles back and says, "Let's see." Then he turns to me and asks, "How did she get on?"

"Very well indeed," I say. "Very comfortable in the water, a great student."

"Okay, well perhaps we'll take another dive in a day or two," Dad says.

"Sure," I say, "just book at the pool like you did before."

"Okay, will do."

"If you do dive again," I say turning to Jane, "we can go a little deeper and for a little longer if you like."

She only smiles and turns to her dad.

Two days later, just before Jane's second DSD, we are studying photographs and indentifying the fish we are most likely to encounter on the dive. I write them on an underwater slate and also bring along an ID slate. She is super keen to know all the fish and all about them and their habits and behaviours. I only wish we had more time. On the dive we spend lots of time at Toilet Reef, and Jane successfully identifies the three species of bream—salema, two-banded, and saddled—and many others besides. We watch as the damsels flit in and out of the safety of the reef, chasing away all those that pass too close to their territories, and I use the signal for "baby" to point out the juveniles with their iridescent blue heads and bodies. The dusky groupers are small here and are now feeding on small mollusks and crustaceans. As they grow, they will rely more and more on fish, and even now one has the posture of a mature adult waiting in ambush as it rests motionless next to a tire.

We see invertebrates too; a stunning nudibranch, its naked gills—hence the name—tiny but clearly visible. The beautiful and fragile-looking feather star is equally mesmerising whether swimming or, in this case, making its way along the bottom. A slightly less fragile fireworm, capable of defending itself by delivering a burning sting, emerges from its refuge under a sink. After twenty minutes, during which I take lots of notes on points to discuss later, we leave Toilet Reef and venture off to explore a little deeper. While still in the shallows on the shelf on our way to deeper water, I give Jane a little more freedom to practice adjusting her own buoyancy before we leave the edge of the slope. We follow the slope down, level off at around thirty feet, and swim effortlessly over gently swaying sea grass beds with a school of salema ever in attendance. After ten minutes, I give the signal to turn and we head back over the sea grass with the slope still in sight but now over our right shoulder toward the statues. I release my hold on Jane's BCD and give her full control of her buoyancy, and she makes the adjustments she needs as we swim above the statues and back up the slope to Toilet Reef and our exit point.

"You know my Advanced Open Water Student?" asks Charlie while we enjoy a cold drink after work. We are on our small but pleasing balcony under a clear sky, one which Charlie, a keen photographer, will later head up the mountains to photograph as the sun sets.

"Yeah, I know him, mate," I answer as I stifle a belch from my Sprite.

"Well he wants to do the fish ID dive," Charlie says.

"Oh yeah?"

"I told him you are a marine biologist and suggested he do that dive with you, if you don't mind?"

"No, of course I don't mind," I say. "Love to, in fact."

"Thought so," he says.

"Okay, we'll talk to Matt tomorrow so he can figure the schedule."

"I guess you would like to be doing more of this stuff, wouldn't you?"

"I would, mate, yeah," I acknowledge.

"This is very different from your last job in the Caribbean."

"It is very—yes, and it was great in many ways, but—you know how that ended," I say.

Charlie shakes his head slightly and releases a low groan.

"Besides, I really enjoy teaching here, it's great isn't it?"

"It is," he says, "it really is. You still want to do more than just teach though, right?"

"Oh yeah, mate, sure, but lots of cool things can be done from within a dive centre."

"For instance?"

"Where do I begin?" I say. "It depends on circumstances, on the location, but lots can be done. More than anything, it depends on willingness, though."

"Willingness?" Charlie is slightly puzzled.

"Well, yeah, I would say all dive operators have a huge opportunity and these days perhaps an obligation to the environment and themselves to offer some form of education and conservation program. Lots do something, but not all," I say.

"To at least look after their own workplace," says Charlie, his eyes widening.

"Exactly, mate. It's too much for some dive centres. But for instance, in a country or region where artisanal fisheries are sustaining the community, outreach projects can be great. First of all, to engage the local community in what you are doing, offer education in schools and jobs and training programs. To help them understand just how important, how fragile and finite their local resource may be and ultimately assist them to manage their fishery and keep it sustainable for generations to come, perhaps with some areas protected or with restricted fishing."

"I see," says Charlie.

"This isn't possible everywhere, I'm not suggesting it is, but offering sessions in schools where children learn all about the reef and its importance is relatively easy and hugely valuable. Taking that a bit further, you could talk more about specific pressures or challenges an area may face, and anyone can organize beach cleanups in places suffering from plastic pollution. It's a great way to engage the locals and tourists alike," I continue. "Or even better for those wanting to get into the water, diving and snorkeling cleanups too."

"Yeah, cleanups are a great idea; I love that," Charlie says enthusiastically. "Education is why you like doing the DSDs and the Bubblemakers with the real young ones?"

"Yeah, that's right, mate, all of them get out of the water having caught at least a little of my enthusiasm and passion," I say.

"They certainly do."

"In the right place, coral restoration projects can be set up as well. Not all ideas are easily initiated from all dive centres, but something certainly can be done. I guess my point is, I am convinced that lots can be accomplished for conservation from within a like-minded dive centre. I firmly believe that education, engagement, and experience can do a hell of a lot to raise awareness of the problems the ocean faces, and in turn change attitudes, outlooks, and behaviours."

"All makes sense to me," Charlie agrees.

The season has passed all too quickly, and now, in late September, things are slowing down. I have had an absolutely wonderful summer with Kos Divers. I have developed as an instructor, taught many courses, and become a Master Scuba Diver Trainer (MSDT). I would like to say there had not been a cloud in the sky for five months, but that wouldn't be exactly true. One morning there were clouds and about thirty seconds of rain before it quickly cleared up again. The only cloud now is the one of having to leave, and it's looming large. But I am also excited about what lies ahead, so it's time to start job hunting again.

Throughout October I am busy with emails and Skype interviews. Then toward the end of October, I apply for a particularly appealing position in the Maldives where dive instructors and marine biologists or ecologists are particularly sought after. I send my CV and a cover letter and am excited to be offered the job without even an interview. All I need to do is send a photograph. Within half an hour, I get a very apologetic email retracting the job offer due to my excessive tattoos. The first step on the road to becoming heavily tattooed was taken as a pick-me-up, but now, thirteen years later the tattoos are having quite the opposite effect. Back in 2002, I never would have thought that a tattoo would keep me from doing anything, but here I am. I had no idea then that I would soon be on a path to becoming a marine ecologist and dive instructor. I wonder if I've been unconsciously sabotaging my chances of living my dream, first criminal record and now tattoos!

"I was offered a job last week, Robin," I say as we sit in our favoured spot outside Costa Coffee in Exeter city centre. It's nicer in the summer but even now it is still pleasant enough in shorts.

"You don't sound happy about it; what's the problem?"

Robin is one of many people over the years who came to Exeter to study and never left, and we met at the gym in 2001. We often spend afternoons here, preferably in the sun, discussing many topics, serious or not. On this cool October day, as High Street shoppers scurry past, I begin to reflect on a past decision and seek Robin's insight.

"The offer was retracted when I sent a photograph," I explain.

"What?"

"Because of the tattoos," I say in a pained voice. "This is the second time it's happened."

"Bloody hell, that surprises me in this day and age. In fact, they can't *do* that," he protests.

"Of course they can, *they* can do whatever they like. I've already accepted the fact."

"They can't though, it's discrimination," he protests.

"Discrimination or not, ultimately they can do what they like. I don't like it, but I don't blame the resort owners for their policies," I say.

"You don't?"

"I think they are silly and misguided, but if that's what they want or don't want and believe their guests think the same way, then that's their choice. I can't change what they think, can I?"

"Well no, perhaps not, but still, it's not right," Robin insists.

"I'm not happy about it, I'm bloody upset about it. I thought I was going to work in the Maldives, and I was really excited."

"I'll bet you were."

Then Robin asks a serious question. "Do you regret having the tattoos?"

"I'm trying not to think like that," I say. "I'm not sure how healthy it is to think too much about regret."

"That's a good point," says Robin, pondering what I have said. Since the news, I have certainly pondered my decision to become tattooed.

"Tattoos aren't so different anymore are they? They're becoming accepted in society nowadays; they're everywhere."

"Not in the Maldives," I say flippantly.

"Sorry, but you know what I mean. I'm surprised to hear such a thing."

"Yes I do, and they are, but when I was collecting tattoos, it was somewhat of a fringe interest. I didn't start getting tattoos because I wanted to be different. But I guess in respect to tattoos at least, I must have been somewhat different in those days. Yes, I liked how my skin looked adorned with art work, and I enjoyed the process. But I have never felt the need to show off my tattoos. In fact, more and more I go out of my way to cover them up."

"You do, and your point is?"

"Collecting tattoos was a personal process, but nowadays people are becoming heavily tattooed as a way to fulfill some preconceived image or to impress," I suggest.

"Okay, hang on, let's see here."

"Go ahead," I say, intrigued by Robin's thought process.

"I used to think being tattooed was a choice to separate yourself from society in some way, or to make some kind of a statement, or perhaps a desire to stand out, or even to intimidate."

"Yes, good points," I say. "I'm sure many would think that way. So what do you think now?"

"Well, like I said, they're everywhere now, it's no big deal."

"Well here's the crux of it, the more popular they have become and the more accepted, the more I dislike it."

"It?" Robin asks.

"The fact that they are accepted."

"You do?" Robin is puzzled.

"You know I do. What do I say every time we see an idiot wearing a T-shirt in mid-winter to show off his arms when everyone else is freezing?"

Walking around in freezing temperatures displaying tattooed arms seems ridiculous to me, and I'm sure it must be to almost everyone. Some will say we shouldn't care what others think, but tattoos can contribute hugely to someone's first impression of us, and we don't get a second chance at that.

"You at least say he's an idiot, which is putting it mildly. But why, and if you don't regret them, why would you rather cover them up?" he asks.

"The way tattoos are worn today makes me cringe, and that dilutes whatever it was I thought I had. I was never one of the people you mentioned before."

"I'm not suggesting you were."

"I know you're not. But more than that, I didn't get tattoos to flaunt them —"

"And walk around freezing in winter," he cuts in.

"Exactly."

"It sounds like regret to me," says Robin. There is a long silence before he asks, "If I had a magic pill that would make all your tattoos disappear overnight, would you take it?"

"Absolutely."

Like the weight training, collecting tattoos was always a personal endeavor. I appreciate this might sound false, as both have very visual results, but both were only for my own benefit. I never sought the approval of others and I certainly have no desire now to be a part of the contemporary tattoo clan. I still maintain that I don't regret my tattoos, but after refusing all opportunities to do so in the past, perhaps I have just grown up a little.

The conversation with Robin reminds me of another conversation, one Darron and I had years earlier.

"When did we stop training together?" asks Darron.

I know the answer to this question without thinking. Darron and I trained together from 1993 to 2000, and I enjoyed every workout. Like the tattoos, working out had nothing to do with what could be seen on the outside. Looking the way I once did was a side effect. I grew to enjoy working out for its own sake, not just as an opportunity to spend time with Dad. By then it had become something more. The process of getting stronger and gaining muscle was an escape and a way of becoming someone else, someone strong and carefree. When I was in the gym, I was tenacious and absolutely refused to admit defeat or surrender to the weights. I loved and hated them.

"In 2000," I say.

"Bloody hell, was it really that long ago?"

I know that Darron is taken aback by yet another frightening reference to the rapid passage of time. It is 2009 now, shortly after my graduation from Plymouth University. We are sitting in Darron's kitchen on a cold November afternoon, but the sliding door remains open to allow the cat to wander in and out as she pleases. Unlike me, Darron still works out hard and is a big muscular guy. His shoulders particularly make it clear to anyone who meets him that he works out intensely. But his muscular exterior says nothing about the man, the man with an intense passion for music, for art, for interior design, for keeping his home immaculate, and for cats, particularly Ophelia.

"That's when you tore your pec off, right?" says Darron, still trying to accept how long ago it was.

"Yep, that's right," I say. "We worked out from 1993 to 2000, with a couple of gaps."

"Yeah, you've had a couple of skinny breaks," says Darron, erupting into a belly laugh at the same time as I do.

When I lost weight in 1997 and again in 1999, I began working out again as a way to regain a sense of normalcy and self, not because I missed the muscles or felt small or insecure. Unlike many of those around me, I didn't care whether I weighed 175 or 225. I remember a conversation where I said something to the effect that "being big and muscular doesn't define me. I don't need the muscles and I am the same without them." After losing lots of weight again after the pec tear in 2000, I maintained an interest in diet and exercise but never tried to regain the serious muscles or weight of the past.

"How's training going anyway?" I ask.

"Not bad, but I don't really train hard anymore," Darron says.

"Come on, you do, you only know one way to train," I remind him.

"Well, you say that, but I don't train anywhere near as hard as we used to."

"Really? I'm surprised."

"No, nothing like it. No one trained like we did, no one," he says nostalgically.

I remember our workouts well. I could swap mental strength for physical strength and, if only for an hour a day, I could be someone else. When I did squats, for example, I would refuse to quit and refuse to replace the bar on the rack at the end of a set. I would finish every set pinned to the floor with the weight still on my back. Only then would I accept I could truly do no more. There is no doubt I gained huge satisfaction from lifting weights and a great sense of achievement, but I didn't need others to see the results, nor did I seek their approval.

"You know something else?" asks Darron abruptly.

"What's that?"

"I think our workouts may well have been a subtle form of self harm." There is a silence while I digest the suggestion for a few seconds.

"Really?" I say, still taking it in.

"We were punishing ourselves, I'm sure."

While Darron is sure, such a thing has never crossed my mind, but he is making me think. If he's right, it was certainly subconscious, but I remember training so hard that it hurt to move for days, and not being satisfied if it wasn't the case.

"Bloody hell, there might be some truth in that," I have to admit.

Suffice to say, losing out on a job because I am presumed to fit a certain stereotype is a real kick in the teeth. In the intervening years, most recently in late 2017, I would be offered two more jobs in the Maldives, only to have them retracted because of my tattoos.

Undeterred I keep applying elsewhere, and in early December I am offered a job on Lake Malawi. Not my favoured ocean water environment, of course, but to a fish nut like me, it's still an absolute dream destination. Lake Malawi is one of the Rift Valley lakes which also borders on Mozambique and Tanzania. Home to hundreds of species of cichlid fish, the huge lake is an exciting prospect, and I can't wait to get there.

Two days later I receive an email retracting the offer because a previous employee wanted to return. Maybe I am being saved for the ocean. As beautiful as Lake Malawi is and as much as I was looking forward to going, the ocean is where my heart is. Undeterred I continue applying.

A few weeks later, in early January 2016, I learn I am one of the final three applicants for a position with a Fiji shark conservation group. They ask if I can head out within a matter of days if I'm offered the position, and I assure them I can. After hearing nothing after a week, I email to check my status but never get a reply.

In late February, after two rounds of interviews for a position in Mexico, I am sitting at the table with my laptop open when I receive an email with "Dive Instructor Position" in the subject line. This could be one of a handful of pending applications that I have titled in this way, but there is a good chance it's from Mexico. The two interviews went well, and I received positive feedback at the time. It is indeed from Mexico, this could be it, and I'm so excited I'm almost shaking, but I also feel confident.

I read a few short introductory lines before getting to the point, which reads: "You were in the top three, but sadly you weren't the one."

Wow, that hurts. I was feeling good about this one, really good, and now it's gone. I won't be going to Mexico any time soon. But it seems to me it's harder to be in the running and get this close than it is to be rejected at the outset. I appreciate that good things often don't come easy, but finding a position in which I can thrive was never meant to be this difficult. So often I have what is required, do well, and get good feedback from interviews. I have the qualifications, the experience, and—something that is often desired—maturity. But something is clearly missing, the X factor I suppose; the face has to fit the team dynamic. I guess it is not just me who is disappointed; in this case there appears to be at least one other.

As the moon and the sun's gravity pull on the oceans, causing the tides, so the oceans continue to tug on me. Sometimes I even torture myself by taking what I call Google Earth holidays. After typing Tofo into the search bar and hitting enter, it takes me mere seconds to zoom out, spin around the planet, and zoom back in again at Tofo. I sit mesmerized as the computer program works its magic and whisks me away to the other side of the globe. I fantasise about actually being able to transport myself in this way as I zoom in and walk the sand roads while listening to a *Café Africa* CD. I long to see the smiling faces of Tofo's people, to be awakened by chattering children on their way to school, to smell the wood fires burning, to taste freshly made matapa, and to feel Africa's rhythm and the scorching sand beneath my bare feet. Now I wouldn't even run from the hot sand, I would let Africa scorch my soles as it has scorched itself into my soul. Unlike a tattoo that fades in the sun, my love for Africa only gets brighter.

I am feeling discouraged, and bedtime becomes my favourite part of the day. I struggle to find the energy to get up and motivate myself. At times like this, I am frustrated and haunted and wondering about the meaning of life, and I feel that ocean tug most strongly.

The tide must be low this morning, for I can smell the seaweed on the exposed rocks as I approach the beach. I cycle under the low, dark railway arch, straight across the tiny roundabout that in summer controls the endless flow of cars in and out of the huge car park to my left. Continuing straight on past the tacky tourist shops, I accelerate to gain enough momentum for the short sharp rise to the lifeguard's hut which, like all the other facilities today, has been abandoned for the winter. Cycling to Dawlish Warren is my favourite bike ride, a twenty-mile round trip that serves two purposes: an hour's exercise out in the fresh air, and an opportunity to sit by the shore and smell the ocean. If it weren't so cold, I could feel it as well.

Sitting on the seawall that prevents the ever-shifting sands of the Warren, as it is known locally, from shifting into the car park, and preserving the dunes behind, I can now not only smell the sea but see it too. It is flat and calm today with barely a hint of white water, the shallow pale green barely managing to lap at the end of the high and dry protective groynes that line the beach. The sun is low and bright and directly in my eyes. I remove my sunglasses for a moment and have to squint. When my eyes are open again, I gaze longingly out to sea, dream of what is over the horizon, and begin to question my dream.

I have been doing everything I could to reach my goal since those first tentative steps over Exeter College's threshold in 2005. It is now 2016, and I graduated for the second time almost five years ago. What have I been doing wrong? Did I give up too easily when I left Utila? As despondent as I was, should I have stayed and fought for my position and, as Kisty urged, waited it out? I would give anything to be there right now. I love diving, I love the ocean and am passionate about its conservation, but I realise the true prize I have been seeking is, depending on your point of view, something much larger or much smaller than I had thought. What I have been seeking all these years is simply contentment, fulfillment, and a sense of value. That's all any of this was ever really about. Some are easily contented, but others, perhaps myself among them, are not and struggle to find their place in the world. I have been seeking it where I believed I had the best chance of finding it, somewhere I have been comfortable giving and receiving love: in the ocean.

Here I am beside the ocean, which seems very near and yet very far away. I certainly feel relaxed near the ocean, but here it also reminds me that I don't really have it. I belong to a tropical species, of that there is no doubt. While I haven't found contentment, at least I know what I am looking for.

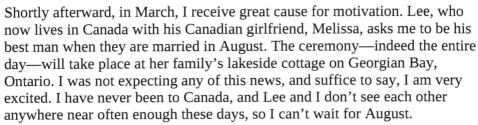

Shortly afterward, in March, I receive great cause for motivation. Lee, who now lives in Canada with his Canadian girlfriend, Melissa, asks me to be his best man when they are married in August. The ceremony—indeed the entire day—will take place at her family's lakeside cottage on Georgian Bay, Ontario. I was not expecting any of this news, and suffice to say, I am very excited. I have never been to Canada, and Lee and I don't see each other anywhere near often enough these days, so I can't wait for August.

Two weeks later, as Lee and I are chatting over Skype, he says, "Why don't you come to Canada for the summer, man."

"For the summer?"

"Yeah, it warms up toward the end of May, so come over any time and stay until after the wedding," he says warmly.

"Oh wow, I would love to, it sounds amazing," I say with great enthusiasm.

"Okay, do it then."

"Are you sure the Stinsons won't mind having a house guest all summer?" I ask, still afraid to get too excited about it.

"Yeah, it's fine, get over here, man," Lee says. "It will do you good."

"Yes it will, dude, it will." I am over the moon, I'm so elated.

"So are you coming then?"

"Yes, okay, I'm coming."

"Cool, man, we'll have a great summer. You'll like it here, it's very nice this side."

"I'm sure I will. Say thanks to the Stinsons, I can't wait, I'm excited already. I'll look at flights for the end of May, shall I?"

"Yes, do it," says Lee as if giving a command. At last I have something to look forward to and to be excited about.

I almost can't believe it, but two weeks later I receive an email from Kostas at Kos Divers inviting me back for the approaching season. I would love to go back; I learned so much and had a great time in 2015. But I have no intention of missing the wedding, or missing the chance to visit Lee and Melissa and meeting her family. So I have to decline, and we agree to talk again when the 2017 season comes around.

Thirteen

Bicycles: Spring 2017

The foam roller I have purchased won't quite fit in my rucksack, so after a quick test ride, I decide I can make the short bike ride home while carrying it at my side. It is a dry, bright, warm spring morning when I exit the roundabout just a minute into the short ride, and in only one month it will be springtime in Kos. I will be working at Kos Divers from the very first day of the season, and I can't wait.

Suddenly there is a jolt, and the front wheel turns violently to the right. I don't have the time or the ability to make a correction—the oversized foam roller has somehow interfered with the steering or become trapped behind the front wheel, I don't know. But either way, I am going over the handlebars. The hard black tarmac stings my hands as they slap and break my fall, but suddenly I forget the sting as focus shifts to my right leg. When I try to stand, I tumble straight back to the tarmac. I lie prone and propped up on my rucksack, gritting my teeth and furiously rubbing my leg and knee in what will prove a futile attempt at easing the discomfort.

"Are you all right, mate?" asks a concerned voice beside me.

"Yes," I reply. "I just need a minute," I say while frantically rubbing.

"You can't stay there," the stranger says as he offers a hand.

"Okay, okay," I say, taking the kindly hand.

No sooner do I attempt to rise again when the discomfort subsides and is quickly replaced by excruciating pain. I am no stranger to pain. I have torn muscles and tendons and dislocated shoulders, all of which are horribly uncomfortable, but this is off the chart. I release my grip and fall back to the relative comfort of the tarmac, resting on my well-placed rucksack.

"No, no, leave me alone," I moan. "Please." I am huffing and puffing and wheezing now like someone deprived of oxygen, and my head is swimming.

"Come on, mate, we have to get you out of the road," says a calm second voice behind me.

"No, no, I can't get up," I reply as I shake my swimming head.

"You can't stay in the road," says the second man as he moves around in front of me. "Come on, we do need to get you up and out of the road."

He extends his arms, and I reluctantly take them. As I am lifted to my feet, the pain reaches a new level and I almost can't cope. Not only is my head swimming, but my stomach is churning as the pain takes over my entire being.

"I'm glad I was going slowly," says the second helper as they lower me to the pavement. "Look," he says, as he points over my right shoulder.

I turn my head just as the first man approaches my bicycle, which lies barely six feet in front of a car bumper.

"I really thought I was going to drive over you," he says, looking shocked and relieved at the same time. "Right, let's get you an ambulance."

I direct him to my phone in the front pocket of my rucksack and say, "Call Graeme for me please, he's a two-minute drive away."

"Are you sure?"

"Yes, he'll be here in two minutes," I manage to say through gritted teeth from my prone but much safer position on the side of the road. I haven't accepted that I need an ambulance; I need help, yes, but I'll soon be fine.

"What the hell have you done now?" asks Graeme, remembering my handful of previous accidents.

"I don't know," I say in my agitated state.

I thought being moved from the road to the pavement was as painful as it could get, but being lifted into the Range Rover is even worse, and I struggle to hold myself together. Passing out would have been a relief, but it doesn't happen. Graeme straps me in and then wrestles my bicycle into the back of the Jeep while I sit there in a bewildered haze of pain.

Just two minutes later we arrive at A and E: Accident and Emergency. Now I have to get out of the vehicle. Graeme runs through the doors and promptly returns with a wheelchair. Despite my agony, I'm put off by the prospect, but as soon as my right leg is lifted from the foot well of the car and my leg is supporting its own weight, my pain is once again off the chart. I can barely utter a word at the check-in desk. Graeme speaks for me as I slump in the wheelchair feeling sick and dizzy and overcome with pain.

I move fairly quickly through the system and advance from triage directly to X-ray. When they try to move me from the wheelchair to the X-ray table, I can't cope and protest with stifled screams. One of the nurses slips out and returns with two more to help make my transition from chair to table a slightly smoother and less painful one. While I'm waiting for the X-ray results, I eventually receive three doses of the painkiller Oramorph, and shortly after the third dose, my pain subsides to a manageable level three. Meanwhile I feel as if I am both asleep and awake, my head detached from my body and looking at myself from afar. The X-ray shows no damage to the bone, and with my head now in the clouds, I am sent home on crutches with instructions to return the following day for an MRI.

The day after my MRI, the consultant informs me I have severed the quadriceps tendon and separated it from the knee, taking the quadriceps muscles with it, muscles that have retracted and now reside bunched high up my leg as if in a pocket.

Surgery goes well, but my recovery is very slow. After a week, I realise I have no chance of being ready to go to Kos in April. Kostas is well aware I prefer the more far-flung locations, but Kos has been my only job offer since my return home from Canada last autumn, and I was looking forward to going back. Reluctantly and with much sadness, I email Kostas once more to say I won't be coming to Kos.

After having my stitches out, my physiotherapy begins. Initially I am simply supposed to tense the thigh muscles and, sitting with my legs straight up on the sofa, simply lift my leg. To begin with, the muscles are nonresponsive, and it takes ten weeks before I get even a glimmer of movement. Attempting to tense and lift with all my might and getting no response whatsoever is frustrating and frightening. Eventually the remnants of my thigh muscles start to slowly and pathetically vibrate, but definitely not tense. My thigh has wasted to almost the same size as my forearm.

At twelve or thirteen weeks, I add therapy bands, incredibly difficult as I can still barely move my leg. Also as part of the physiotherapy, I am walking every day, though with the aid of a brace and crutches. I try to walk faster in an attempt to force the thigh muscles to respond more quickly, but my leg regularly gives out as it struggles to catch up with what I need it to do. In late June, Lee once again provides motivation for recovery by inviting me to return to Canada as soon as I feel I am fit and strong enough.

By late July, I nervously dispense with the crutches and am using only the brace. My leg is still terribly weak, and I don't trust it at all, but if it is to get stronger, the crutches have to go. Over the course of the next two weeks, my leg begins to improve, though it is far from reliable. But at this time, and with much encouragement from Lee, I book a flight to Canada and will leave in two weeks.

Walking up and down the sand slope between the beach and the cottage at Georgian Bay proves great for rehabilitation, strengthening, and much-needed confidence. Then, after being in Canada for a week, I take what feels like a huge step and remove the brace.

Walking on the sand and up the slope is harder both mentally and physically without the brace. I am aware I have come to rely on the brace and feel vulnerable and much weaker without it, but if I am to get stronger, then I must push. The next step is to go for a dive in the lake. I feel certain that once I am in the water and neutrally buoyant, I will be fine. The challenge will be managing the heavy dive equipment.

Lee carries all my gear down the slope and into the water, where I put it on as I float. Easy. As I suspected, swimming is no problem and feels like good resistance exercise pushing against the broad flat fins. Afterward my leg aches more than it normally does, but it feels like a good ache, so I do it again.

After a few days, I tackle the sand slope carrying a scuba tank. I'm wobbly and apprehensive as my feeble, unstable leg barely responds in time to support each new step, but I manage it without incident.

A week later, after slowly building up, I am ready to tackle the walk down the slope while wearing all my dive gear, heavy weight belt included. Like the beach, the view out across the lake could easily be mistaken for a tropical one. The water is clean and clear and a surprisingly warm seventy-five degrees. A light breeze blows onshore, just enough for the windsurfers and small sailing yachts farther out in the bay to make some headway. Everything is still and quiet on the beach. I hear the occasional low purr of a small outboard, but more often a kayak or paddle boarder will leisurely pass by without making a sound. I stand up, inhale deeply and deliberately, and take my first step wearing all my heavy dive gear. The slope is gradual at first, and I walk slower than Nan used to walk. If Olive, my dear departed Nan, could see me now, she would follow me every step of the way with encouraging words. As the slope gets steeper, I feel the delay in the muscles' reaction and concentrate hard on each step. Chipmunks taunt me as they scamper around a tree with great speed and agility, both of which I lack. I reach the bottom of the slope and walk onto the flat sand with a sigh of relief. I'm beginning to feel like a diver again.

With confidence in my leg now growing every day, I begin applying for jobs once more.

Unlike the recent past, things start to happen quickly. I have a Skype interview and email exchange for a position in the Cook Islands with a September start date, which is very exciting and perfect timing. I am not quite offered the position but receive an email asking if I am available immediately, as a staff member has left unexpectedly. I don't feel comfortable leaving Canada right after arriving, and my leg still needs more rehab time, so I reluctantly reply that I'm unavailable until September. Shortly afterwards, I have an interview with a dive centre in the very exotic and exciting dive destination of Timor Leste. Things are going well, and I have already looked a little more into it including flights, the cheapest of which is £1900. I am offered the position but feel I have to decline this one too.

It's late August now, the temperature outside is rapidly approaching eighty-five degrees but it is a cool seventy in the house, and the smell of late morning coffee fills the kitchen along with the fresh golden rays of the sun.

"Dude," I call to Lee, "when do you want to head out to Pita Pit for lunch?"

"No rush," he replies. "Why, you hungry already?" He sounds surprised, knowing my usual eating habits.

"Ha!" I snigger. "No, there are a couple of good jobs on the PADI site; I want to get my CV and cover letter in straightaway, that's all."

"Carry on, dude," he says approvingly.

I modify my cover letter slightly to relate to the specifics of the job and send it, along with my CV, to Chris Davies at Octopus Divers on the Caribbean island of Saint Martin.

"How you getting on?" asks Lee.

"Just want to send off one more application, and then we'll head out if you like," I say.

I am partway through the next application when I receive an email:

Hey Mark,
It's a small world as I'm from Plymouth.
I'd be interested talking to you today on the phone.
WhatsApp works for me.
I'm on the boat now and back in an hour.
Chat soon?

Wow, I've received a few quick responses before, but this is the quickest by far. I can't believe it, this is really exciting.

"Dooooood, I have an interview Dooooood," I call to Lee in the manner in which we address each other when we're excited about something.

"Nice, who with?" he asks enthusiastically.

"The job I just applied for," I say in mock nonchalance and a shrug. Actually, I'm thrilled.

He laughs. "He's on it, that's incredible."

"Interview's in an hour," I add.

"Nice one, man, where is it?"

Lee will love this. When he worked on Sint Eustatius, affectionately known as Statia, he had to fly through Saint Martin and didn't like the airport landing at all.

"Wait for it, dude. Saint Martin, your favourite airport," I say with glee.

"Oh bloody hell, is it?" Lee pulls a face.

"When were you working on Statia?" I ask, thinking about how he met his wife, Melissa, there.

"In 2008."

"Wow, time flies. I'm just going to do a bit of research and be ready to talk to Chris in an hour."

"Cool, I'll go for a run and see you in a bit. Good luck, dude."

Like others of the past, the call soon turns into more of a chat than a formal job interview. I explain that I am still recovering from knee surgery, and while my leg remains in a weakened state, I am functional now and able to dive and manage my equipment.

After we've talked for about a half hour, Chris abruptly asks, "Do you want the job then?"

I am taken aback, but do not hesitate to say, "Yes please."

"When can you get here?" Chris asks. "I need someone ASAP."

I really can't think straight, I am so excited. I am supposed to be here in Canada for another two weeks yet. So on the spot and with no real time to think I say, "I need to go to the UK and grab all my dive gear, so is eight or nine days okay?"

"Sure, just send me a copy of your flight details as soon as you've booked and I'll be at the airport to pick you up."

"Okay, great. I'll let you know as soon as I have a flight, in a day or so."

I can't believe how easy this was. After such a long time with no job offers, I'm finally back in the game.

"Okay, great, speak to you soon," Chris says casually.

"Okay, thanks and look forward to seeing you," I say as we both hang up.

I hear Lee returning from his run, and I jump from my seat yelling, "I have the job, dude, I'm off to El Caribe."

Lee appears from the adjoining room beaming. "Nice one, when do you start?" I am elated that, after far too long and so many disappointments, letdowns, and accidents, I am finally getting back out into the world of diving where I belong.

"Eight or nine days from now," I say.

"Nice, Pita Pit to celebrate?"

"Let's go."

Fourteen

Saint Martin: September 2017

I leave London Gatwick's South Terminal at ten thirty and, seven and a half hours later at two o'clock local time, I land at VC Bird International Airport, Antigua. After a two and a half hour wait, during which I am asked if I am in the movies by the guy at the check-in desk—whatever was he thinking?—I am on my way to Saint Martin.

I arrive into Princess Juliana International Airport at 17.20 on an island shared by two nations and bearing two names, Sint Maarten and Saint Martin. Sint Maarten, on the south side, has been an independent country since 2010 within the Kingdom of the Netherlands and is not considered European territory. The northern two-thirds of the island is Saint Martin, one of the departments of France, and technically a part of Europe and the EU. The island is separated from the British territory of Anguilla four miles to the north by the Anguilla Channel. It is approximately nine miles from east to west and eight miles from north to south, the total land area being around thirty-four square miles and the smaller Dutch side being the more heavily populated. The two island nations affectionately refer to the island as SXM, the international airport's code name, or by its nickname, the Friendly Island. Both sides of the island have mountainous peaks but no rivers. The highest peak, Pic Paradis on the French side, rises 1390 feet into the Caribbean sky.

SXM is world famous for its dramatic and spectacular takeoffs and landings, and many tourists flock to Maho Beach to feel the jet blast and witness the spectacle of Boeing 747s and Airbus A340s skimming only feet above the beach before touching down on the tarmac moments later. Unfortunately, as I arrived from Antigua on a much smaller craft, I missed the opportunity of a window seat view of this dramatic landing over sea, beach, and road to the landing strip.

A warning on the fencing surrounding the airport reads: JET BLAST OF DEPARTING AND ARRIVING AIRCRAFT CAN CAUSE SEVERE PHYSICAL HARM RESULTING IN EXTREME BODILY HARM AND/OR DEATH. The signs do nothing to deter thrill seekers from clinging to the fence during takeoffs where they get blasted from the engines, nor those on the beach who get a free sand blast exfoliation treatment while their belongings are scattered into the sea.

It is a warm and sunny Wednesday evening when I arrive, and Chris is at the airport to meet me. He greets me with a warm handshake and grabs the larger of my two bags. We walk across the car park and sling the bags into the back of Chris's bright white new Toyota Hilux truck. The sound of my bags slapping the floor of the truck with a *whump* reminds me that I am where I am meant to be, just like the fly screens in place of glass windows, and not wearing shoes, and an open-back truck. All is well in my world.

During the twenty-minute drive to the dive centre in the town of Grand Case on the French side, I get my first opportunity to see a little of the island. The passage from the Dutch to the French side is seamless. There is no obvious boundary between the two, and only the very keen-eyed would notice the discreet signs and monuments that delineate the border between the two territories.

Chris stops the truck on the main road that is barely wide enough for two cars to pass and points to a narrow street to my left. "Here you go, this is your spot," he says. "You'll see Les Alizes apartments just down the alley on the right. I've booked you in, and Mr. Hodge, the owner, is expecting you."

I jump out quickly, grab my bags from the back, and return to the passenger side window where I lean in and say a quick, "Thanks, mate. I'll drop my bags and see you at the dive centre shortly. Where exactly is it again?"

"Straight ahead, three-minute walk."

"Okay, cool, see you in about ten minutes," I say and tap the roof of the truck with the palm of my hand.

As Chris pulls away and I head toward the alley with my bags, I realise there was no need to rush. There still isn't another car in sight.

My bags are heavy, and I struggle with them despite the short walk down the alley between private residences on the left and an apartment block on the right. My dive gear bag particularly is far too heavy and causes me to limp on my still recovering right leg; I really need a bag with wheels. I find the entrance to Les Alizes just past the apartment block and, as I had hoped, it is an oceanfront property. I am happy to see a tiled floor inside and gladly drag the heavy dive gear bag to the office where I am met by Mr. Hodge. He is an accommodating, elderly Saint Martiner who also happens to be a reverend. He shows me to my ground floor, oceanfront apartment which has a balcony and, of course, a view.

"This is your room, number four," he says with a hint of pride.

"Thank you," I reply with a smile.

"I have had friends of Chris here before, so if you want to stay long term, we can talk about a deal."

"Okay, great, can we talk about that later?"

"Sure we can." He gives me another big smile.

It is a small but functional open floor plan apartment with a large firm bed, adequate kitchenette, en suite shower and bathroom, and air conditioning that Mr. Hodge has turned on in anticipation of my arrival. I drop my bags in the room, switch off the air conditioner, and head straight back out to the balcony where I sit and take it all in.

There are no real beaches in this part of Grand Case, but the water laps the building just a few feet below me and looks to be about three feet deep. All along the front I see the same: buildings essentially form a seawall with occasional gaps between them affording access straight into the clean, clear warm Caribbean Sea. Only a short time ago, I would have gazed at such a tranquil, idyllic picture longingly, but now I am here. The brilliant white boats moored in the bay do not appear to even be moving, and there is barely a sound from the water lapping against the wall directly below me and offering a calming reassurance, like a gentle touch from a friend.

I reluctantly leave my balcony and head out to meet Chris.

It's a three-minute walk to the dive centre, and only the Grand Case Beach Club, nestled in the corner of the bay, lies beyond it. Grand Case is a small, typical Creole town with a single main street which has many oceanfront restaurants and bars that bustle with life. Walking barefoot along that tarred road without the shackles that are shoes, I feel light and am almost floating. My feet have blistered before on tarred roads, and they will blister again; shoes are way behind me now. I have not even brought any with me, and until my feet toughen up, I wear those blisters as a reminder that I am free and where I'm supposed to be. Even flip-flops slow me down here, and although I have them, they won't see daylight for a long time. I get to the corner where the road heads inland leading to Grand Case L'Esperance Airport half a mile away just as a plane is coming in to land. Its low rumble and roar as it hits the tarmac momentarily distracts my gaze from the hillside ahead. Scattered with trees large and small and completely decked in green, Saint Martin really is a Caribbean paradise. The hillside is also dotted with occasional properties offering what must be an even better view than mine.

Just one minute later, I arrive at the gates of Octopus Divers where Chris is waiting. He is taller than me, a little over six feet. He is lean but not skinny, with a full head of hair, and I'm guessing he's six or seven years younger than I.

"So this is it then," I say, "Octopus Divers, Grand Case branch."

"Yep, this is it, our little piece of paradise," he says proudly.

"Do you live on site?" I ask. "Looks like a house there."

"Yes that's right, no commute for me," Chris says with a smile.

"Perfect, mine is about three minutes," I say in mock protest.

"You'll get used to it."

"I'm sure I will," I say, and I mean it. Even at this ridiculously early stage, I feel very welcome here.

"I'll save showing you around until tomorrow. You must be hungry."

"I am actually, yeah, thanks," I confirm.

"There is a really nice French pizza place about five minutes away, fancy that?"

With a rumble in my stomach I answer, "Sounds good to me."

We order our food and chat casually in the relative cool of the early evening while we wait for our meals. Chris suggests not talking too much about the job, as there will be plenty of time for this. So instead we spend an hour chatting like two old friends. Chris, though originally from Plymouth, just an hour from my home town of Exeter, rarely visits the UK these days and has essentially left it long behind him. While he doesn't appear to have picked up a French accent from the locals, he has for the most part lost his Devonshire one. Chris is an engineer and, unlike me, he loves compressors and outboard motors. Along with all his personal dive equipment, he prides himself on keeping it all in perfect working order. I sense from this that he likes everything in order in respect to work and his work force. This suits me, as I don't like ambiguity. He makes it clear he is busy working between the two dive centres here on Saint Martin and other projects as well, and will soon expect me to be self sufficient and make decisions in his absence. He also expects his staff to treat all equipment as carefully as he does, and dive safety is at the top of his list. We are on the same page here; above all I always strive for a safe, comfortable, stress-free dive environment for new and seasoned divers alike. I am sure I will get on and work well with Chris; he strikes me as an open, honest, and trusting person who gives and expects a lot.

"Do you want to work tomorrow, or do you need time to settle in?" asks Chris with a slight shrug as he drops me off on the corner.

"I'm ready to work, for sure; I can't wait to get started."

"Okay, great, see you at the dive centre in the morning, at seven?"

"Perfect, see you at seven." I'm positively beaming. "I can't wait."

I don't ask what I will be doing tomorrow, I'll find out in the morning. We have established that I need a good recap on skippering the boat; it has been a while for me, so maybe we'll start there, we'll see. It is only eight thirty, but I set an alarm for six, climb straight into bed, and fall asleep.

At ten to seven I leave my room and set out on a warm and sunny Caribbean morning. Even at this early hour, many are out and about, and I am greeted with many a "good morning." I arrive with a smile at the dive centre shortly before seven and am met once again by Chris at the front gate.

He gestures for me to come in and says, as he turns to walk briskly away, "Follow me and I'll introduce you to the other two."

It's not yet seven and the other two are here already. I thought I was keen. I like being early and on time, and it seems as if the others do too. Great, it feels like we're all on the same page.

"This is Chris, and this is Jenn," he says.

I lean in and shake Chris by the hand, "Good morning, nice to meet you."

"You too, welcome to Saint Martin," he says with a warm smile.

"Chris works in the dive shop and on the boat, and the two of you will soon be working together a lot," says Chris.

"Okay, great," I say with a smile. "Nice to meet you too mate." I take Jenn's proffered hand.

"Hello, welcome," she says a little shyly.

"Thank you, how are you?" I ask.

"I'm good, thanks."

"Great, how long have you been here?"

"Three weeks," she says almost proudly, and she sounds and looks settled in already.

"Oh not too long then. You're waiting for your divemaster training, is that right?"

"Yeah, I am," she says with a broad grin, "and I can't wait."

"Chris mentioned it when I spoke to him last week. You'll soon be well under way now," I say confidently.

Chris interrupts to say, "See you guys in a few minutes, I'll just show Mark around."

"See you in a bit," I say cheerfully to Chris and to Jenn as I turn to follow Chris while thinking how excited I am to be training and mentoring my first divemaster.

Octopus Divers occupies a large seafront lot with ample parking behind its large gate. Alongside the gate is a wide, open entrance that leads directly into the dive shop where you will normally find, let's call him, local Chris waiting to greet the day's divers, dealing with telephone and walk-in enquiries, and taking bookings. The shop sells a large range of souvenir T-shirts and some dive and snorkel equipment. Its oversized refrigerator is stocked full of cold drinks and a selection of snacks including chocolate and cereal bars. Directly behind the shop is a small shipping container that has been modified to function as a service workshop for all the dive equipment. It has been fitted with large windows, plenty of shelves, and a large work surface. On the outside, the wooden cladding hides its origins, and it is in exact keeping with the rustic nature of the dive shop. There are three shipping containers in all, all cleverly disguised with the same wooden cladding. The rear door of the dive shop leads customers neatly into the dive centre grounds; a modest path is bordered on the right by a low wooden fence that separates the dive centre from Chris's house and garden. The path leads you past the second container, which is full of all kinds of spare dive equipment, many power tools, and household and garden tools of every imaginable type.

Beside the second container is a wooden building where all the snorkel gear is kept and where the staff store their dive equipment.

"Take a look at this," says Chris, looking pleased as punch with himself as he opens the door to the third container.

I am intrigued and ask, "What do you have hiding in here then?"

"It's the compressor room," says Chris with a smile.

Compressor rooms are the least exciting element of diving for me, so as the door swings open wide, I struggle to summon some enthusiasm.

"It's fully insulated, really well ventilated, and can barely be heard from outside," Chris continues with arms outstretched as if revealing something amazing. Being insulated is great for anyone normally within earshot, but it's still a horribly noisy and oppressive environment for the person filling the tanks, and I'm still not overly enthused, until I notice something unique.

"Oh wow," I say as I see the fill hoses exiting through the back of the container. "This is more like it, great."

Normally scuba tanks are filled directly beside the compressor, where the filler must remain to monitor the tanks as they fill. Even with ear protection against the racket, filling tanks is an essential but very unpleasant chore.

"I'll show you where the tanks are filled."

The extra long hoses leave the back of the container, and we follow them out the way we came in, turn to our left, walk a few paces, and then up two wooden steps to a decking area. From here I can see the hoses running neatly along the top of the wall that forms the boundary to the neighboring property. The decking area has plenty of shaded bench seats, and built on top of the decking that backs onto the container is the all-wood dive equipment room. One side of this is simply a screen that allows gear to be hung up to dry inside, out of damaging direct sunlight but with the benefit of a drying breeze. We walk across the decking and down two more steps, and just beyond sit all the tanks on a concrete platform under the shade of one of the many large trees on the property. Here dive tanks can be filled in comfort and with a view out over the bay.

The steps from the decking also mark the end of the fence and the separation between the two areas of the property. Now we are in the spacious seafront garden with a coconut palm and large shade trees. In the garden and directly opposite the compressor room is Chris's house. It is typical of many in the Caribbean, a single story with single-skin concrete block walls and a roof consisting of sheets of plywood covered with corrugated zinc. The rear of the house has a wooden extension, half of which is Chris's office and the other half an open decking area facing the ocean. From the tank-filling platform, it is just ten paces to the seawall and then a walk down half a dozen steps that, depending on the minimal tide, will lead you either straight into ankle-deep water or onto a narrow strip of sand where the dive boat *Octopussy* awaits you just off the beach.

"What's going on today, Chris, and what do you need me to do?" I ask in anticipation as we walk back to Jenn and local Chris.

"We have three French certified divers this morning doing a two-tank trip. You can lead the dives, Jenn will monitor the group from the back, and I'll skipper the boat," he says as he bounces his cell phone up and down in his hand.

I am happy to do this, but I want to give the divers the best experience, and I'm not sure I will be able to deliver without knowing the dive sites.

"Shouldn't I learn the sites first? I'd hate to be the one to make us look bad, especially today," I say.

"It's no problem, the sites are easy," Chris assures me. "I'll give the briefing and include everything you need to know too, while trying not to make it obvious it's your first day."

"Okay, cool."

By the time the guests arrive at eight o'clock, we are all prepped and ready. Local Chris greets the divers and introduces everyone, while neglecting to mention it is their dive guide's first day. He leads the guests through the garden to the steps at the concrete seawall. Already the sun is working its magic, and I intermittently feel it warming my back through my rash vest as I move in and out of the shade of the ample trees. At the bottom of the steps this morning there is barely an eight- to ten-foot strip of compacted wet sand before reaching the water's edge. Twenty-one years ago at Kennack Sands in Cornwall, my oversized beach towel lay on similar sand. There's no need for towels here, as the water is at least eighty degrees, and the sun will dry you quicker than any towel, damp or otherwise.

As we make our way to the dive site, Jenn and I set up our own dive equipment and that of the guests while chatting and getting to know one other.

"How long have you been diving?" she asks with a hint of envy in anticipation of my reply.

"Since 1998, but it's not as great as it sounds. Unfortunately, I've have not been diving consistently."

"How many dives have you done?"

"Just about five hundred," I reply while thinking being here and diving regularly, I should soon reach a thousand.

"I've not been diving very long, but I love it," Jenn says beaming. "I really, really want to be a divemaster."

"Well you're in the right place, and you soon will be," I say cheerfully.

Jenn sounds a little dejected as she adds, "I've not been diving long, and I've made a few mistakes."

This strikes me as a very open and honest thing to say to someone you have just met. Perhaps like me, Jenn is someone who needs time to become confident in her own ability. This is a strength in itself, in my eyes.

"Don't worry about that. Making mistakes is fine now, it's a part of learning," I say, hoping to offer some reassurance.

"I don't just want to be a divemaster, I want to be a good one," she says.

"Are you comfortable and confident in the water?"

"Yes, I am," Jenn answers with more confidence this time.

"Well fine, everything else will fall into place, and I'm sure you will soon be the divemaster you want to be. I'll make sure you learn everything you need to."

Jenn is very likeable, and I'm sure everyone she works with will find her so. As a divemaster it is important that divers look up to you both as a person and as a professional. With time and growing confidence, I'm sure that will be the case with Jenn.

"How long are you planning to be in Saint Martin?" I ask, with her divemaster internship in mind.

"About five months."

"Perfect, that's a good amount of time. You will have learned all you need to know in that time. Don't worry about anything; you'll soon be well on your way."

We will be diving on the wreck of a small tugboat measuring about fifty feet in length that was intentionally sunk about fifteen years ago. I listen particularly carefully to Chris's dive briefing while doing my best to look and sound as if I have been on St Martin longer than fifteen hours. I think I get away with it, as none of the guests seem suspicious of my distinct lack of experience on the island. We all kit up, check our gear, and descend into the blue for my first dive on Saint Martin.

No sooner is my face in the water than I can see the tug boat around fifty feet below me. During its time under water, it has become well covered in coral and has attracted plenty of colourful reef fish. After doing a couple of laps of the tug, I rise to the wheelhouse where I find a large turtle quietly resting. After a few minutes, following Chris's briefing, I swim the eighty or so feet out across the sand and find the reef wall rising from the sandy bottom. As soon as we reach the wall we drift with the gentle current and see two more turtles, plenty of reef fish, and lots of healthy coral. As we drift, I slowly ascend until after a total time of forty-five minutes, we are in shallow water on top of the wall. We ascend to around fifteen feet and make our three-minute safety stop, and I send up a marker buoy to alert Chris we will soon be at the surface.

At the surface, we find Chris and *Octopussy* just a hundred feet away. I have surfaced where he expected me to. After less than twenty-four hours on the island, I feel settled in already. As Chris said, this certainly isn't difficult, and I feel as comfortable and confident and as ever, despite a long break from guiding.

The second site is Japanese Garden; this time the boat will remain on the mooring so I have to make sure I get us back to it. No pressure then. We make our way down the mooring line and find it attached to a huge concrete block in thirty feet of water. I follow a sand groove into deeper water where, unlike on the previous dive, I now have options in terms of depth and direction. I follow the reef down to about fifty feet and then decide to turn left and follow the reef.

We see a large stingray, a blacktip reef shark, plenty of reef fish, and again an abundance of healthy coral. I successfully lead us back to the concrete block and can see our boat waiting for us above.

Back on the boat, Jenn quietly announces, "I can't believe we got back to the boat. I'm amazed, how did you do that?"

"Thanks," I chuckle.

"I've been here a few times, and I didn't know where we were," she admits.

"Well, it's quite easy when you know how," I say. "I'll tell you later."

"So how did you do it then," Jenn asks once the guests have left.

"Ahh, the navigation?"

"Yes, come on, tell me. I'm sure you didn't use a compass."

"You're right, I didn't. A compass is useful and an essential part of your kit, but you don't always need to use it."

"You don't?" she sounds surprised.

"No, other techniques are much more useful sometimes," I say. "Different techniques and combinations will work better in different places and situations."

"So, what did you do at Japanese Gardens?"

"I used depth and time, that's all," I say.

"Depth and time," Jenn repeats, sounding a bit puzzled.

"Okay, so how much water was the mooring block in?"

"I don't know."

"It was thirty feet," I say.

"Sounds about right."

"Okay, so that's the first thing, I needed to know the depth of our entry and exit point," I explain.

"Okay."

"Then I found the sand groove."

"Yes, I do know that part."

"Then I followed it until I decided to stop. I stopped at fifty feet and decided to turn left," I explain as Jenn listens intently now.

"So when I turned left, I checked the dive time and remembered it," I explain.

"Right."

"It took about four minutes."

"Okay."

"Then I just made sure I followed the fifty-foot contour until we were at the mid-point of the dive."

"How did you decide that?"

"When the first person reached half a tank of air," I say.

"Ahh, yes, yes," Jenn says.

"Then, I checked the dive time again and figured out how long we'd been following the fifty-foot contour, twenty minutes. Then turned left again and kept swimming at the same pace, which for me is slowly, until we were back up to thirty feet. Then turned left again and kept swimming for around twenty minutes. When the time got close, I knew to start looking for the mooring block, and then we bumped right into it."

"We did, it was brilliant," she says.

"You have to remember to keep the same pace for the time to work accurately, which is easy for me—super slow—and to consider any stops you might make. You need to remember to figure the time and distance you swim to fit with your total planned dive time, and remember dive time works in conjunction with air consumption. If you have a dive time as your turnaround signal but someone reaches half a tank before that time, then that's when you turn regardless."

"Yes."

"You might not do it exactly like this on every dive, it will be situational, but this worked well for the site today. You try it next time," I suggest.

"Yes." She beams.

I am glad to be Jenn's mentor and am looking forward to helping her become the divemaster she so wants to be.

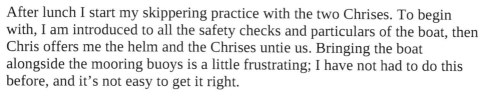

After lunch I start my skippering practice with the two Chrises. To begin with, I am introduced to all the safety checks and particulars of the boat, then Chris offers me the helm and the Chrises untie us. Bringing the boat alongside the mooring buoys is a little frustrating; I have not had to do this before, and it's not easy to get it right.

"Long, slow lazy turns," repeats Chris throughout the session as I make my approach to different buoys. At times on dive boats, I have witnessed frantic activity when the time comes to pick up a mooring, but Chris stresses the importance of slowing down and getting it right the first time.

Considering it has been a while, driving the boat itself comes back to me easily, but picking up moorings needs more work.

"Slow your approach; long, slow, and lazy, remember, and line her up a bit differently this time, use the outside rail," Chris advises.

"Ahh, I've been using the bow and then adjusting as I get close."

"Thought so, keep the buoy on the rail," he repeats.

"Right, will do," I say as I make my lazy turn.

"Got it," shouts local Chris. "Perfect."

"Okay, drop it and I'll reverse us clear," I shout back, just loud enough so he can hear.

"Clear," he shouts back.

I move into forward feeling pleased with myself, and Chris points out another buoy farther offshore. Without hesitation, I open the twin outboards up a little and feel perfectly at home at the wheel.

"Just remember to look over your shoulder at your motors when you're making adjustments," Chris reminds me. "Sometimes it will be fine, but if it goes wrong, you'll get in a state, so get in the habit now."

"Yep, will do."

"Right, trim the motors and open her up," says Chris grinning.

I need no further encouragement and we are soon up to cruising speed, and it feels great. This is it, this is what it's all about.

Listening to the tips and with a little more practice, I hear "I got it," over and over as we pick up the moorings with ease, until enough is enough and we take *Octopussy* for another high-speed excursion outside the bay.

Fifteen

The Storm

L ocal Chris, Jenn, and I meet at seven o'clock on another perfect morning
in paradise. Like the day before, the sun is already warm, there is barely
a cloud in the sky, and I can't wait to get back out on the water. Local Chris
and I head out on the boat to carry on where we left off the previous day
while Jenn stays to look after the dive shop, much to her disappointment.

During the course of the morning, local Chris makes reference to an
approaching storm in a very matter-of-fact way and appears not at all
concerned.

"There's a storm headed this way, but I'm sure it will be okay. We have
not had a bad storm here for twenty-two years, so we don't need to worry,"
he says with quiet confidence.

On that note, no one says any more about it. In his mid-twenties, Chris has
not experienced a bad storm, not one that he can remember at least. He would
have been barely a toddler when Luis shook the island in September 1995
with tropical-storm-force winds lasting for twenty-one hours and hurricane-
force winds lasting for eight hours. The storm moved forward slowly at
between seven and nine knots and consequentially stayed around the island
for hours, damaging 60 percent of the buildings.

When we get back to the dive centre at lunch time, I meet another local lad,
Pepe. He is thirteen years old and works at the dive centre when he's not at
school. Local Chris introduces him as an annoying kid, to which Pepe shrugs
and offers a broad cheeky grin. The four of us look at the different hurricane

websites and find the storm is currently rated a Category 4 and has been shifting between Category 3 and 4 for a couple of days. Some models show the storm heading for Saint Martin while others predict it will turn away.

"Should we be worried?" Jenn asks. She already sounds worried.

"No one else seems to be, so I guess we shouldn't be either," I reply, ever the optimist. "All we can do is keep an eye on it and hope it turns away from us, I guess."

I am not the person to ask, really, as I don't seem to have the capacity to overly worry about things until I am confronted with them. Not because I am blasé, brave, or in denial. I just don't seem to be able to face up to things until they slap me across the face. Then I know something is real, and that's when I start worrying.

"Hi, guys," says Chris as he walks into the dive shop. "Listen, just to be safe, we're gonna put the boat into safe harbour at Simpsons Bay Marina, on the Dutch side. That's about a twenty-minute ride away. We'll have to close for a few days with no boat."

Jenn gives me a look that says perhaps we *do* need to be worried.

"There's no need to be worried, it's just a precaution, guys," Chris reassures us. "Mark, you can take the boat around this afternoon with Chris and Pepe. They both know where the marina is, and I'll drive around in the truck and meet you there."

I really don't know what to think, despite Chris's reassurance. The fact that after only two days I am taking the boat to safe harbour rather than to dive sites doesn't feel right.

"When do you want us to head off, Chris?" I ask.

"No hurry," he says "we'll have lunch now and you can leave in an hour or so."

"Okay, sure," I say.

"We'll collect it again next Thursday when the threat will have long since passed," Chris adds.

"Okay, Pepe, you ready to go? Where's Chris?" I ask.

"Chris or Black Chris?"

"Black Chris, I guess," I say. I have just learned that, in order to eliminate confusion, local Chris is referred to by all as Black Chris. This may not be politically correct, but I find it somewhat refreshing.

We board the boat, and I take the thin hot stainless steel wheel in my hand while Pepe unties the stern lines from their concrete block moorings. Black Chris pulls the lines in and secures them on the rear deck. Pepe climbs up the ladder, secures it in place, and gives the word that all is safe. I lower the motors and start them one at a time. The keys barely need turning before the motors grumble into life. While still in neutral, Chris frees us from our mooring at the bow and throws the line clear; I put one engine into reverse and ease gently back and away from the mooring. Chris gives the word when we are clear, I slip the one motor into forward, and we gently make our way out of the bay.

With the wheel in my left hand and throttle in my right, I feel whole, where I am meant to be. Despite the fact that I am driving the boat into safe harbour, I don't have a care in the world. The inviting blue expanse of the Caribbean is laid out before me all the way to the horizon, the impossible to reach horizon, and the ocean goes on and on like the pleasure she gives us. She is fickle, though, and we know and accept this. When she is happy, she welcomes us into her warm blue embrace, but when she is unhappy, we must listen, heed her warnings, and not trouble her with our presence. We must not dive on that day, nor swim, nor venture out; we must wait until the next day when we will be welcome once more. The carpet of blue before me offers more excitement, allure, and sense of achievement than any red carpet could ever do.

We are up to cruising speed now and the sound of the motors changes to a clean, crisp, slightly high-pitched *waaa*. It would perhaps be nicer without a noisy outboard motor, but the singing outboard is part of the experience. This is a dream come true, I am at the helm on a perfect day, and life doesn't get any better than this. It is impossible to imagine what is to come.

It is midday, and Chris is headed to the airport on his way to Columbia. He has a prearranged holiday, and before he heads off, he gives us a list of things to do in preparation for the storm. Again, *just in case* it does pass our way.

Probably not necessary, we are reassured, but better to be prepared. The list consists of things to do to make the dive centre, equipment, and property as safe as we can, as well as sprucing up the place in preparation for the approaching high season. Sprucing up the place is a clear indication that Chris is sure there is no need to be concerned, so all this work is just a brief diversion from the real reason for being here. We needn't worry.

Black Chris and I set about moving all the dive tanks from the outside filling station into the gear room. Meanwhile Jenn and Pepe pack all the T-shirts from the dive shop into boxes and move everything into the container with the tools. Next we move all the wetsuits and BCDs from their airy gear room and put them with staff equipment. Apparently cleaning all the dive gear, even after a mild storm, is a real pain in the backside. The screen wall of the gear room serves well to dry everything but provides no protection from flying vegetation and leaves, and everything ends up covered in sticky stubborn sap.

We finish up early today, and the next morning at eight, we will start cutting back trees close to the house that might lose branches and potentially cause damage.

"If you stand on the bottom step, Jenn, I'll climb up and start cutting," I say as I ascend the ladder into a relatively low and squat, but dense tree.

"Yep."

The tree is close to the house, and over the years has grown its way around what look like two sets of power lines, one of which might be a telephone cable.

After pushing branches aside and trying to figure out which branch to cut first without bringing the lines down, I am ready to begin.

"Right, I'm going to start cutting now," I say.

"Okay, shall I move out the way?"

"Not just yet. I'll stop when it's almost through and you can get out the way. If I stand on this branch, can you reach it and pull it down a bit?" I ask.

"Think so, but I'll have to get off the ladder," says Jenn.

"Okay, go on, I'm halfway through the branch, but the saw is stuck."

"This one?" she says as she reaches up on tiptoe to grab a handful of small branches.

"That's it, pull more, yes, go on, more," I say as the sticky, sap-ridden branch begins to loosen its grip on the new shiny red bow saw.

"I can't pull any more," Jenn says, straining against the first of many branches.

"That's it, that's perfect, hold it there," I say somewhat excitedly as the saw is freed and I can recommence sawing. "Right, it's almost through. Can you see if it's free of the cable?"

"It looks like it is."

"Okay, get ready to pull it free and jump out of the way," I warn.

"Yep, I'm ready, cut the rest."

After a few more strokes, the first branch is on the ground, and Jenn drags it out of the way to the gate.

"Okay, next," she says.

I move a little higher into the tree and leave the ladder behind to reach the next branch. "Can you go up a step or two and pull this one down please?"

"Yeah," she says, and I start cutting again.

"Where did these bees come from?" I ask as I look down just in time to see Jenn looking up at me.

"Don't know, but they're all around your head."

"Ahh, shit, they're not happy either." I yelp as I feel the first of numerous stings. "Bloody hell, jump out the way, I need to get down quick! Argh, bloody hell, vicious bastards, argh!" I do my best to make a quick exit without falling as I grope for the top of the ladder with my naked foot.

"Are you okay?" Jenn asks. She sounds sincere, and I have to admit I would probably be stifling a laugh if our positions were reversed.

"It stings like hell, but I'm okay, ta."

After taking five minutes for the stings to calm down, I slip on a hat and my rash guard and venture back up the tree, but the stings smart.

"Do you fancy cutting, mate?" I suggest to Jenn.

"You're all right, thanks, I'll stay put."

The first tree is soon finished with power lines exposed and free and clear from threatening branches.

At around four o'clock, after a hot sweaty day of cutting and then dragging branches to the patch of waste ground a challenging five-minute slog away, we are done.

"Beer at Lolo's anyone?" Black Chris suggests.

No further encouragement is needed; we lock up and walk the five minutes to Lolo's.

The next morning before we do anything else, we check on the storm. During the past twenty-four hours it has been moved up to a Category 5 then down to a 3 or 4 and back up to 5 again. We don't know what to think, but it seems surreal, as if we are looking at a situation someone else is facing. I for one just cannot believe or mentally prepare for the worst. Everything is perfect here. Surely nothing will take that away, will it?

Before he left for Columbia, I'm sure Chris didn't really believe anything bad would happen. I base this on the fact that our list of things to do included staining all the outside woodwork and sprucing it up for the approaching high season. Thinking positively ourselves, the four of us happily spend most of the day staining, a welcome change from the previous day's hot, sweaty, and stinging tree cutting.

We accomplished a lot the day Chris left, but there are still plenty of trees on the property that need to be trimmed. So after an easy day of staining yesterday, we once again set about cutting back the trees and dragging the branches away to the patch of waste ground. Black Chris and I cut while Pepe and Jenn drag. After a couple of hours, there is a huge pile of branches on the ground, so Chris and I stop cutting, and we all start dragging.

We break for lunch around one, and after Chris suggests a takeaway from Lolo's, he takes everyone's orders and heads off to collect it.

"Nice one, Chris," I say as he returns with lunch. "What do I owe you?"

"Nothing, this is on me."

"You sure?"

"Yeah absolutely."

"Thanks very much, mate."

"You're welcome."

After sweating all morning, we assemble on a heavily shaded bench under one of the shrinking trees. We don't talk about the storm at all.

"Where have you been diving?" Jenn asks.

"Quite a few places. South Africa and Mozambique are amazing, and I love Mexico too," I say, remembering them fondly.

"I would love to go to Mexico," Jenn says longingly.

"You should go. It's great, and the people are great too. What about you, where did you dive before here?"

"Philippines," she says with a smile.

"Oh I would love to go, the corals must be amazing there."

"Yeah it was great, I loved it, and I'll definitely go back one day."

"I would love to visit Malapascua Island to see thresher sharks. Did you go there?" I ask, hoping to hear firsthand how great it is.

"I didn't, I stayed on Cebu, and it was amazing."

"I have to go," I repeat.

"Where else have you been?" Jenn asks.

"Sipadan was absolutely incredible," I say.

"Yes, I've heard of it. Borneo, right, with lots of turtles?"

"That's the place, every dive was incredible. There's so much to see and, yes, lots and lots of turtles. One day as we ascended up through a school of jacks, they came in closer and closer and swirled all around until we could look into their eyes. We were in the centre of a jack tornado, incredible."

"Wow, I've seen pictures like that. I wanna go."

"Make sure you do, maybe get a job there some day," I suggest.

"Oh, yeah, how great would that be?"

I wish I could remember the details, but as a break from all the dive talk, Black Chris enlightens us all on his understanding of women. Whether he is right or wrong I don't know, but once again he sounds older than his years. Interestingly, Pepe claims to understand Chris's thoughts on women and even offers some advice of his own. Jenn and I exchange glances with raised eyebrows and can't help grinning broadly.

After our long, late lunch, so entertaining and enlightening, we don't do any more work. Chris and Pepe go home while Jenn and I walk the mile or so to the large supermarket to collect the suggested two-day supply of emergency food and water. The supermarket is very busy, and bottled water is in scant supply. We quickly scoop up twelve one-and-a-half litre bottles between us and something to eat. On our way back, we've only walked a few minutes before we're offered a lift. We accept gladly and return to Chris's house where Pepe, Jenn, and I will spend the next night. Storm night.

"We're in for a direct hit," Black Chris says in an uncharacteristically somber tone as Jenn and I walk into the bare looking dive shop.

It is eight o'clock on the day of the storm, and Chris delivers the news without even a good morning. "Guys, I hate to tell you, but this is serious now, and we have to prepare for the worst."

"Really, mate," I say, as Jenn just stands silently.

"My family and I have been monitoring the storm and listening to reports, and it's going to be a really bad one."

"What can we do, Chris?" Jenn is clearly worried.

"Not much more than we have done already. Try and stay safe, look after each other, and be prepared to go without power for a day or two. You both bought some food and water yesterday afternoon right?"

"Yes, mate, we did," I say.

Pepe suddenly appears and delivers a message from Chris in Columbia. With a deadpan face as if he were a foreman instructing his workforce, he says, "Chris says we have to severely cut back the trees now," and then quickly disappears.

Okay, it's no longer *just in case*. We are about to face a hurricane, not that it has really sunk in, and I still don't fully appreciate what it means.

"Well, let's get on with it then," I say matter-of-factly. I thought we had seen the last of the tree cutting, but it seems not, even though we're sick to death of it.

Black Chris looks dejected at the prospect, while Jenn says, "I'm fed up with this. What's going to happen?"

It seems to me that this threat has suddenly become very real to her, and she looks afraid.

"Let's look at the Cyclocane website," says Chris, "and you can see for yourselves what's going on."

The laptop is one of the very few things left in the once busy, inviting, vibrant, well-stocked dive shop. It is now almost completely empty and characterless. All that remain, apart from the laptop, are the fridge, well stocked with Fanta, Sprite, bottled water, Snickers, and cereal bars, and two split-ring connectors clipped together and hanging on a nail just inside the door.

"Look, this is us right here," says Chris pointing to Saint Martin on the Cyclocane map. "You see the different lines? Well, they are predicting the storm's path under different models, and every one shows Saint Martin getting a direct hit, no matter what happens." Chris does a good job of explaining this without sounding too dramatic.

"Okay," I say, as Jenn and I look at each other aghast. I'm still trying to absorb the news.

"Might it be wrong?" Jenn asks hopefully.

"No, not at all," says Chris. "Whatever happens now, we are getting a direct hit around midnight tonight."

"Well, let's get on with it then," says Jenn, her shoulders slumped. She is clearly resigned to a further day of sweat and toil, cutting and dragging branches—and then facing a hurricane.

As the morning progresses, we are so engrossed in sawing and dragging branches to the waste ground that we say nothing more about the storm for hours. Somehow the hard work of preparing for the storm distracts us from the fact that we are, in fact, preparing for a direct hit from a Category 5 hurricane!

Eventually we finish cutting and dragging branches. The final job of the day is to fill sixty bags with sand and put them in front of the house and dive shop. There is a good chance the storm drains will become blocked, potentially flooding the property, so we set about building a sandbag wall. As usual it is super hot and sunny, and we are all sweating like crazy. Chris and Pepe are filling bags from a tiny neighboring beach while Jenn and I are lugging the full bags 250 feet or so to the border of the property. My right leg is really struggling today and gives out regularly, but I do my best to fight it and try to think of the work as intensive rehabilitation.

We finish around three o' clock and celebrate with cold drinks while checking Cyclocane once more. There's no change, the storm is still a Category 5 and is forecast to stay that way. No matter what happens, Saint Martin will get a direct hit.

It is slowly beginning to sink in, but all we do in acknowledgement is turn to look at each other with almost blank expressions.

Suddenly Jenn lifts the mood when she cheerfully suggests, "We should go for a swim."

We need no further encouragement but all head hastily to the sea. Swimming, floating, and diving about in the chest-deep, clear, warm water under a cloudless sky makes the news that we have only just assimilated and almost accepted seem impossible. The horizon shows no hint of the trouble to come. We cannot fathom the approaching chaos and how it is raging somewhere right now merely eight or nine hours away. There is nothing useful in my head; I have no reference, no barometer for such a thing. What is a Category 5 hurricane like? Will we be safe? Should we worry?

After a refreshing, pleasant, and distracting dip, Jenn and I set about making a bean chili. Chris's house consists of an open floor plan with a living room and kitchen at the front and two bedrooms and a bathroom at the rear. On the living-room side is a large patio door–sized opening that leads to the wooden extension which serves as an office. On the kitchen side are double glass patio doors that lead to the other half of the extension and a covered wooden deck.

Pepe turns up just in time for chili, and as the sun slowly sinks away, it illuminates the sky with a dazzling display of red and orange. Ordinarily stunning, tonight this sunset takes on a sinister appearance, but we still we have no idea what we are about to face.

Jenn suggests a movie, and the three of us get comfortable on the sofa with Pepe's biscuits, and of all things, we watch *Twister*. Oddly, like the tree cutting, the movie choice serves as a distraction. At around nine when the film is over, the atmosphere changes, and we sit and wait in near silence while an unspoken tension builds between us.

"Listen to this from Chris," Pepe breaks in. "This will be the worst storm in Atlantic history, with sustained winds of 185 mph and gusts up to 220 mph."

Jenn and I turn and look at each other, while Pepe excitedly squeals, "It's gonna be crazy."

A while later Pepe reads another message: "Chris thinks we should move into the storage container. He says we can clear the shelves and find somewhere to lie down and wait it out in there."

I'm not sure about this, but the three of us go and take a look in the dark. The floor space and the shelves in the container are full of tools and all kinds of junk including sharp objects.

"How will we close and lock the door from the inside?" asks Jenn sounding stressed.

"Exactly mate, we can't, this is ridiculous. Come on, let's get back in the house," I insist.

"But Chris thinks it might be safer," Pepe insists back.

"Then Chris can stay in there," I snap. "Look, Pepe," I say in a hushed tone, "it's no good, mate, we can't secure the door. We have to go back to the house." Once we do, messages of concern and offers of advice keep coming in.

"Listen guys," says Pepe, "Chris thinks the dive shop might be safer than the house, or perhaps Jenn's apartment."

I realise Chris is concerned, but the messages are becoming frustrating to me.

"We are here in the house, and that's it," I insist. "None of us wants to be here, but we are, this is our lot, and it's too late to be messing about. We're staying in the house."

At around eleven I'm tired and ready for bed. Pepe is already asleep on the sofa. Jenn is as tired as I but insists I use the spare room to go lie down for a while, and she will stay on the sofa with Pepe. It is windy now, but no more so than on a wet and miserable windy night in November at home, so I go and lie down. I don't sleep properly but doze in and out of a mild slumber while I listen to the wind. At around one it seems really windy, and I get up just as Jenn knocks on the door and says, "The bathroom ceiling has been partially blown away."

"Okay, let's see," I say.

There is a large hole through which rain is pouring in. It's not great, but it's not the end of the world either.

"We'll be okay if that's all we have to deal with," I say, though I really don't know.

"Yeah," replies Jenn nervously.

We close the door and return to the sofa together. We sit in silence, and all the while the wind ever so slowly increases in intensity. Here we remain for over an hour, ever quiet, ever waiting—but for what? It seems very windy now, so is this it? We remain in silence hoping the wind will soon start to subside.

Water is dripping through the ceiling in many places now, and Pepe starts laying out towels and pots and pans to catch the drips. At two o'clock, it is extremely windy, and I believe it surely can't get much worse. I don't have a reference, but a hurricane at night seems worse than one in the daytime. A look through the patio doors in the kitchen or the large window from the office doesn't reveal much more than violently swaying trees—what's left of them—and driving rain. All the while we can hear what sounds like the roof of our one-story shelter flapping in the wind and occasional dull thumps that can only be flying objects hitting the house. At three o'clock, curtains of water pour in at numerous locations. Like perfectly manicured and picturesque waterfalls in miniature, they cascade to the floor, rendering the towels and pots and pans useless. Pepe springs into action again and finds plastic food bags, the ones with the good seal, and offers them to Jenn and me.

"Put your phones in here," he says with a wry smile.

"Nice one, Pepe," I say.

For the next hour, the roar of the wind and what can only be the flapping roof and flying objects hitting the house intensify in volume, frequency, and eeriness. The roar continues to build.

Now I don't know how and when this is going to end. I have stopped thinking we will soon be through it and am now wondering if we will come through unscathed. The sound of the flapping roof and thumping of objects hitting the house are putting the three of us more and more on edge. The occasional huge crash makes us jump, and we remain silent while the monstrous noise continues to threaten us.

I don't know why, but around this time Jenn leaves the confines of the sofa and takes to standing in the kitchen, leaning against the work surface.

"What are you doing over there?" I shout over the cacophony.

"I don't know, I just feel better here somehow," she hollers back.

Meanwhile Pepe is pacing up and down between the kitchen and the sofa. His excited screaming in response to the louder thumps and cracks have stopped, and he is completely silent. He wears a face like a small petrified animal facing death.

Jenn shouldn't be standing on her own, so I get up to join her just as Pepe pulls back the curtain covering the kitchen door to the decking and presses his face against the glass. The glass appears to be flexing, or maybe it's the entire door. I didn't think glass had any flexibility; but in any case, it doesn't look right.

"Get away from the glass, Pepe," I shout, almost exasperated at how stupid he's being.

"Look at the trees," he yells back.

"Never mind the bloody trees, look at the glass. I don't want to be patching you up if it breaks, now get away from it."

He pulls the curtains closed and together we overturn the dining table and rest it against the doors as a makeshift barrier against the inevitable breaking glass. We join Jenn in the kitchen leaning against the work surface, and five minutes later there is a new and more immediate noise. The window in the living room has been blown in. Glass, frame, and all has smashed through the television, bounced off the sofa, and come to rest on the floor. I just turn toward Jenn. We say nothing as we look at each other with eyes wide, but I think, *Good move, Jenn*. Neither of us would have done too well if we'd been struck by that. So the bathroom ceiling has blown away, we have lost a window, and the storm has been blowing hard for a few hours now. This must be the height, so surely it will soon pass, we'll be fine, and that will be that.

But still the storm rages, and we are trapped in time with no idea when it will stop. Surely it has peaked now; surely it can't get any worse? But no, unbelievably, the storm continues to intensify. The howling gets louder, the thumps more regular, and we have not uttered a word to each other in an hour. We remain motionless, staring across the open floor plan house toward the open window as rain pours in and the curtain coils on itself and spins like a sodden flag on a pole.

I am beginning to feel as if this will never end and the worst is yet to come. I am beginning to understand what it is like to be afraid, and not just of Irma, who is real now, with form and personality and a name. She is here, there's no escaping her, and she has come to wreak havoc. But I am also afraid of the unknown.

I'm sure the roof is being ripped off the building. Yet for now, despite the violent flapping of the ceiling, it continues to hold. While the objects— whatever they are—thumping into the side of the house cause it to shudder and shake, I wait for something to crash through the walls. I had no idea fear could be so prolonged. A sustained fear is exhausting. I can't imagine the scene outside, and I try not to think about it. The kitchen ceiling and the ceiling fan are jumping up and down like a canvas tent roof flapping and rippling in the wind. The waterfalls have become a mass of cascading torrents, and any surreal beauty they once had has vanished as the water pours in and thrashes around the room, exacerbated by the wind that pours though the shattered window.

The three of us are soaked through by the warm thrashing water which, judging from the stinging in my eyes, is more sea water than rain. It's as if we are in our own film, but unlike actors, we have no stunt doubles. Irma's howl is more monstrous and terrifying than ever, and the sense of foreboding is excruciating. This is not stopping, and it is becoming ever clearer that we've seen nothing yet. I want to scream at the top of my lungs, "If you've come to take us then take us, don't make us wait any longer!" I can only compare the monstrous noise to a jet engine as I try to quash the terrible sense of impending doom and mounting hatred for our tormentor. It strikes me as odd now that Saint Martin is where thrill-seekers seek out a jet blast at the airport fence.

Then somehow the fear slaps me across the face, finds its peak, and moves beyond frightening. Momentarily I don't know quite what it is I feel. I am chilled to the bone, and a terrible panic seizes me, penetrating to my very core. I have no idea what an explosion sounds like, but I hear and feel what I think an explosion must *be* like. I am momentarily frozen to the spot as you might be out in the bush and hearing the roar of a nearby lion.

Although the three of us are together, each of us is feeling exposed and alone with our own versions of fear, panic, and dread. The senses are completely overwhelmed and time stops. My eyes are stinging even more now, and I can barely see. It is definitely sea water that is being hurled into my face. Not only does the salt sting, but the water is hitting my face so hard that it hurts, as if I'm riding a motorcycle in the rain without a visor.

The sound is different now, as well, and I can not only hear the wind, but I can feel it. It is thumping and pounding at my chest in a way that anyone who has stood too close to a speaker at a concert will recognise. This is different, because Irma offers no rhythm, no joy, no pleasure. She pins me to the work surface and beats on my chest like a crazed primate. Surely this is a bad dream, and if I blink I will wake up. In the confusion, it takes a few seconds to realise we are surrounded by sheet metal and wood, the roof has disappeared, and we are exposed to the elements, to Irma and all her might and wrath. Then a further terrifying crunch and an awful snapping and tearing sound fills my ears even above the terrifying howl. I squint and struggle to see Chris's office in the dark as the storm thumps at my chest and forces me back against the work surface. It looks different somehow, and I realise the wooden extension is gone and I am looking directly outside. The office— along with Chris's computer, printer, and all his business files—has disappeared, as has all the wooden decking. The glass door and curtains are no longer there, leaving two patio door–sized openings, so essentially the back wall of the house is gone, along with the roof.

One of the wooden roofing sheets has fallen lengthways in front of the fridge to our right and rests on the kitchen work surface right next to me. The angle has created a small gap between the board and the kitchen cabinets. Pepe is the first to squeeze between the end of the board and the cabinets, followed by Jenn and then me. We all grip the board and pull it toward us, bracing it at Pepe's end against the fridge and at my end against the edge of the work surface and the end of a wall cabinet.

"Are you hurt?" I scream to Jenn and Pepe.

Pepe shakes his head, and Jenn screams back, "No I don't think so."

Miraculously no one is injured. I don't know how we escaped without a scratch while sheet metal, wood planking, and glass flew all around us. For now, our conveniently placed wooden roofing sheet is a shield against everything that is being tossed and smashed around the room. Here we remain in stunned silence.

I was afraid before, but now I'm petrified. What next? Will our makeshift shield be enough to protect us, or will it be torn away from us? Will our single layer of concrete blocks remain? I am waiting for the entire house to collapse, leaving us entirely exposed with no refuge, no shelter. We will have no chance against Irma but will be dashed and thrashed around like ragdolls. I am certain this is our fate, but I try not to show it as we huddle behind our flimsy barrier.

Then, screaming into my ear over the terrifying cacophony, Jenn asks, "Are we going to die?"

I truly believe we are, and I'm sure she does too. I look into her eyes momentarily and see my fear reflected back. I want to be strong, to be positive, but I answer rather feebly, "I hope not."

Some will ask me later, did I find a new faith in God at this time, did I pray? The answer is that it never occurred to me. Petrified and cowering in the corner of the room with the storm raging all around and buckets of seawater being hurled in my face, I close my stinging eyes, trying to block out Irma's terrifying two-hundred-mile-an-hour howl, and wonder, how did I get *here*?

Looking back on this time shortly afterwards, I will feel as if I let Jenn down in what I believed were her final minutes on this planet. I should have been more reassuring and protective, but I had nothing to give. I didn't even offer a hug. I didn't quite know how. True, in those moments I was powerless to do anything, but I feel I should have done more. Not since my childhood have I felt so helpless and utterly useless.

We have holed up in our corner for about half an hour now, and still Irma howls all around us. The pressure changes are agonizing. Those familiar with scuba diving and the need to equalize the pressure in your ears as you descend will understand best, as the feeling is like being suddenly dropped down to thirty feet, then yanked back up again, then down again with no sign of letting up. The few words we exchange have to be shouted directly into the listener's ear. It is a scene of complete chaos, and there is no way out.

Pepe remains totally silent and looks ever more terrified, if that is possible. Yet he continues to grip his end of the wedged board as if clinging to life itself and keeps it pulled in tight against the fridge, shoring up his end of our barrier like a real trooper as it bends and buckles in the ferocious wind. We are all soaking wet, half blind, helpless, and terrified. I have resigned myself to my fate and truly believe that we will remain in limbo until the end finally comes.

We pass what feels like an eternity cowering in our corner, listening to what sounds like a band of medieval attackers attempting to break in with a battering ram. Yet somehow the rest of the house remains intact. I have been in a confused state of exhaustion and high alert for what seems like an age. A new day is dawning on Saint Martin as it slowly begins to get lighter, yet still Irma refuses to leave us in peace. I can't imagine what the rising sun will reveal outside. Some time later it is light. We are still behind our shield, and still I wonder when Irma will release her grip on us. We have made it this far. Dare we let ourselves relax a little? I thought the house would have given up long ago, but it holds fast as the chaos continues all around us. I'd hoped the dawning of a new day would provide some comfort, but it has been light for a couple hours now, and the black skies above provide no such solace. We might as well be on another planet.

Perhaps another half an hour passes, and the storm appears to be calming. Does this mean the end is in sight?

"We have to get out of here," Jenn says, her voice panicky. Despite the relative calm, it is still extremely windy, and we need to shout to be heard.

Pepe looks keen to do the same and says, "Yeah, let's go."

"Go where?" I ask. "It's not safe to go outside."

Jenn insists, "We can't stay here."

They both are very keen to bolt. This period of relative calm seems like a pressure cooker letting out the steam of panic they have both held in for so long.

"We've been safe here, haven't we? Let's try and stay calm now. We're okay here," I say slowly and deliberately.

"We can go to our neighbors' house," suggests Jenn.

"We have to wait, it's not safe to go outside," I insist.

Jenn seems ready to panic. "I want to get out."

"We will," I say, trying to be reassuring. Gradually over the next ten minutes, the spells of relative calm increase in duration from a few seconds to half a minute. I try to monitor the changes and look for an escape route.

"Let's go now," calls Jenn.

"No, wait, we need to wait," I insist. Jenn and Pepe both want to leave, but each time I insist we must wait, and each time the wind picks up to full force again. I monitor the spells of calm, and soon I start to have more confidence in them. Finally I'm as certain as I can be. It feels like a huge risk, but they are both desperate to get out, and they stare at me, waiting for the signal.

"Okay, let's go," I shout. Pepe pushes the board aside slightly at his end and squeezes out. Jenn clambers over right behind him as I stand in her place poised for my turn. Pepe is almost at the back of the house amid the rubble when I start to squeeze past the board. I am slow to clamber over the obstacle course, and by the time I am barely a step into it, Pepe and Jenn are outside.

I reach the back of the house and jump down to where the office and decking used to be. By now the other two are out of sight, and there is even more to clamber over. I get around the side of the house and see them at the neighbors' house just sixty or seventy feet away. I catch up with them under the porch just as the neighbor appears in his doorway, which no longer has a door, looking somewhat startled to see callers in the middle of a hurricane.

"Come in, come in," he says in a bewildered tone.

Jenn says quickly, "We've come from Chris's house next door."

"Oh, where's Chris?" he asks, looking over our shoulders.

"He's away," say Pepe and Jenn in unison, as we slosh our way into the kitchen, ankle-deep in water.

We are truly in the eye of the hurricane. Irma has passed directly over us and just five minutes later, the wind begins to pick up yet again to its former strength, and we get Irma Part Two. Like Chris's house, his neighbors' house is a single-story building with two bedrooms, a living room, kitchen, and bathroom. It is a little smaller but differs primarily in its construction; it is a poured reinforced concrete house with a poured concrete flat roof.

We join the three members of the family in their bathroom, and as the wind begins to build once more, we feel relatively safe in our concrete chamber. Pepe has been diligently monitoring the time since the power went out, apparently at three in the morning. Chris wants to know this to have an idea of how long food might last in his fridge and freezer. Apparently the roof disappeared at five o'clock, and it is seven thirty now, so we spent two and a half hours huddled in that corner. I guess we have another two hours at least before the worst has passed. Standing in the shower on tiptoe, I can see outside through the tiny bathroom window. I periodically look out into the dark gray morning and watch as all kinds of objects fly by.

Sixteen

The Aftermath

T he neighbors' house is still standing, structure intact, yet I doubt much will be salvageable inside. All the windows and the door have been blown out, and the entire house is flooded. Their belongings are saturated and strewn about, and everything appears to be smashed beyond repair.

"Where's the stove?" our neighbor asks as we survey the battered and bruised house.

"Don't know," I say with a shrug.

"It was right here by the door." He is astonished not to see it.

Judging by the space it has left behind and the missing door frame, it would appear it was blown around the kitchen until it smashed its way out the door.

At around ten o'clock, Pepe, Jenn, and I tentatively leave the carnage inside the neighbors' house and peer around like nervous cubs emerging for the first time from their den. We see a surreal scene of almost total destruction. On the way here just a few hours earlier and still in a state of high alert, I had not paid much attention. Now it is like walking into a once familiar setting long since changed, or struggling to recognise the face of an old friend after many years.

The dive shop is just twenty paces away, but I can't see it. It's gone, and all that remains is a pile of rubble. We walk slowly toward it while climbing over electric cables, telephone poles, and pieces of wood of all shapes and sizes. The three of us stand in horror as we simultaneously realise that, had we been in the dive shop, we would surely have been blown away and smashed like ragdolls. The large fridge is gone. In the coming days we search the local area numerous times but never find it. The staff equipment room where we stored all the wetsuits is partly intact, and the wetsuits are piled up in a wet, pathetic heap at the back. The equipment room where we put all the tanks is gone, vanished without a trace, as have forty scuba tanks. The decking is also gone, and looking around the garden, we observe that our tree cutting was futile.

Three trees have been blown down, including the palm which lies sad and dying on the lawn. The trees still standing have bare, stubby limbs, as if someone has tried to bonsai them. The frayed limbs emerge from the trunks looking sorry and afraid, with their insides exposed and sore. Looking at the house is frightening. The decking and office have gone, leaving the two patio door-sized holes. The entire roof is gone as is the entire back wall of the house. A look inside and our eyes are drawn to the corner, our corner, where we huddled alone and afraid. Waiting.

We leave the house and return to the pile of wetsuits. I climb over the heap of junk and throw the suits to Jenn and Pepe, who hang them in the service room container.

Grand Case has been obliterated, destroyed. Every turn of the head fills me with dismay, and everything around me looks like something from a post-apocalyptic movie or the aftermath of a bombing raid. But in truth, the scene is not *like* anything; it looks exactly like what it is, the aftermath of a Category 5 hurricane. Walking the streets is both awkward and heartbreaking. This once charming island town has had its face ripped off. Every window in the buildings that remain has been smashed. Most of the buildings have no roofs. The front of one concrete house has collapsed, and we can see people inside throwing their smashed belongings out into the street, making it even more impassable. We climb over heaps of power lines, poles, wooden beams and sheets, sheet metal, smashed cars, fallen trees, and all kinds of building material and broken household items.

I turn to look over my shoulder at the lush hillside, but it is lush no more but bare and brown, more like desert than Caribbean. The only things that break up the image are sheets of coloured metal and wood that litter that once lush backdrop like giant graffiti. Nature will recover, the trees will grow again, but right now the brown stumps sticking from the ground on the hillside at varying heights don't look like trees at all. I see a hillside of jagged crucifixes. Struggling on through Grand Case, we see many buildings, seemingly much better constructed than ours, that have been utterly destroyed. Lolo's no longer exists, and the only clue it was ever there is a concrete platform littered with broken material. Steel railings lie twisted in the street, and entire roofs have been picked up and tossed hundreds of feet from their respective buildings. These roofs are clearly built of sturdier stuff; large bolts hold the thick heavy roofing material to the wooden frame. While these roofs were not torn apart, they were still ripped from their buildings intact and tossed aside. Seeing all this and appreciating Irma's power from a different perspective makes me wonder again how on earth we survived.

There is an eerie silence and stillness in Grand Case, and unlike previous visits, there is not a bird to be seen or heard, nor is there a single iguana in sight. Community spirit is high though. As we struggle down the street like people at a funeral who don't quite know what to say to the bereaved, we exchange subtle nods of recognition. "How are you," asks a gentleman sitting in front of what remains of his house.

Jenn is quick to reply, "We are fine, thank you. How are you, is everyone okay?

"Yes we are okay," he says with a reluctant smile. "Do you need anything?"

"We're fine," I reply. "We have water and some food. Do you need anything?"

"We are okay, thank you."

An elderly lady is standing at the roadside unable to pass. She looks heartbroken.

"Are you okay?" I ask, while looking around for her companion.

Suddenly she perks up somewhat and says, "Yes, I'm fine."

"Do you have anyone with you?"

"My son is back there," she says, pointing over her shoulder down a small alleyway.

"Okay, that's good."

"Do *you* need some help?" she asks, as her eyes move between the three of us.

"We are okay, thank you," Jenn answers.

"Are you guys okay?" asks a lady as we step aside to allow her and her two children to pass.

"We are good, thanks," Jenn replies, "but how about you guys?"

"We'll be fine," she says almost cheerfully.

The exchanges are all brief but meaningful. People are genuinely concerned about each other's well being. Those we don't speak to either nod, raise a hand, or smile slightly. The sheer bewilderment and shock that everyone feels is displayed more openly by those who remain silent.

We return to Jenn's apartment and find it soaking wet and filthy. The walls, floor, work surfaces, and furniture are drenched and look as if a raging, muddy torrent has passed though and left its tidal mark. The bedroom has a small step down to it and is four inches deep in water, and the bed is saturated. Rather frighteningly the air conditioner has been blown through the wall across the room and has come to rest in the centre of the bed. Despite the carnage in Chris' house, I'm certain we did the right thing in staying there. The dive shop is gone, and I dread to think what would have happened if someone had been hit by that flying A/C unit. The reason the apartment is so wet and filthy is revealed when we climb upstairs to the top apartment. It's gone, completely gone. The floor of the upstairs apartment is now just a flat roof ceiling for Jenn's apartment below.

Amile, the landlord, and his nephew turn up and assure us the occupants of the top apartment had moved out the day before and are safe. According to Amile, Hurricane Luis, twenty-two years ago, was a baby in comparison to Irma. He goes on to say we are lucky that Irma was traveling more quickly than Luis. If she had stayed any longer, there would be nothing left at all.

Jenn, Pepe, and I, along with Amile and his nephew, muck in and bail the water out of the bedroom, and Amile boards up the opening left by the A/C unit. Jenn begins washing all her filthy clothes and bedding in buckets using the one plentiful commodity, stirred up, sandy sea water. The mattress is also soaked, so we drag it outside to the open stairwell and then jump across the small gap to a neighboring flat roof and leave it there to dry.

At around five in the afternoon, Jenn suggests trying my phone, and I am astonished to see we are picking up a signal from neighboring Anguilla.

"Can I use your phone to call my mum?"

"Yes, of course you can," I reply immediately as I hand her the phone with a smile.

Jenn gets through to her mum, but unfortunately they get cut off after about a minute or so. Jenn is upset and crying while talking to her. She is understandably scared and just wants to go home. The heart has been ripped out of this place, and it's a mess. I want to make Jenn feel better and give her a hug, but I still don't know how. I'm so bad at this stuff, and it's hard to know if she would be receptive. I have to be strong now and make her feel safe and get her out of here.

I feel hugely responsible for the young divemaster trainee I met only five days ago. We have been forced together in extraordinary circumstances, and she is rightly afraid and desperate to get home.

We go to bed early, me on the sofa in the living room and Jenn and Pepe in the bedroom.

I don't know the time, but I hear people on the stairs shouting, "Pepe, Pepe, Pepe."

I rise from the sofa as one voice becomes even louder. It is a female voice, so perhaps it is his mother. She must have been worrying about him all last night and today. I join in the chorus and call to Pepe myself, but neither he nor Jenn stirs. I open the door and see two figures heading up the staircase toward what is now the flat roof. I can barely make out a face in the dark, and I ask rhetorically, "Are you looking for Pepe?"

"Yes!" comes the animated reply.

"He's in here," I say, "and he's fine."

I invite them into the dark house and call once again to Pepe, who soon appears bleary eyed, followed by Jenn. His mother pounces on him, gives him a crushing hug, and speaks rapidly in French. She looks and sounds incredibly relieved to have found her son.

"Would you all like to stay here for the night?" Jenn offers.

"No, no, it's okay, we can walk back."

"Are you sure?" I ask. "Walking around in the dark must be a nightmare."

"We have a flashlight, we'll be okay. Come on, Pepe, let's go."

With that the three of them make their way into the dark and broken streets.

I am awakened by a plane that must be landing at the airport just half a mile away. It's not a sound I expected to hear today.

"Was that a plane?" Jenn calls from the bedroom.

"It was, and it was definitely landing."

"We should go and check it out," she says.

Normally at seven thirty in the morning, the town is coming alive, people are going about their daily routines, and the odd motorcycle or scooter will pass and the occasional car, but not today. Now a handful of people are clambering over the tangled heaps in the streets while also navigating the tangled mess the storm has made of their minds. People still stand and stare in confusion and disbelief. Someone is sitting upstairs in a house with no wall. Yesterday he may well have been sitting at his kitchen table, but now he sits and stares down upon someone else's in pieces in the street. Five minutes later we approach the site where we dumped all the tree limbs and see two scuba tanks lying at the side of the road. It is hard to imagine those tanks flying down the street like torpedoes smashing anything in their path and threatening life where normally they sustain it. A little further on, our heaps of tree cuttings are gone. In their place, we see the two large shipping containers spun around more than ninety degrees, and the pleated side of the container resembles the ventral grooves or folds on a humpback whale's throat. The image is a perfect and startling example of the juxtaposition of beauty and the destructive power of nature in its extremes.

We find French soldiers at the airport gates and, despite some language difficulties, we ascertain the planes have been transporting in the French military who are here to secure the airport. We decide to go back to the dive centre to try and retrieve some food and water. There is not a cloud in the flawless blue sky and just a hint of a breeze to cool our sun-drenched skins. It would ordinarily be a glorious day, but all around is devastation, loss, and heartbreak in the wake of Irma's terrible wrath. What has the island done to deserve this? The answer of course is nothing. Nature and her forces can be beautiful, awe inspiring, and powerful, but they are also terrifying and destructive beyond imagination. We humans may have risen to the top of the food chain among this planet's inhabitants, but we remain powerless against the planet.

Hunting around in the mess inside the house for food and water is difficult and more than a little bizarre. We find two bottles of water and a food can without a label. Then we remember the stock of Pringles and cereal bars, Corona and Sprite in the container. We scramble out of the house and pick our way through the garden to the container. We grab everything and take half of it to our neighbors, so we now have half a box of cereal bars, six mini-packs of Pringles, eight cans of Sprite, and about half a case of Coronas. As we walk back to the apartment, we hand out bottles of Corona to the few people we encounter in the street.

Jenn sets about washing the rest of her wet, stinking clothes, and I open my bag to find a similar soggy mess inside. All my belongings are completely soaked, including my passport. I secure my passport with a concrete block and empty the contents of my bag onto the flat roof to dry in what is now a gentle, cooling breeze.

"Are you okay here if I dash back and try and find some more water?" I ask. "There must be more somewhere."

"Yeah, sure, go."

"I'll be straight back, ten minutes."

"Okay, see you in a bit. I'll be fine."

I smile, head out of the apartment, and clamber up the road as fast as my injured leg will allow. After five minutes of rummaging around, I find a single bottle of water. As I'm climbing out the back of the house through what was once Chris's bedroom wall, I see Black Chris. He has a momentary look of complete relief on his face, as he says, "There you are." His expression quickly changes and in a hushed tone, he says, "Where's Jenn?"

"She's fine, mate," I say. "Don't worry, she's at her apartment." His expression is again one of relief, and he flashes a brief but sweet smile.

"How is your family, mate? How about your house, is everything okay?" I enquire, hoping for the best.

"Everyone is fine, thank you. Where's Pepe?"

"His mum came and collected him from Jenn's place last night."

"Last night?" he asks, surprised.

"Yeah, late too, we were all asleep."

"Are they all okay?"

"Yes, apparently so, mate," I assure him.

"How did you survive in that house? I was here earlier, and it's a complete ruin."

"I really don't know, mate. For a while, I truly thought we were done for."

"Where exactly were you in the house?" he asks with an air of disbelief.

"Huddled in the corner right beside the fridge, behind a sheet of roofing board," I say, not quite believing it myself.

"Well it seems to me like you are all very lucky to be here."

It's strange to hear such a statement and to know only hours before you really didn't think you would survive.

"Yeah," I say weakly.

"There's another problem now though," says Chris.

"What?" I say, afraid to hear the answer.

"People are fighting over food, and there are looters everywhere."

"Surely not, mate?" I say.

"They don't care," he says emphatically, "and they are carrying weapons —machetes mostly, but some have guns."

"What?" I just can't believe this. What happened to the community spirit? I thought everyone was helping one another.

"You should take the machete from the container, just in case."

Just in case, those words again. Still, I don't want to need a machete, least of all here on the Friendly Island.

"Really, how can it have come to this," I say rhetorically and with slumped shoulders and a glum expression. I leave the machete, and we both hurry back to the apartment. Jenn is as relieved to see Chris alive and well as he is to see her. He gives her a hug, and she begins to cry.

The three of us briefly discuss what Chris has said about looters and decide that the machete may as well be here with us as sitting in the container, waiting for someone to break in and steal it. So reluctantly we both go back to the dive centre to retrieve it as Chris heads back home to Marigot.

"Machete or pick axe handle, Jenn?" I ask with a smirk.

"Pick axe handle, please," she says, almost without thinking and with a smirk much like mine.

We walk to the apartment, Jenn with the pick axe handle slung over her shoulder and with a wry "don't mess with me" smile on her face, as I rapidly swish the machete around in fake combat moves before tucking it under my T-shirt. All this forced humor serves to distract us from the scary reality that we need to arm ourselves in what was, just a few days ago, a Caribbean paradise where neither of us had a care in the world.

"I'm sorry I got upset before," says Jenn.

"Don't be silly, there's no need to apologize," I reply.

"It's just that I can't believe what happened, and I was relieved to see Chris was okay," Jenn explains.

"I know, of course, don't worry," I say. "We'll get out of here, and I'll make sure no harm comes to you."

"Thank you," she says quietly.

We switch on the phone at midday, Jenn texts her mum, and there is a text from Ian in reply to one I sent him yesterday letting him know I'm safe.

Ian 12.03: Thank goodness for that, good news, mate. Good to hear from you, stay safe, mate. There's another one coming your way. Good luck, mate. Speak soon.

"Shall we go for a walk and see if the small store down the street is open?" I suggest.

"Yeah, come on let's go, you never know," is her prompt reply.

The walk to the store would normally have taken three or four minutes, but today it is more like fifteen. We can't take more than a few steps before needing to climb over telephone poles, trees, tangles of wires, beds and mattresses, smashed cars, and building material. When we arrive, the shop looks intact, wedged in the middle of a terrace of small business premises, but it is also closed.

"Do you know if the shop has been open at all?" I ask a lady in the street.

"No it hasn't, but it has been looted. Look, they climbed up there and got in through the roof."

"Oh I see." I am disappointed, not because I can't buy anything but to have the report of the looting confirmed. We head back to the apartment empty handed. On the way back, we swing by the airport again, hoping for some better news. We learn that the Red Cross might be organizing evacuations, but at the moment the only people being taken out of Grand Case airport will be the sick, injured, elderly, and children. For now we have no chance whatsoever of going anywhere.

The two of us spend another hour or so washing and rinsing more clothes, with regular trips to the small slipway for fresh supplies of sandy salt water. When all the clothes have finally been washed and rinsed, to the best of our ability, we switch on the phone again to find text messages from Ian, Jenn's mum, and an unknown number.

Ian 14.58: I hope you are as well as can be. Don't know if you're getting any news, but the other storm is a Category 4, due to hit Barbuda on Saturday morning. Whatever you did last time, whoever you were with, do the same thing if it's safe or find somewhere safer if there is such a place. Stay together, take no chances, keep your wits about you, and stay strong. Everyone here sends their love, stay safe, good luck to you all. Good luck, mate.

Mark 15.05: Thanks for the update on the other storm. We will be somewhere else this time. I have quite a story to tell, the house broke apart around us, and stuff was flying everywhere, and it was touch and go for a while and really scary. Try to find out about the airport and if we will be evacuated. Cheers.

Mum 15.11: People are getting evacuated from Grand Case to Guadalupe, that's all I know. X

Unknown Number 15.20: Hi, it's Natalie. Glad to hear you are okay. Well as okay as you can be. Trying to keep up on the news with what is going on. I hope you have supplies now.

Hope it's not too much longer before it's safer over there and you can get out. Thinking of you. XXX

Natalie is my sister, and getting her message is a real shock to me as we are quite estranged. I would be willing to bet that I have seen her perhaps twenty times in as many years, and apart from a brief period when she was around four years old, I have never been a brother to her. Despite the fact that I don't really know her and *he* is her father, I have always considered her my sister, but I have not been her brother. All of a sudden I am aware of this, and I go straight to the small bag I keep my passport in. In it is a small wooden fish—it was a key ring until the clasp broke—that Natalie gave me twenty years earlier, and it travels with me everywhere. Where did those years go? How do I behave from here on? Should I apologize for not having been a brother to her? If so, how on earth do I do it, and will she even care?

On my eighteenth birthday, Mother tells me she is two months pregnant with *his* child. I am disgusted beyond belief. How could she want a child with this excuse for a man, never mind actually make one? I feel a mixture of shock and horror.

"Didn't you tell me not long ago that you hated him?" I ask feeling very confused.

"Yes, I did and I do," she says matter-of-factly.

"How on earth can you want to have a baby with him? It makes no sense."

"I don't want to be on my own. I made that mistake before, and I want a daughter."

"What mistake?" As I say it, I know what she means, but I ask anyway. "You mean letting Dad go?"

"Yes."

"So you let my dad go, but you will keep that excuse for a human being and have his child?"

"Yes." It hurt me to my core that she confessed to this. Suffice to say when the baby came along I had nothing to do with her, and felt nothing very much at all until Natalie was four or five years old, I believe.

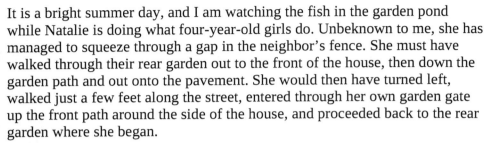

It is a bright summer day, and I am watching the fish in the garden pond while Natalie is doing what four-year-old girls do. Unbeknown to me, she has managed to squeeze through a gap in the neighbor's fence. She must have walked through their rear garden out to the front of the house, then down the garden path and out onto the pavement. She would then have turned left, walked just a few feet along the street, entered through her own garden gate up the front path around the side of the house, and proceeded back to the rear garden where she began.

"Where's Natalie?" Mother asks me.

"I don't know," I say with a shrug.

"Well she was out here with you; she's not in the house."

I have nothing to suggest. Then Natalie appears behind Mother with a proud, beaming, almost smug expression, one you might expect to see on the face of someone who has just completed a hike with a complicated map to follow for the first time.

"Where have you been?" Mother says in an accusatory tone of voice.

Natalie then proudly explains her little adventure. Mother perhaps has had a fright, but her response to the child who believes she has done well is to thrash her bare legs over and over. Natalie is in complete shock and has no idea why she is being treated in such a way. I stand by in disbelief and feel tears welling up in my eyes, and I quickly go to my room to let them flow.

It must have been shortly after this day that I began to show Natalie a little more attention. I enjoyed playing music for her and also watching her imitate the musicians on rock and heavy metal music videos. She would jump up and down and shake her ringlet hair in front of the TV. When not educating herself musically, Natalie began proudly reading to me from picture books. One day, and much to her annoyance, I covered the pictures from random pages and asked her to continue reading. Reluctant and upset at first, she gave it a go. Not long after she had progressed to chapter books.

When Jo and I separated in 1999, and she was no longer encouraging me to visit, I simply stopped going to my mother's house. At this time I had no feelings at all, or if I did, they were buried deep and I had no desire to unearth them. I'm sure I told myself it didn't matter if Natalie and I saw each other. Now very suddenly I am all too aware that twenty years have passed and I don't know my sister.

My thoughts are interrupted when Jenn exclaims, "I've just had an idea. We could plug the phone into Chris's truck and try to charge it up a bit."

"Oh, yeah, great idea," I say.

When we emerged from our neighbors' house after the second half of the storm, we could hear the truck's alarm as a mere whimper, so now we hope there is still some power left in the battery.

"Are you ready to go now?" I ask.

"I am."

"Okay, let's go check it out," I say.

We make our way to the once shiny white Nissan truck. It is almost new, but it is now a write-off for sure and looks as if it has been in a terrible accident. Somehow it is still in the same place, but the front bumper has been torn off, all the lights are broken, all but one of the windows are smashed, and there is a length of wood protruding from the windshield. The front and one side in particular look like someone has attacked them with a sledge hammer. Inside, the seats are covered in glass, and it looks like someone has left the windows open at a safari park, allowing a troupe of monkeys to not only pull apart the windshield wipers but also completely destroy the interior.

We use a piece of wood to sweep most of the glass from the seats, and then we clamber in and gingerly sit down. I insert the key and turn it with anticipation, and I'm very excited when the dashboard illuminates. Jenn plugs in the phone and it begins charging. We are sucking life from the truck, just as Irma has sucked life from the island. I'm not sure why but I try to start it. The engine turns over but refuses to catch. I don't try again; I save the power for the phone. We sit in the demolished truck for an hour. When the phone stops charging, we give up and head back to the apartment. We stop briefly and stand over the wreckage that was the dive shop, and I spot the two lanyards, inexplicably still hanging from their nail.

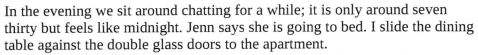

In the evening we sit around chatting for a while; it is only around seven thirty but feels like midnight. Jenn says she is going to bed. I slide the dining table against the double glass doors to the apartment.

"Why are you doing that?" asks Jenn, who sounds disconcerted.

Shit, I think, perhaps I should have saved that for later. "Well at least if someone tries to get in, we'll hear a noise and there will be some kind of an obstacle," I say.

"Do you think we need to worry about that?" Now she looks really concerned.

"I really hope not, but let me worry about that."

I move the sofa bed so it's at an angle to the smaller side window that offers a frosted view down the corridor toward the stairwell entrance. I sit there and do my best to stay awake but doze most of the night. I have no idea what time it is when the first light flashes around the room. Silently it wafts back and forth on our frosted glass door, probing in the dark for an opportunity. I reach for the bright dive flashlight and direct it back, illuminating the room and casting strange shadows all around me as I subtly wave it across the door. I don't hear a sound, but when I cover my light with my hand, I see two intruders with flashlights making their way up the stairs to what is now the rooftop. They soon return, and I uncover my dive light and again hear nothing. Moments later I switch it off and all is dark once more as my heart rate slowly returns to normal. At least a flashlight beam and the presence of someone inside is enough to deter the prowlers, as it will need to once more before daybreak. I can't help wondering how long a light from an unknown source will prove enough to make them look elsewhere for whatever it is they are looking for. I hate myself for thinking it, but I wonder how quickly society will deteriorate and how far people will go. It is disheartening to see how easily people have taken to looting and robbing their neighbors. I had no idea it would be like this. I expected the community spirit to continue to grow. Maybe I am naive. Suffice to say, I am not letting Jenn out of my sight. I hate the thought, but I must consider that, for one reason or another, we really may need to defend ourselves.

Seventeen

Bad to Worse

Ian 8.18: The other storm is due to hit Barbuda tomorrow afternoon, Barbuda is being evacuated. They have not said it will be like the one you've just had, but from the news and weather models, it is on its way. You hopefully won't get a direct hit, but it looks like it's not going to be good; it is a Category 4. There is no ETA on other islands, but you're not that far away. Sorry, mate, but it might be with you through the night and early hours of Sunday morning. It is not as big as what you have just seen, Irma was 460 miles across, this one is nothing like that but still a good storm. Sorry, mate, I just want you to be prepared as you can be. After what you have just been through, it is the last thing you or any of the islands need. It is complete devastation throughout, still going on too, on its way to Florida now. The storm of the century. Take your battery out, it is still running otherwise. Look after each other. Be safe.

Mark 8.18: Can you get in touch with Jenn's mum, the girl I am with; here's the number.

"Bloody hell, Ian says Irma was 460 miles across," I say out of nowhere.

"What, that's crazy."

"Here take a look," I say as I hand the phone to Jenn.

"Ian has texted again," she says as she is only partway through reading the previous one.

"Read it to me."

Ian 8.19: Hello, mate, it looks like you will get a glancing blow from the next storm, but don't take it lightly; if you can, get to an official shelter. If and when you see any officials, play on your dodgy leg. Planes are leaving from St. Kitts, if you can get off, get off. Even if the flights are to the States just go, they can kick you out and send you home from there.

"We can't take another storm," says Jenn, looking scared all over again.

"We survived the storm of the century. Nothing can hurt us now," I say with a smile and a touch of fake bravado.

"Yes we did, didn't we?" she agrees with confidence. "Shall we go to the house again in a minute and try and find some more food or water?"

"Yeah, good idea, we still haven't looked for our dive gear yet either," I say.

"Okay, shall we go now?"

"Yeah, come on, let's go."

Once again we set off picking our way through the mess on the streets. At the junction leading to the airport, a bulldozer is working to push debris and a huge fallen tree to the side of the road. We arrive at the dive centre property six or seven minutes after setting off and are met by two strange bicycles in the garden. We exchange glances, but don't need to say anything. Looters!

"Okay, stay close to me," I say as we creep through the garden past Chris's battered truck. I can see into the house through the missing back wall, and as I get closer I see and hear no one.

"I don't hear anything, I'm not sure they are in the house," I say hoping.

"They can't be far away can they? Their bikes are here," Jenn says cautiously.

"Yeah. Stay here, I'll go into the house and take a proper look around."

"Okay," Jenn whispers.

I clamber up into the house and into the bedroom through the open wall and can see that drawers that were previously closed are now open. Turning toward Jenn I raise a hand to reinforce what I just said and move though the bedroom out into the small corridor. A look to my right toward the second bedroom reveals no one. I struggle in my flip-flops over the broken material and mess of household items while looking out for nails and into the open main area of the house.

"Come in, Jenn," I call, "there's no one here."

"Okay, coming."

Jenn immediately says, "Oh look, someone *has* been here, all the drawers are turned out."

"Yeah, but where are they?"

"We should take any of Chris's valuables we can find and wash and dry his clothes," Jenn suggests.

"Yeah, we should, you're right. Let's see what we can find, hopefully they haven't taken everything of value."

After a few minutes of rummaging around, Jenn somehow finds a laptop hidden under all the mess. Then she produces an old fashioned–looking box that simply says "Chris's Life" on the side. I remember the Nitrox analyzer that was on a small shelf in our corner refuge, and it's still there, so I grab that too. Just as I walk back into the bedroom I see two guys in the garden.

"There they are," I exclaim.

"Oh yeah," Jenn says, with a what-do-we-do now look on her face.

One is carrying a television set, not ours, which is smashed under the sofa now, and the other has a medium-sized clear plastic storage box.

"What are you going to do?"

"Don't know," I reply as I stumble and stagger over the debris back toward the open wall.

The two lads, who are maybe in their late teens or early twenties, stand nonchalantly looking in our direction, still holding their ill-gotten gains, as we climb down back into the garden.

"What did you steal from this house?" I yell when I'm within earshot.

"Nothing," one replies defiantly.

"Bullshit, your bikes are here, and we know you've been in the house."

"We've taken nothing," says the other.

"What the hell is wrong with you, stealing from people at a time like this?" I can feel myself getting wound up now, first because I'm sure they're lying and second for doing what they're doing. One must sense my mounting anger and quickly backs away with the television set under his arm. He half stumbles on all the broken material.

I move toward him as quickly as I can while shouting, "What is wrong with you, you horrible thieving bastards? A TV set, what are you going to do with that, you idiots?"

"Screw you, man," the one carrying the TV set replies from a safe distance, as he retreats further into the street.

He is much more nimble than I am and is soon more than a safe distance away. He puts the TV on the ground and then becomes extra brave and begins yelling all kinds of abuse.

"Come back here and say that and I'll crack your skull, you piece of shit!" I scream.

Looking over my shoulder I see his mate still standing in the same place, just behind me among all the scattered broken wood.

"You're bloody mad!" he screeches, his face screwed up like a bulldog.

He's right. I *am* mad, I feel really bloody mad, and I want to hurt them both. "I'll show you mad, you twat," I yell as I skip the few paces toward him.

Like his partner, he is more agile than I and takes off quickly, but not without one fall along the way. He picks himself up though and makes it to the seawall which he quickly scales. Then he stops, and turns to face me, and shouts, "You're crazy, we'll be back."

"Good, come back now, you piece of shit, and I'll break both your bloody necks."

He disappears along the seawall and we don't see either of them again.

"Sorry about that," I say as I turn to face Jenn, who is standing motionless, almost to attention.

"It's okay," she says, relaxing, "but where did that come from?"

"Sorry," I say again.

"No, it's okay; someone needs to stand up to people like that."

"Yes, I think someone does," I agree. "I hate people like that, taking advantage of others at their weakest."

"You really shocked me for a minute, that's all."

"I don't think they'll be back, despite what he said," I assure her.

"No, neither do I," she says with a broad smile and a chuckle.

"We only have two bottles of water don't we, so we should go look for more before we head off."

"Yeah come on," I say, "I'm sure we'll be fine now."

After ten minutes of rooting around, we are triumphant, as we now have another two bottles of water, three anonymous cans, half a packet of soggy biscuits, and some honey. Jenn has also found an iPad and some dive gear. Fortunately the two guys were not very thorough. It looks like they quickly turned out drawers rather than going through the mess on the floor as Jenn has so diligently done.

"Let's put these bits and pieces in the container, shall we," she says.

"Yep, come on."

No sooner have we done so than another new face appears, and a man moves purposely toward us, as purposely as anyone can under the circumstances and with a hand extended in warm greeting.

"Hi, I'm Don."

"Oh yes, hi," I say, glad to see a friendly face. "Chris spoke about you before he left for Columbia."

Don is a very good friend of Chris's and, to use his words, a very good man.

"Hello again, Jenn, how are you?" he says.

"We're okay," she says. "How are you?"

"I'm okay." There is a subtle but telling pause. "Thanks. This place is a mess," he acknowledges, turning the attention back to us. "Do you guys need anything?"

"Yes it is, but we're doing okay. We're staying at my apartment at Amile's now," replies Jenn.

"Oh, I see," says Don, "you're sure?"

"Thanks, yes," I say. "We have just put some valuables in the container, computers and files and a few other bits and pieces."

"I can take it; it will be safer at my place."

"Can you? Okay, great," I say.

"We were going to take all Chris's clothes too," Jenn adds.

"I'll come back and grab all those later as well," Don assures us.

"Are you sure?" says Jenn. "We were going to wash and dry everything."

"Yeah, it's fine; I'll come back this afternoon. Bulldozers are clearing the roads now, so I should be able to drive back later today or tomorrow."

"Yeah, okay, we might see you later then. Here's a spare padlock key," I say, handing it to him.

Don heads off and we clamber over everything that was once the staff gear room, now essentially broken in half, with just the back wall and a partial side wall remaining. We find our gear bags where we left them wedged in the corner right at the back, close to where all the wetsuits were. All of my gear is there except my fins.

As soon as we get back to the apartment, I switch on the phone again.

Ian 9.59: Can you see aircraft on the ground; the French airport is probably your best way out. This storm should be a glancing blow, but still going to be horrid. Stay out of the way of the sea surge. It's going to be with you overnight, so you must get to safety.

Natalie has been speaking to your employer. He's doing what he can to try and arrange rescue efforts from Columbia. Efforts are being made. Dad says there are helicopters and planes on the ground in Grand Case, you must be able to see them coming in and out. PLAY ON YOUR LEG and get home. Don't need to worry even about passports, there is talk of sorting all that out after. Chris said if you need to as a last option, you can take one of the boats to Antigua.

There is a plane on the Dutch side, but the Dutch won't let it leave. Now the Yanks are saying they won't take anyone but Yanks, bloody politics. So it looks like Grand Case airport might be your best chance. Will contact Jenn's mum now. Be safe, good luck to you all, mate.

Ian 10.03: Just spoke to her mum and let her know she's okay. Your dive man is organizing a rescue effort, more news as we get it.

Mark: 10.37: We are staying at Amile's apartments.

Ian 11.39: Good that you have somewhere to go, will you be safer there? After this storm has passed I think there will be more of an effort to get people out. Be safe.

Ian 11.39 Jenn's mum said she's glad to know that she's in good company. She said don't worry about money for tickets, just get yourselves out. Easier said than done, I know. Everyone is on your side. Stay safe.

Later in the afternoon, we head to the airport again. Irma has had a huge influence on Grand Case. The obvious physical damage aside, there is an air of distrust in the community now. On Thursday morning everyone was neighborly, helpful, and concerned for everyone else. It's not like that any more. People look afraid and anxious and regard each other with suspicion. I can't help but wonder what it would take and how long for this to spiral out of control?

As far as we can see up and down the street, it has been made passable and the mess is now piled high at the side of the road. French soldiers are in the street now as security, and the scene at the airport is chaotic to say the least. The sick and elderly along with parents with young children form very disorderly loose lines at the airport gates. We speak to someone and, suffice to say, there is no chance of us going anywhere from Grand Case airport, and no one is able to give even a hint as to when we might. We leave, but for some reason we take a short walk past the airport gates and soon notice a soldier lying on the ground in the grass. He has a rifle in front of him, and when we look carefully, we see many soldiers adopting the same sniper posture. The airport fencing has disappeared completely, and in its place are snipers lying on their bellies.

A short while later, back at the apartment, Black Chris comes to visit us again from Marigot.

The door is ajar and he pokes his head around and wakes me from an afternoon nap. "Hi guys, how are you doing?"

Startled, I jump up immediately and shake him by the hand. "Hello mate, how are you?"

"Not bad," he replies. "Are you guys okay, do you have food?"

"We're pretty good. We have some water, a few cereal bars, a small tub of Pringles, some cans, biscuits, and honey."

Then Jenn comes out of the bedroom and Chris turns very serious.

"Listen guys, you need to be really careful of looters now. Many are going around in gangs with guns and stealing food directly from other people now, not just looting stores and empty houses."

Saint Martin really is a paradise lost. It sounds like the island has fallen into almost complete lawlessness. Jenn and I eye each other now with guilty faces, which Chris notices, and his eyes dart between the two of us.

"What? What's up with you two?"

Jenn and I look at each other again while deciding who is going to speak up on my behalf. Jenn breaks the monotony and says, "We found looters today."

"Found them?" Chris is puzzled.

"At the house, when we went looking for food and water," Jenn continues.

I join in and say, "We turned up and found two bicycles in the garden. I went into the house but no one was there. Then a few minutes later they appeared outside from somewhere."

"What? What happened?" Chris is shocked.

Between us, Jenn and I tell him the story. When we are done, I get a bit of a telling off for confronting them.

"Yeah, I understand, mate," I say in response to the rebuke, "but sometimes someone has to make a stand."

"Yeah, well fine, but please don't do it again."

"Okay, mate. I won't."

"What are you going to do tonight?" asks Chris, changing the subject to more immediate matters and the second approaching storm.

"We are going to put all our belongings in the small corridor to the bedroom," I say as I point to it, "take the duvet and pillows, and hide there."

"I see, I suppose there's more support there in that little area."

"Yeah, that's what we thought, and this place survived Irma, so I think we'll be okay."

"It might not be great, but I'm sure you'll be okay."

The three of us hang around just chatting for a couple of hours, including about whether we should stay.

Jenn brings it up when she asks Chris, "What do you think about us wanting to leave the island?"

"What do you mean?"

"Well, we're not sure we should really be trying to leave, Chris. Are we?" Jenn turns to me.

"No we're not; it's all a bit confusing. We think we should be leaving one minute, and then we think we should stay and help rebuild."

"Listen, you're foreigners here right?"

"Yeah," we say.

"Well wanting to help is great, but the best way you can help is to leave," he says decisively.

We both look puzzled at him and each for a second or two. Then he continues, "This island and its people belong here, you don't. This isn't your home, it's theirs. All you are doing really is using up valuable food and water resources."

I hadn't even considered that angle, and once again Jenn and I simply look at each other.

"Look, you both came here to work with tourists and to enjoy yourselves. None of that will be happening here in Grand Case for a long time."

"No, I guess not," I reply.

"But isn't there something we can do to help work toward that soon?" Jenn asks.

"Yeah, there is. Leave."

I can't help but splutter a laugh when he says this. "Okay, we'll get out of your hair," I say in mock offense.

"You know I don't mean it like that."

"I know, mate, I'm only winding you up."

Chris continues, "Besides, your friends and families will all want to see you after living through everything you have. Don't worry; you guys need to go home, it's the right thing to do."

An hour or so later after Chris heads off back to Marigot, I am sitting on the sofa bed, and I raise one arm above my head as I often do and flop my forearm over my head. I catch a pungent whiff of body odor and for some reason move in for a thorough check, just as Jenn comes out of the bathroom.

I look up in her direction and say, "I stink, do you?"

"Ha, yeah, I do a bit," she says with a huge grin.

"I've not had a shower for days and could really do with one now. I'm sure I didn't shower after we finished lugging the branches and sandbags, did you?"

"No, I didn't," she says as she walks toward me.

"Bloody hell, you do stink," I say cheekily.

She only laughs and her eyes light up as she says, "Let's go have a bath in the sea."

"Yes, I love it, let's go." I get some soap and a shower sponge, Jenn grabs shower gel and shampoo, and off we go.

The gap in the seawall to the water is just fifty feet down the path from the apartment. The path is still a mess of broken material and cables, so we tiptoe our way toward the sea.

The water has calmed down considerably now, and there is barely a ripple, but the bottom is still stirred up and it remains cloudy and almost milky looking. We wade out into just over waist-deep water and immediately float on our backs and then swim a few strokes still clutching our toiletries. The water is warm and reassuring, and for a few minutes we almost forget about the situation that has been thrust upon us.

Perhaps surprisingly, the salty bath is very refreshing, and afterwards we both feel as clean as new pins. As we come out of the water, we are greeted by an iguana sitting on the rocks immediately to our right. This is the first wildlife we have seen since the storm. It is colourless, an insipid very pale brown, and somehow it looks petrified. It is nice to see it alive, though, and we hope it will recover soon. Iguanas were plentiful before the storm; I saw at least half a dozen in just a few days. Hopefully many more have found refuge and will soon be out and about and thriving again. Just before the entrance to Jenn's apartment block, I see another iguana, a huge one sitting on top of the head-height wall that forms the alleyway. I notice him just as I pass, and as I do he pulls his tail back away from me. Cocked and ready to strike.

"Be careful," I say, "there is a huge iguana there, and he doesn't look happy."

"Ohh, so there is," Jenn says as she takes a half-step backwards, startled as it looks over its shoulder toward her.

"He just cocked his tail back and looks ready to whip whoever he can. That'll be you," I say as I laugh.

"Thanks," she says as she looks for a route that will avoid the terrified but ready-for-action lizard.

He—I'm sure it is a he, as he has the huge head and swollen cheeks characteristic of mature males—is definitely on high alert and ready to attack his next perceived threat, Jenn.

"Do you think it will reach me if I climb up here?" Jenn asks she grabs the neighbor's railings and pulls herself up onto their two steps.

"Nah," I say as she begins to shuffle along the steps toward him with her back turned and facing me. "Actually I don't know, he's pretty big," I say with a grin.

Jenn stops and crouches down quickly as she loudly says, "Shut up."

"Shush, you'll make him angry," I say, laughing more.

Jenn gives me a you're-supposed-to-be-helping look from her prone position.

"It's fine, keep going," I say.

"Is it?"

"Yes," I chuckle, "it is, come on."

As she moves barely past him, I say, "Another step and you can jump down."

She looks back over her other shoulder to check his position, and as she does, sure enough, the big tail whips around. She is safely out of range but is still startled and lets out a scream. It is great to see wildlife emerging, even if it is edgy and trying to whip us.

Back in the apartment, I have the bright idea of listening to some music on my laptop. We listen to the Chili Peppers for an hour until the battery dies and then decide it's time for bed. I assure Jenn I will wake her up if she is asleep when the storm starts, and we will move to our little hidey hole. I rearrange all the furniture again, prop myself up in my nighttime position, and remain there neither asleep nor awake for the majority of the night.

I was really angry when I confronted the looters. I have not felt that angry since I was very nearly knocked from my bicycle seven or eight years ago. A artic lorry passed me at a distance of no more than a few inches on a narrow bend, only to need to stop for oncoming traffic. I passed him as he stopped in traffic and then he caught up to me once more and drove six feet from my back wheel while blaring his horn.

I had to stop at traffic lights and turned to ask him if he actually wanted to flatten me in his truck. He then gestured he would get out, and I was already boiling and then I spilled over. I begged him to get out of his cab and I already knew what I was going to do. I visualized grabbing his legs as he attempted to climb down and pulling him headlong into the road and then giving him a beating. I was screaming at him, and my vision began to blur. If you ask anyone who knows me, they will say I am quiet and laid-back and easygoing. But I believe there is a deep anger bubbling away below the surface. I have been aware of it for a while but have not really given it any serious thought until now. It takes a lot for it to surface but it is there. If I stop and think about it now, it seems Reese was right all those years ago and I do have anger in me. But why?

On two definite occasions I am disturbed again by prowlers, despite the fact we have been told there is a curfew. All through the night there are windy spells, which I believe must mark the beginning of the storm. But each time they fade after a few minutes, and as morning approaches, I am certain this storm has missed us. It's getting light now, and I don't believe the storm can be this late.

I just sit around waiting for Jenn to wake up and to share in the relief of being spared a second storm.

"Morning," she says as she emerges from the bedroom.

"Morning."

"The storm can't have been that bad, then, but how did I miss it?"

"It never happened," I say. "Well not for us, at least."

"It must still be on its way then." She sounds agitated rather than relieved at the news.

"No, no, it's missed us, I'm certain. It can't be this late; it was meant to be here last night wasn't it?" I'm trying to sound reassuring.

"How can it miss us?" says Jenn, sounding more worried now than she was last night.

"It was only going to be a glancing blow for us, remember?" I say still trying to reassure her.

"Yeah, but it must still be coming."

"I don't know, but honestly, I'm sure it has missed us. Come on," I say, "let's go sit outside and get some fresh air."

"Okay, yeah. What time is it?" she asks, finally calming down.

"Seven thirty."

Outside we are greeted by an already warm and gloriously sunny Caribbean morning. We can see the ocean from here, and it looks like it has settled down a little more. In less than a week, I'm sure it will be perfectly clean and clear once more.

Ian 7.40: Alright, mate, good to see the other storm turned away. I assume you got away with that and all is okay? There are Royal Caribbean cruise ships on the way, and one is going to Saint Martin apparently. On the web it says the cruise ships dock on the Dutch side. Keep your eyes open. Jenn's mum has registered you with the French authorities as a couple. I have spoken to Lee and Menno, and they are trying to organize a private plane through someone they know to get you both off. I have said you won't leave Jenn there. I'd like to think you'll be off in twenty-four hours. Hope you are both well. Good luck. Allegedly people have got guns and machetes and are looting hotels for TVs and whatever they can get their hands on. Crazy! Be careful and don't get wrapped up in that nonsense. Be safe.

"Oh, listen to this," I say as I read the first line of Ian's message aloud.

A big beaming smile of relief is Jenn's response, and the only one needed.

"Blimey, now listen to *this*," I exclaim. "Lee and Menno are trying to organize a plane for us."

"What? That's amazing."

"I know, isn't it?"

"Who are Lee and Menno?"

"Lee is a good friend; we've worked together and have done lots of dives together over the years in a few places. Menno is a friend he worked with a few years ago on Sint Eustatius. He's a great guy too. I met him last year at Lee's wedding."

"Who's got the plane then?"

"I am guessing it is a mate of Menno's who must still be on Statia. Wouldn't it be amazing if they could sort that out?"

"Really amazing," Jenn says with a bright beaming smile.

We can't help but allow ourselves to get a bit excited at the prospect of being picked up by a private plane, but the fact that people are doing so much to try to help makes me realise how fortunate I am to have such good friends around me.

"I'll just go to the loo and we'll get straight over to the airport," I say.

"Yep," says Jenn, looking much happier.

The scene at the airport gate is no different than on previous visits. Confused, harassed, and somewhat helpless looking soldiers do their best to reassure, organize, and herd those eligible for evacuation through the gate and onto the tarmac to wait for a plane when their turn comes. Their need is certainly greater than ours, but feeling trapped on an island in turmoil, its society deteriorating, and not knowing when we might leave is stressful, to say the least. We are told the same as before, that we have no chance of going anywhere anytime soon.

"Do you fancy going for a walk through Grand Case?" Jenn asks.

"Yeah, why not," I say.

We walk further than we have before, all the way to the junction to the main road. As we approach the junction we see people milling about frantically and shouting.

"What's going on here?" I say, in anticipation of another ugly scene. A small truck at the end of the road seems to be the focus of the attention. Then the crowd parts slightly and one, two, three, then four people emerge from the crowd carrying bottles of water, shrink-wrapped together in six-packs.

"Ooh, water," sings Jenn as she quickens her pace.

We try to stand in line in a crowd that is pushing and shoving and jostling for position as the two soldiers in the back of the truck try to distribute the water evenly. It doesn't take us long to work out that if we stand here politely for much longer, we won't get anything. With a bit more gumption we eventually make it to the back of the truck and are handed six one-litre bottles of water each. This is an absolute boon and it is cooler than what we have become used to. What we have been drinking is very lukewarm. That's not a bad thing, as it has stopped us from drinking too much at a time, which helps the rationing.

We don't get too far back up the street en route to the apartment when someone sees us and exclaims, "Water!"

We point back down the street and shout, "Soldiers are handing it out just on the corner," and the person takes off running.

A little further on, we're asked again about water and realise that the water might all have been handed out by now. Jenn hands over two of her bottles without thinking. Then an elderly lady sees us and her eyes light up, so I give her two of my bottles. When we get back to the apartment, we have three bottles between us from our original dozen. At the rate we have been drinking it, we now have enough for perhaps two more days.

At around two o'clock, we switch the phone on again.

Ian 14.32: I have been talking to Lee, and he has a friend who can fly you out. He's only an hour away. Go to the airport and ask for landing clearance and then let the pilot know, he's called Fred Welsh. No: 945 444 555. The plane is a Cessna Twin with a capacity of four. It's a shot in the dark, but they may allow it. Also been on the phone to the British Consulate, and they are letting the French authorities know you are waiting and what the situation is there, but they can't give me any news on potential evacuation. Sorry, mate, stay in touch if you can, be safe.

Ian 14.32: I've been speaking to the British Consulate in France to see if they can get landing clearance or can give me numbers to ring to pressure for clearance. Keep you posted. Good luck.

So, off we go to the airport once again, this time excited and overwhelmed by all the help and support we are getting and all the effort being made on our behalf. When we ask about getting permission for a private plane to land, a soldier tells us that they are not in contact with the air traffic control and that they won't contact anyone on our behalf. We plead with a couple more soldiers, sure that someone can help us, but we get the same response each time. We leave and head back to the apartment feeling despondent. We won't be leaving any time soon, private plane waiting or not.

At around five thirty, we open the three anonymous cans we found. They contain chopped tomatoes, kidney beans, and corn. Jenn has some black pepper and mixed herbs in the cupboard, so we mix it all together, and it looks pretty good. Eating it is a real treat, it's real food, even though it's cold, and something we would normally turn our noses up at. But we feel as if we are eating like royalty. Next is a dessert of slightly soggy cookies and honey. We are in heaven now. Compared with the cereal bar and Pringles of the past few days, it's gourmet fare. Shortly after dinner we retire, and I spend yet another night unable to relax, in and out of sleep, flashlight in hand. The machete on the floor beside me, and the pick axe handle in plain sight by the door, serves as a stark reminder of our current situation.

Eighteen

Escape

Ian 8.20: Have you received any aid, food and water?

Mark 8.28: Just some water yesterday, we have enough for a day or two, we have some food. We have been eating cans of beans and corn, and crisps. Any news about the Dutch airport or the cruise ship?

Ian 10.53: Apparently the French might be starting flights out, that's what they were trying to contact you for, again no promises.

Mark 10.56: Who was trying to contact us? We will go to the airport again.

Ian 10.56: Home office has been on the phone. They are releasing a plane and trying to get hold of you to instruct you to get on the plane. I believe your names are on the list. Good luck, take what ever option comes first to get you to safety. Don't worry about the American thing. If they're taking you there, go there; sort the other nonsense out after. Worst they can do is kick you out and send you home. Again, good luck, maybe just be close to the airport.

Ian 10.56: It's the British Embassy that's trying to contact you, not the Home Office. No news on ships. Take the first option and bail out. Good luck.

Mark 10.58: Tell them to text not call; the phone is on and off. I have no choice. Phone is 15 percent now. Which airport will it be from, we are on the French side, and it's not easy to get to the Dutch side.

Ian 11.06: It was the British Embassy, just to say that the French might be starting flights out, that's all it was, mate. Sorry I did tell them to text. Paul has just seen on Facebook that a Canadian airline is supposed to be doing a flight out today from Saint Martin's airport at one thirty. It's West Jet 4905, and they're asking people to register for the flight on

Facebook. Paul is registering you both, so be at Saint Martin's airport French side for one thirty. If you see a plane coming in, your names should be on it. Forget the embassy, it was nonsense. Good luck.

Mark 11.11: Shit, okay, we will go check it out.

Ian 11.18: Yes, that's your best bet at the moment. Not sure how the money will work, but there's a handful of us ready to pay, tell them money is not an issue. Good luck.

We walk the ten minutes to the airport and make enquiries. I can barely see the phone with the brightness turned right down but it is cloudy now and I just manage to send a text.

Mark 11.43: At airport now and not getting any help, no one here knows anything about it and are saying they don't believe it. I want to scream. Is it the French side for sure? Is it real or not? Uncertainty is killing us. Can you call West Jet and get the details? Landing and take off time, as much as you can? No one at the airport believes it and no one is helping.

The phone almost immediately beeps and vibrates into life, but the sun has come out again, and I can't see the message even when I huddle on the ground to try to make shade. We stay at the airport for close to half an hour and speak to a different soldier who has better English, but he knows nothing about a Canadian flight. I am messing with the phone trying to turn the brightness up, but I can't do it, argh!

We head back to the apartment. Jenn stops just up the street to talk to a lady while I go into the apartment to read the last few messages that have come in the last half an hour or so.

Ian 11.43: Sorry, mate, secondhand info. It's on the Dutch side. Canadian airlines, you've got to be at the airport for 1:30, it leaves at 3:30 for Canada. They have asked for your phone number, and Paul has given it to them, and they know you have limited power. If a number is ringing from Canada, it's the airline. Paul is registering you now.

Ian 12.15: They have asked for your final destination, Paul said UK, but Canada is good for now. You could maybe stay with Lee for a day or two. Jenn's sister has seen this on Facebook too, and her mum has called me as well, so I think it must be true. Relax, mate, and stay calm. I know that's easier said than done. As far as I can tell, it's real.

Ian 12.16: Jenn's mum has just texted and said it's Princess Juliana Airport on the Dutch side and said it leaves at 3:50, so slight difference but supposedly it's on. Just waiting to hear from Paul to confirm. Turn off and on again in half an hour, and hopefully I can give you more solid news. Good luck, stay calm, there is a lot of effort being made our end. Trying everything.

Ian 12.18: Paul has just had an email from the airline, it said, please tell Mark to get to the airport on the Dutch side. It's on. You're registered; if you can get there you're on the plane. Go steady but get there; keep it to yourselves, because there will be riots otherwise. They may try to contact you, they know the full story of power etc. Go go go.

Ian 12.18: I will call Lee and let him know you are on your way if all goes well. Let me know when you board. Email said, tell Mark to get to the airport, Jenn is registered with you, and we have said you have friends in Canada too. You're on the list, you have to be there for 1:30 your time. Good luck, mate. X

"Jenn," I shout down the street, interrupting her conversation.

"I'll be there in a minute," she calls back.

"No, you have to come now," I shout frantically.

"What is it?"

"Come on, we have to go," I say, as she trots toward me with a what's-so-important look on her face.

"Quick, come upstairs and read these messages. It looks like we have a flight."

"What, really? Amazing!" she says, with a look of complete surprise and utter disbelief.

"Here, read for yourself," I say as we walk into the apartment.

Our bags are already packed, and we need only a few minutes to gather our belongings before we head out the door, fully laden. I struggle back down the alley I struggled up less than two weeks ago. I was filled with hope and excitement that day. Now I am being forced to go back to the airport to try and escape a paradise lost.

There are a few cars moving around the streets now, and it is not long before we stop someone to ask for a lift. The driver says no, he has to stay in Grand Case because his family is here. We ask the French soldiers, but they also refuse. Our bags are heavy and not made for carrying any great distance, and we are both struggling. I have one on my back and balance a larger bag on top of my head. Jenn stops after a few minutes, exhausted and frustrated. Her bags are dragging along the ground and bashing her in the shins with each step.

"You go and look for a ride and I'll wait here," Jenn says.

"No way," I say. "Here, give me one of your bags."

I lower my large hold-all bag from my head and grab one of Jenn's that is similar. I alternately swing them in front of me like ungainly forty-pound walking sticks. It is slow, hard work but we are making progress through the sad and broken, hot and sweaty streets of Grand Case.

After another five minutes of cursing heavy dive gear and sweating unbelievably, Jenn asks a lady for a lift and she kindly agrees to help. She is French and speaks very little English, and unfortunately we speak no French. But we bundle ourselves and our bags into the small car with her and her son, and the first thing they do is offer us water. We politely refuse; we have one large bottle left, which will be enough for today.

Once we get onto the main road, it is slow going due to heavy traffic. After about ten minutes of stop-and-go driving, we are just stopped. Every minute or so we move forward a few places until eventually we can see the source of the delay. There is a huge shipping container in the middle of the road, twice the size of the ones on the dive centre property. How on earth did our small ones stay in place?

We make it to the airport just before two. Our kindly French driver drops us off on the main road right next to the car park. I open my wallet and offer her something, but she will not accept any money and backs away, waving her hands in refusal. We are so grateful and cannot thank her enough, and even though she does not speak English, I'm sure she gets the message. She seems very happy to have helped us.

The sun is blazing hot today, the hottest day of the past two weeks. It beats down relentlessly on the car park and everyone in it, and the black tarmac radiates heat back up at us. The scene at SXM is one of organized chaos. There must be a couple thousand people here at least. We struggle once again with our bags and approach a now Dutch soldier for help. He directs us to someone nearby who is dealing with the flight to Canada. We approach the official and tell him we are booked on the flight to Canada.

"Are you guys Canadians?" he asks.

"No, we're not."

"Are you sure you're on *this* flight?"

"Yes, mate," I say, "we are. My brother booked us on it, and we received a message telling us to come here right away."

"Well I'm not sure, but the line is right there, go and stand beside it for now."

"Beside the line?" I repeat.

"Please, for now," he says.

Discouraged, we stand beside the line. It is soon clear we are not the last to arrive, and the line grows behind us. I try to send a text to Ian to let him know we are at the airport, but it will not send.

Mark: At airport, still much confusion. Where are we flying into in Canada?

I never shy away from the sun, I love the sun, I love to feel its hot tingle on my bare skin, like a snake warming itself. I come alive in the sun. I'm not lethargic like many. But now the sun feels different. Just days before, I was sweating and toiling in its heat cutting trees in a futile gesture. I felt tired, but not due to the sun; it was hard work, sawing and dragging huge limbs. But now the sun seems to be sapping my strength instead of giving me strength. It seems hot and malicious. Irma has taken my dreams and now the sun is taking what little strength I have left. Maybe it is punishing me for leaving? Everyone here looks alone, there is little interaction. Everyone looks desperate to escape, and there is no doubt we are fleeing an island in turmoil.

I can't help but wonder who all these people are: tourists, locals, I don't know. It is not high season here yet, so I believe there must be lots of local people, both French and Dutch, I suppose. Where are they going and why? Have they lost everything? Are they returning to family and friends back at home, and if so, where is home? Why are we leaving?

I have thought about what makes home before and I'm thinking about it again. I believed Saint Martin was to be my home, for a good while at least.

But what would have made it so? I believe it would have been a combination of being on, in, under, or near the ocean every day, being around like-minded people, sharing underwater experiences and my passion for the ocean with others, and instilling a bit of that passion in them. I have said home was a place of safety and comfort, where healthy strong relationships thrive, where people care and share and listen and look out for one another. So could home now be considered a collection of people with shared interests and experiences and a healthy attitude toward each others' feelings at a given time and place? I think home and happiness might be one and the same.

We can see the runway from the car park and have been looking for a West Jet plane for almost two hours now. We have finished our litre of steamy water, and fortunately we have been given another small bottle of much cooler water by an official. At around four o'clock, we see a West Jet plane coming in to land.

"Look, West Jet," I exclaim.

"Do you think we'll get on it?" Jenn asks. She doesn't sound very confident.

"I'm sure we will, we're booked on it, aren't we? Even if the guy here doesn't seem to know, I'm sure the people on the plane will. Don't worry; we'll get out of here soon."

Shortly after the plane lands, the line is moved past the barriers to a second set right on the edge of what I believe is called "air side," right next to the runways.

"Can we join the end of the line now over there?" I ask the official.

"Yes, go through," he says, somewhat more cheerily. Hearing that is a relief. We're at the back, but I'm sure there's plenty of room on board for us. I have never felt so tense in my life, I really want to leave here now, and being so close to a way out has my stomach tied in knots. After what seems like an eternity, we eventually reach the head of the line.

"Passports please? You're not Canadian."

"No, we're not," I answer, "but my brother booked us on this flight."

"This flight is for Canadians," the woman says abruptly.

"You have our names; my brother booked us on and he received an email telling him to tell us to get to the airport for West Jet flight 4905."

"There are no bookings."

"We are booked on, how else would I know the flight number?" I ask in protest.

"Show me the email then," she demands.

"I don't have it, he didn't forward it to me, and I have not had a signal since we left Grand Case, so can't check for it now," I say, hoping for understanding.

The lady simply shrugs and says, "See," as if accusing me of lying.

I can't believe her attitude. "How would we even know the flight number if we weren't booked on it?"

"You're not getting on this flight," she says.

We are standing almost on the edge of the runway, and we *are* booked on the flight, but we might as well be miles away. I see another lady with a clipboard and decide she might be a better person to speak to. She is hovering just the other side of the final barrier. I can see the plane and others boarding just feet away. I get her attention and repeat our story and ask her to please check with someone.

"We are doing all we can in difficult circumstances," she says in an irritated tone.

I don't say it, but I think, bloody hell, you've only been here half an hour and you'll be heading off again soon. Who is really in difficult circumstances here? She confirms what her colleague said, that we will not be allowed on the flight. Our spirits are shattered, and Jenn bursts into tears.

At last I give her a long overdue hug, one that I need as much as she does. Since my time at Plymouth University, I have come to accept hugs now and again, but I am still slow to offer them. Now it feels easy, natural, warm, and comforting.

We hang around the barrier like desperate refugees, shuffling and pacing up and down. One soldier is particularly kind and tells us, "The plane will not be going anywhere for a while, because all the bags are being opened and checked. So you never know, there's still a chance."

Thirty minutes later, someone in a green army uniform approaches and asks Jenn, "Where are you going?"

"We were meant to be going to Canada, but they won't let us on board."

"Do you want to go to France?" he asks.

At almost exactly the same time, another person says to me, "See that lady over there, she knows about your booking." He points to the lady with the clipboard I had spoken to earlier.

"Really, are we on this flight then?" I am astonished and frustrated.

"Where do you *want* to go?" asks the soldier, upon overhearing the Canadian deliver the news.

"We don't care where we go, we just want to leave," Jenn says to the soldier as she looks toward me for help.

A second later, the lady with the clipboard arrives and says, "You are on the flight," in a much friendlier tone.

"We don't mind where we go," Jenn repeats.

"Well, come to France then," says the same soldier with a big smile, as he moves the railing aside. His slightly mocking tone implies that we had been delaying making a decision and messing him around all afternoon.

We stop just paces through the barrier, still confused as to what to do, when the Canadian lady says, "well, are you coming to Canada or not?"

We turn to look at each other, not knowing what to do. The idea of going back to Canada is great, but it seems wrong to turn down a place on a flight we were offered when we had nothing. We spend a few confusing moments in limbo, and when the soldier gestures for us to follow, we do without even thinking. I have one bag still on my back and one in each hand, in awkward walking stick-style, until very quickly someone scoops up one end of one of the bags and we carry it together while I swing the other.

It soon becomes apparent we are heading toward a huge green Lockheed Hercules, the back of which is open like a huge dark cavern. The sun is in our faces and the entrance to the Hercules is dark, but as we slowly trudge up the ramp with our bags, the interior is slowly revealed to us.

There is a row of gray mesh suspended seats with red racing car style–seat belts along each wall of the plane facing toward the centre. There are no hostesses on this flight, only French soldiers who take our bags and tie them down in the middle of the aircraft under thick wide luggage straps. I wonder if these are the same straps they use to tie down things like tanks? We strap ourselves into the webbed seats that hang suspended from the ceiling. I can't quite take it all in. This is certainly a no-frills aircraft experience. The walls are covered in gun metal gray paint, and the frame of the plane is visible save for a few panels here and there. Cables and ducting are secured to the ceiling and walls, and in the strange light it looks like something out of an *Alien* film. I say no frills, but it is thrilling, because this is a plane I have always wanted to jump out of. Jenn sits next to me beaming. I wonder if she has dreamed about jumping out of one of these too. Or maybe she is distracted by the French soldiers and their short shorts? It is strange not to have any windows at all.

The cavernous door slowly closes, the engines and props rumble into life, and it feels as if we are doing slow laps back and forth around the airstrip until eventually the engines begin to roar. The soldiers who have no seats position themselves on the floor and hook their feet under a spare strap. They seem to be enjoying leaning back and holding onto the strap as the plane heaves itself from the tarmac and wobbles and rocks and rolls into the hot humid Caribbean sky. It is a different and slightly disorientating flying experience aboard the Hercules. It seems to not quite fly but to float up and down and groans as it does so, a little like the way a pigeon sometimes undulates in flight.

About an hour after takeoff I am sure we are descending, and Jenn shouts over the din, "It feels like we are going to land."

"Yeah I'm sure you're right, my ears have been popping for ten minutes now." Shortly afterwards, we do indeed, and the huge cavernous doors at the back of the aircraft open and slowly reveal a strange new world.

Nineteen

Martinique

"Are we in France?"

"No, we can't be, not after an hour. Maybe we've stopped for fuel?" I suggest. The ramp is fully open now and our bags are being untied and others are untying their belts and getting to their feet.

"I guess we're getting off here then," I say.

The soldiers help people with their bags and we help each other and we file off back down the ramp into a strange twilight world. Just to the right, the tarmac is bordered with a dense green, and I can smell and see vegetation all around. Trees of varying heights line the runway and sway in the gentle breeze; wherever we are is green, lush, vibrant, and alive. In the fading light, our surroundings somehow take on an eerie beauty. It has only been five days, yet the real world—or is it the Garden of Eden?—looks strange and mysterious and alluring. As I look around in wonder, I feel as if I am learning about it all over again. Just an hour's flight away and here, wherever *here* is, seems unaffected by Irma.

As we approach a building just a hundred feet from our flying savior, Jenn asks one of our accompanying soldiers what we are both wondering: "Where are we?"

"France," comes the swift reply.

"We can't be in France," I say, puzzled.

"Well, Martinique, it's still France," he says proudly.

"Oh," Jenn and I say in unison.

All of us aboard file into a sterile, bright, and clinical-looking square room. Long buffet-style tables have been pushed haphazardly to one side of the room, and two rows of chairs line the wall on the opposite side. A quick glance around confirms everyone is as bewildered as we are, and we watch as people shuffle about, not knowing whether to sit or stand. There is another door opposite the one we came in, and a serious looking man in uniform stands there as if on guard. I guess he is a police officer or perhaps an immigration officer. He seems to be eyeing the room rather suspiciously as he stands to near attention. Jenn and I each take a chair and wait to learn what is going on. The scraping of tables and chairs and dumping of heavy bags continues until four or five casually dressed people clutching clipboards stacked with sheets of paper enter the room. As people settle down, the room's chatter and hustle and bustle begin to slow and to hush. The whole time, a man and a woman with lanyards containing what must be ID cards of some kind shuffle about at a desk next to the uniformed man, until finally the man with the lanyard speaks up.

He is speaking in French, so unfortunately neither Jenn nor I know what he is saying. Soon he stops, and the woman introduces herself and repeats his words in English.

"Welcome to Martinique everyone," she says with a sympathetic smile. "Very soon we will transport you all by bus to a hotel, but before we do, psychologists will come and speak to each of you."

I look around the room and those with clipboards who just entered the room all raise a hand and smile in greeting. Psychologists, I think, wow, these people are really concerned about our wellbeing. The man speaks in French again, and then shortly afterward we learn what he said from his colleague.

"When everyone has spoken to a psychologist we will take passport details and then drive you to the hotel. You are all refugees here and can stay for as long as you want or need to. Your accommodation and three meals a day are provided by the French government free of charge. Please be patient and wait until everyone has had a chance to speak to one of the team."

I can't believe what I am hearing. This is nothing short of amazing. I had no idea where we were going or what we would find, or how we would be treated, but being looked after like this is quite something.

"Can you believe all this, Jenn?"

"I know, it's crazy, we are refugees!"

Mark 18.08: Ended up in Martinique, think we are on our way to France. Explain later. Please let everyone know, for me and for Jenn.

Ian 18.09: Get in, get in get in. Well done, mate. So happy, I'm talking to Lee right now.

Mark 18.10: Thanks for everything, mate, we just had a ride in a Hercules. It was a mess at the airport, so we took what we could get in the end.

Ian 18.12: Of course I will, yes, well done, we're so chuffed mate.

Mark 18.13: Let you know when we are leaving here and where we are going if battery lasts.

"Hello guys, is it just the two of you together?" says a friendly lady.

"Yes, that's right," Jenn replies as I nod.

"Are you happy to speak to me?"

"Yes," Jenn replies quickly.

"How are you both feeling?" she asks.

We look at each other but don't answer; I think, like me, Jenn doesn't know what or how she feels.

"Not really sure," I say, breaking the silence and sounding as uncertain as I feel.

"Well, you've been through a lot," she acknowledges without really knowing. "How was your experience, do you mind telling me?"

Jenn and I quickly retell parts of what happened to us on Saint Martin, while she listens intently.

"It sounds terrible. Please remember that while you might be confused now and unsure of how you feel, you can have delayed reactions to this type of thing. It is important to talk about it and not bottle anything up. Stress and anxiety can come later and cause problems."

"Okay," we both say. "We understand," I add.

We talk a little more, and she reinforces how important talking is if we feel upset or stressed and that someone will be at the hotel every day if we need them.

"Please take one of these forms, sorry it's in French," she says.

"That's okay," we say again in unison.

"If you ever need help you can call one of the numbers. Don't worry too much about the form; it really just repeats what I've said."

"Thank you, we will," says Jenn with a slight smile.

"Okay, I'll leave you now," the lady says as she rises to her feet.

"Thank you very much."

Half an hour later we arrive at the hotel and all file into the busy reception to wait our turn. While it is crowded and noisy, it is relatively calm by comparison to Saint Martin. There are four receptionists working as quickly as they can, and as our turn draws nearer, I ask, "Do you want to get separate rooms?"

"No, we can share a room," Jenn says.

"Are you sure you don't want your own space?" I ask, not wanting it to be awkward in any way, but hoping for her company.

"No, we'll get a room together; it's fine," she says.

I'm so glad she said that. I really want the company and I'm not ready to let her out of my sight yet.

"Are you awake?" I ask early the following morning.

"I am," comes Jenn's reply. "Did you sleep well?"

"I think I did, thanks. Did you?"

"On and off, but okay I guess," Jenn says.

"Here, check the messages, there are some from your sister," I say as I toss her the phone.

"Did you read them?"

"No, you read them first."

"Oh cool," exclaims Jenn, "my sister has found a flight to France on Thursday and needs our passport details."

"Has she? That's great, saves us looking. I'll find my passport," I say as I get out of bed.

"She says the flights will be her gift to us as well."

"Really? Oh, wow, tell her thanks very much."

"I will. Breakfast?"

"Yeah, come on, let's go," I say.

We take the short walk through the hotel grounds, past lush lawns and perfect gardens, accompanied by a morning chorus of birds.

"This is how the Caribbean is meant to be," I say. "Nature is so powerful," I add, thinking how just an hour away back on Saint Martin, everything has been reduced to rubble and sorrow.

"Yeah," says Jenn, "it's all a bit surreal, isn't it?"

"I can't imagine how long it will take to put right," I muse.

"So cruel."

We walk the next three or four minutes in silence, and as we approach the restaurant, Jenn says, "Go sit down, I'll just call my sister and catch up with you in a minute."

"Sure, say thanks very much from me," I say with a smile.

"Will do."

Five minutes later Jenn joins me with a grin on her face and says, "Guess what?"

"What is it?" I can't help but grin back.

"My sister has booked us business-class seats."

"No way," I say.

"Yep."

"Wow, that's amazing." I am astonished.

"I know, isn't it? We deserve it," she said.

"Wow, you'll have to thank her again for me."

"No need, you'll see her at the airport. She is going to drive from Switzerland to meet us at Paris Orly Airport and take me back with her for a few days. Then I'll go to Ireland to see my parents."

"Great," I say, "I look forward to meeting her."

The previous night's attempt at an evening meal was pathetic, and we barely ate a thing. But this morning we make up for it. For someone who normally doesn't eat breakfast, I do very well indeed.

After breakfast, we go check out the beach and then take up residence poolside. Trying to relax on a lounger and soak up the rays is difficult, as my mind is full of Saint Martin. What is happening there? How is everyone? These thoughts interfere with my relaxation. When we head to the restaurant for lunch, we are surrounded by other refugees from Saint Martin. No one really talks to anyone much at all. Jenn spoke to one lady who asked about her experience, but she didn't seem to believe Jenn's story. I have said good morning or good afternoon to people, but not much more than that. It seems everyone here is walking around in their own little bubble. While we are eating our dessert, I have an idea and say, "Let's go to reception and ask if there's a dive centre nearby."

Jenn says with eyes wide, "Oh yeah, shall we?"

"Yeah, come on," I say. "We should do something while we're here. A dive would be perfect." I rise from my chair.

"Yes," says Jenn, as her chair too drags across the tiled floor of the restaurant.

There is indeed a dive centre, in the town, about a thirty-minute walk along the beach. We set off immediately and book a dive for the next day.

At eight the following morning, we walk back into town for our dive trip. The owners of the dive centre are very nice people and are taking the boat out with only Jenn and me aboard. Many dive operators would not organize a trip with only two passengers, so they make us feel quite special. It is another perfectly sunny day as we head out to the dive site. As we are setting up our gear, I have a strange feeling that I can't quite identify. When it is time to get into my wetsuit, I realise that the strange feeling I have is nerves. What on earth am I nervous about and why? Why now? I have not been nervous before a dive for years. Certainly not in clear warm water to a depth of thirty feet or so in a perfectly calm sea. Yet, here I am.

I am so apprehensive I could easily stay right here on the boat, but I won't do that. I hold in my true feelings and take the plunge, as it were, put my regulator in and jump in. When I put my face in the water, straightaway my breathing is erratic, even more so than when I took those first underwater breaths in 1998. Rather than the usual long, slow, almost lazy breaths in and out, my breathing is more like a stutter as I take three or four short, sharp inhales in rapid succession. Now I am upset about being nervous, which just makes things worse. I turn my back slightly to Jenn and our dive guide, not wanting them to notice my problem. They are slowly descending to the bottom now, just thirty feet below, and the water is warm, clear, and inviting and already full of life. Yet I am not the same dive instructor I was before the storm. Today I can't do what I did then. What's going on? I feel terrible, but I have to fight it. I so want to get back on the boat, but if I give in, when will I get back into the water?

I wait thirty seconds, and my breathing hasn't changed; the other two are on the bottom while I remain above. I silently urge them not to notice. In anger and frustration, I force myself to release the air from my BCD and slowly to descend, not into my place of calm and tranquility, but into one of stress and anxiety and threat. This was meant to be relaxing, a way to normalise and a respite from all the chaos we have seen on land, yet I'm really struggling. Usually everything melts away in the water like an ice cube thrown into a boiling kettle. Yet here I am, struggling to leave the surface when I should already be on the bottom. Why do I feel this way? Trying to understand is making me even more stressed. Finally I reach the bottom. I'm fighting not to spiral deeper into anxiety and I'm doing my best to cover up my feelings as I struggle to relax. My breathing is still rapid and erratic. This can't be happening, yet it is.

I try to concentrate harder on my breathing, to take ever longer, slower breaths, and to calm myself. After perhaps four minutes on the bottom, I am beginning to relax. A minute later and I feel much better and manage to enjoy the rest of the dive. Back on the boat after the dive, I say nothing of my experience and focus on talking about what we saw underwater. I want to forget it, but I am afraid it may happen again. As much as I hate to admit it, I am happy we are doing just the one dive today, and that alone really hurts. I have never felt stressed or nervous about diving, except perhaps in Australia when I dove alone with an unknown buddy for the first time. Or my first few dives on Protea Banks in South Africa with Trevor. I expected that mild degree of apprehension. It was healthy and helped me focus, pay attention, learn, and grow in confidence. This was different. I just felt nervous and didn't want to be in the water, and I hated that feeling. I *always* want to be in the water. I wonder if this a delayed stress response to Irma, manifest in diving? If so, will it happen again?

We get back to the hotel around one, and after lunch we attend another meeting where we learn that the French government has organized a free flight for everyone on Friday. We don't have to take it, but it is there if we want it. We are already being so well cared for here, and now to have free flights home, I can't believe it! Jenn calls her sister to find out if she can get a refund on the flight she has booked, but she insists we keep the flight and return on Thursday.

Twenty

Going Home

I remain as fascinated with air travel as I was the first time I stepped into an aircraft. No matter how many times I step from that air-conditioned aluminum tube after a flight, I am amazed. Somehow flying feels like time travel to me. As soon as the aircraft doors open, the time aboard melts away, and I feel as if I have walked on, sat down, stood right up again, and walked off into a new climate, another time, another culture, another language. Yes, the ocean is my biggest pull, but I am fascinated by our planet as well, and being out and about in it feels right. I will never get used to air travel and will never stop being enchanted by it.

Melting into the ample and luxurious comfort of the Air France business class seat is bittersweet. As we settle into our elegant accommodations, a young girl walks down the aisle and lets out a drawn-out, "Wow," summing up how we feel, at least in part.

We turn to each other and laugh loudly for a moment until we realise we are leaving behind hopes and dreams and newfound friends on a broken island.

Nine hours later and very well rested, we arrive at Orly Airport and are greeted by Jenn's sister and her partner. It feels strange that this crazy experience is over.

"Thanks for being there for me," says Jenn as we approach airport security for my short flight to the UK.

"You're welcome," I say. "I'm glad I was."

"So am I," Jenn replies.

I let out a sigh and simply say, "Crazy."

"Everything happens for a reason."

"I guess so," I say, but I'm unconvinced.

I have always struggled with this concept and finding comfort in it. But if my reason was to look after Jenn, I am comfortable with that. In fact, more than that, as I said to Jenn, I am *glad* I was there to look after her. We hug again, and I walk to join the line at security. I turn and see the three of them standing in the same spot. I smile and raise a hand. I turn to smile and wave many times until I pass all the way through and out of sight. I feel very emotional and am trying not to let it show.

I should be relieved to be home, but relief is not what I feel. Irma is still roaring around in my head, and she refuses to move on. It feels as if I have been suddenly physically removed from all the chaos, as if someone has waved a magic wand, and here I am in what should be the calm of Exeter. Yet mentally I am still in Saint Martin, and the thoughts spinning in my head will not leave me. I can't stop them for more than a moment. I think about all the people left behind on Saint Martin, particularly our neighbors. I wonder how they are and what they might be doing. Have they received any food? Any water? I feel terrible for leaving them and all the other good people of Grand Case. I turn on a tap and water comes out. I have a fridge, and when I open it food is there. If not, it's a short walk to a supermarket that offers everything I could possibly need or want. In Grand Case there is nothing. Black Chris reassured us both that leaving was the right thing to do, for Grand Case, for the island, and for ourselves. But right now it doesn't feel that way, it feels as if I have run when I should have stayed and fought. Fought for the island, for Grand Case, and last and by no means least, for Chris and for Octopus Divers.

I keep reliving the storm and trying to work out how we survived. My brain just goes over and over it, putting me back in the midst of the chaos. Despite being at home now, it feels as if I have been removed from the situation all in a flash and have not had time to process the change. I listen to music to relax, but I can't enjoy it. Irma howls around in my head, and struggling to enjoy music takes me back many years and to another time when I also found music hard to enjoy.

While I was growing up, I needed to tiptoe around Mother when she was angry. At other times, of course, she would be like a normal mum. I'm not sure exactly when, but this drastic contrast led me to an astonishing belief: my mum had been kidnapped by aliens and replaced at times with an evil clone. This was so real to me that I could hear her calling to me through the speakers in my bedroom while I was listening to music. It was many years later when I realised perhaps this must have been a way for me to justify her erratic behaviour.

Maybe the strangest feeling of all is how very uncomfortable it is not having Jenn around. We barely knew each other before the storm hit; we went on two dives together, spent a few days sweating and toiling on the hurricane prep, and then bam! We were thrown together under terrifying circumstances. Where's Jenn? The phrase pops into my head and gives me a start three or four times a day. As soon as I look around or jump from my seat, I snap back to reality and remind myself she is safe with her sister. I know she's not in Exeter, and I know I am not on Saint Martin, yet I have no control over my irrational thoughts. There is a bond between that will make us friends for life.

Just two days after returning to Exeter, I have to move out of the flat I have been living in, as it has been sold. Before I left for Saint Martin, I packed all my things and put them into storage. Now that I am here, I will help Graeme with the rest of the move. The process of packing up the last of the flat begins, and though my body is here in Exeter, my mind remains on Saint Martin, and it is really hard to concentrate on the simplest of tasks.

How I make it through the day without breaking down or screaming I don't know. Wrapping delicate crockery in newspaper and carefully packing and moving CDs, stereos, and TVs are incredibly difficult. Why do we own all these things, and why do we treasure them so? They can all be taken away in an instant and for the most part are so unimportant. Wrapping delicate glassware is the worst. I feel dizzy, and my head swims with images of Grand Case, of Chris's and particularly our neighbors' house with all their belongings smashed beyond recognition. They flash in and out of my head like a haunting strobe. I want to smash the glasses on the ground and turn them to dust, to sand. The whole process seems ridiculous and unimportant, when just a few hours across the Atlantic, people are living in rubble and hoping for food parcels.

I don't believe anyone will understand how I feel and will think I am just looking for an excuse to get out of walking up and down the fifty-nine stairs to the flat. I reluctantly carry on and work hard to concentrate, but my head is still swimming.

Mark: Do you know if Hurricane Maria affected Saint Martin? I have been looking and can't find clear information. I texted Black Chris this morning, and it looks like the message has not been delivered. X

Jenn: I'm really not sure, I texted the Dominican guy and Chris and Pepe, but none have been delivered. X

Jenn: I think it must have hit. X

Mark: Bloody hell, I feared that too. Now I'm crying. X

Jenn: Me too. I'm heartbroken once again! I'm trying to ring one of them, but it's not going through.

Mark: The island really can't take any more. Makes me feel sad thinking about all those people on Saint Martin and elsewhere. X

Jenn: Me too. X

Jenn: I feel so helpless.

Mark: Yesterday I couldn't stop thinking about everything we have been through and what we saw in the aftermath. Moving house and looking after silly household things seemed ridiculous. In my spinning head, I was in Saint Martin all day. X

Mark: Yes, it's an awful feeling.

Jenn: It's very surreal. I feel heartbroken and like I should be there. I would give anything to be back there helping out with everything. But at the time, it was the right thing to do, and realistically it was too.

Jenn: I can't sleep at night because I keep having flashbacks. Do you?

Mark: Black Chris said again the other day that we were right to leave. There were more resources for the islanders, and seeing our nearest and dearest was important.

Jenn: Yes, definitely.

Jenn: It's just hard when you connected with people and hearing what they are going through.

Jenn: Knowing they have no food and water, and here we are eating and drinking like it's okay, and they have nothing.

Mark: Oh Jenn, that's awful. I'm okay at night, but in the daytime, particularly yesterday, I can't switch off.

Mark: Yes, I only met a few people in my short time, but they are real nice people, and I think about them all the time. X

Mark: Do you think you should talk to someone? I am going to, I think, someone is arranging something for me. X

Mark: You can talk to me, of course, and I'm sure your parents will listen. Just please don't bottle things up and try to deal with them on your own. X

Jenn: Are you? That's good, I'm glad you're taking that step. It will help you a lot. Someone who really doesn't know what's going on is good to talk to. Yes, likewise, Mark. I'm going to get back on my antidepressants, I think. I hate taking them, but they do help. X

Mark: I used them many years ago, and they helped me too. I'm not sure it's great to rely on pills, but they definitely have a role to play. Could you take them and talk to someone as well? X

Jenn: No, that's why I hate taking them, because I hate relying on them. Yeah I think I will. Let me know how it goes please. How do you feel inside, honestly?

Mark: Honestly, mixed up. I think about the storm a lot, and after looking around Grand Case afterwards, I don't understand how we survived. For a while I thought we wouldn't make it, and I think I should have done more to make you and Pepe feel safe. I feel bad for not being stronger. When I think about that, which I do too much, the scared and useless feeling comes back. I know leaving was right, but I can't stop thinking about those left behind. You have said how you feel at night, but is there anything else? X

Jenn: I know we were very, very lucky, and that's what we need to think about. And please don't feel bad, because you were my rock, and I'm so glad I had you by my side through everything we went through. And I haven't thanked you enough, but I am extremely grateful. You were very strong, even if you don't feel like it. And I know Pepe will feel like you did everything you could. Speaking to someone will definitely help you and help you manage your feelings. I suffer from depression quite bad, and I feel it slowly coming back and just can't sleep at night. I feel like you, just thinking about all the people still there and feeling a lot of guilt. But I still feel complete shock too, like it hasn't sunk in and it's going to hit me hard. So, yeah, I'm going to take your advice and speak to someone because I think that's the best thing to do. And like I've said before, you can talk to me anytime, even if it's the middle of the night. XX

Mark: Thank you for saying that, Jenn. It makes me feel better knowing that I helped you. I know I have said it before, but I truly am glad I was there with you. I did my best, but I think at times I should have done more.

Mark: Please do talk to someone. I would hate it if your depression came back really bad. X

Mark: Same goes here as well. I am here for you always. X

Jenn: You did your best, and that's all you have to think. I think it's hard as well because I'm not keeping busy because my mum and dad live in the middle of nowhere, so I'm constantly thinking about it. XX

Mark: I felt I did at the time, and I felt strong, but reflecting on it, I don't feel so strong. Keeping busy is important sometimes; perhaps you will when you leave Ireland. Hope you sleep better tonight. X

Mark: Night. X

Jenn: Thank you. Yeah, when I get working again. Night night. X

I wake up the next day and begin to feel angry at Irma for taking something away from me. I only lost a pair of fins—and what would have been a great job and life with great people on an even better island. Why did Irma have to take everything away so quickly, so cruelly and without compassion? I can't imagine how the people who lost everything must feel—their homes, their livelihoods, businesses, their possessions, and terribly for some, family members. When I think about how frightening she was, I believe she is still out there. It plays on my mind, and one evening just after dark I call the only person in the world who will understand.

"Hi, Mark, how are you?"

"Okay, you? Are you sleeping any better, Jenn?"

"I'm okay, but no, I'm still not sleeping so well."

"Are you not? I'm sorry, I was hoping you might be now," I say, feeling bad for her. "I'm so lucky at night. It's during the day that I struggle."

"I'm not sure which is worse," Jenn says sympathetically.

I exhale and say, "I think you have it worse; at least I'm sleeping."

"True," she has to admit.

"I can't stop thinking about Saint Martin and what might be happening there."

"I know, so do I. It's so weird being here and thinking about there."

"I think Irma is still out there somewhere as well. Is that weird?"

"No, no it's not," she says quickly.

"She was so frightening; I can't see how she can just disappear," I add.

"I know, I know what you mean."

"I feel bad for being pissed off with her for my own sake too. I only lost the job, but so many lost so much more," I say.

"Yeah, but you can't feel bad about that. We all lost something, and it's not always that easy to measure. If you feel Irma took something from you, you are entitled to resent that, so don't feel bad," she says.

"I'm glad you understand what I mean, no one else could," I say, feeling a bit better for getting it off my chest.

Even now it is impossible to reconcile that a storm so powerful, so vengeful, and so cruel can now have vanished. How can something that powerful just disappear? To me it can't; she will always exist. She is out there somewhere.

After being in Exeter for almost two weeks and feeling lost once more in my home town, I realise I have no real right to feel bitter and upset, because I have lost nothing irreplaceable, and with that in mind I start applying for scuba instructor jobs again. Autumn is often a busy time for recruiting, and there are plenty of good jobs on the PADI website, one of which is on Grand Cayman. This is a place I would love to live and work, so I send my CV and cover letter. I hear back from Grand Cayman quickly, and a few days later I have a Skype interview. It goes well, and I'm sure I have a chance.

There is something else that needs to be done too, to go and visit Mother. I want to go, but it also feels like something I *have* to do. Having a life-threatening experience makes us question many things, especially relationships. I have been asked in the past if I want to fix things between Mother and me and improve our relationship, but I have never been able to give a straight answer. I just don't know, and meanwhile time keeps ticking along. Even if I did, I would have no idea how to go about it. Somehow now it feels like there is pressure on me to do better and behave as if nothing is wrong between us. We talk amicably enough on the rare occasions we see each other, but we are far from close.

Natalie will be there too, which makes me happy. It will be good to see and talk to her, even if it has taken a hurricane to make it happen. Apparently I am an uncle too, and I am really nervous about meeting two nieces for the first time. I hope they don't ask me any uncomfortable questions. Who are you? Why don't we know you? I have no idea what anyone has said to them about me. Hopefully nothing, and I can just appear out of the woodwork simply as Mark.

I tap on the kitchen door feeling even more awkward than usual here. I don't have to wait long before it opens, and I step over the threshold.

"Hello," says Mother, "come in." Two strange faces appear behind her.

"Hello," I say, looking down at the two young faces.

"Hello," they echo.

"Natalie's in the living room, so let's go sit down," Mother says, leading the way.

"How are you?" I ask the two girls, while wondering how I'm going to manage this.

"Hi," says Natalie, as I plonk myself on the sofa beside her.

"Thanks for all your help," I say.

Natalie is almost apologetic. "Couldn't do much from here."

"Don't be daft, you did what you could, thanks."

"Well, I'm just glad you're okay and you got out of there."

"It sounds terrible," says Mother. "It must have been a nightmare."

"It was, yes," I agree, while the youngest of the two girls waves a ball in my face.

"Leave him alone," Mother says, trying to help.

But playing with a ball is the easier option and perhaps a way to break the ice. I take the ball, and my niece immediately jumps back to a reasonable ball-catching distance, her hands out in front of her in readiness.

"What was it like during the storm?" Natalie asks.

I exhale and say, "Where do I start?" as I turn to catch the ball.

"It must have been awful," Mother says.

I try to explain how it was during the storm while continuing to throw the ball back and forth between the two girls who squabble for catching rights. When my story is over for the most part, the younger of the two has become bored with the ball and is desperate to play cards. She asks me if I know how to play a game I've never heard of.

"She makes up card games all the time," Mother says. Then she attempts to come to my rescue. "He doesn't want to play, leave him alone."

"No, it's fine, let's play cards," I say.

The card games go as well as card games with no clear rules can, but what goes better is getting to know them. After the first game, I feel quite relaxed as Natalie and I chat about her work, school, and a common bugbear, the weather. When I leave, I feel I know her much better already.

It turns out I was the only one who was awkward about today.

A few days later, I am offered the job in Grand Cayman. This is another near-perfect place for a marine ecologist/dive instructor to work. The diving is world renowned and the attitude toward the environment and conservation is a healthy one. I complete all the Cayman Islands work visa documents and wait for a police check form to arrive in the post. When I receive it, it states, No Live Trace. The accompanying document explains this means I once had a criminal record that is now deemed irrelevant. Okay, great. I feel I should let my employer know, though, so I mail him to explain everything. He gets straight back to me and says he is not bothered about something twenty years ago and is sure the authorities will be fine.

I am super excited and can't wait to get back out into the world, a world in which I feel at home. Then on Friday, October 6th, I hear from Tom, the dive centre owner, that my work visa has been denied. I can't believe it. I foolishly allowed myself to get excited, and now I feel something is not right. The decision has been made very quickly, too quickly. I know this because I received notification from UPS when my documents arrived at the dive centre in Grand Cayman, and I have this news less than twenty-four hours later. When I call the Department of Immigration from Robin's house to speak to someone about my application, I learn they never received it. So immediately I call the dive centre.

"Good morning, dive centre."

"Good morning, is that Tom?" I ask, certain that it is.

"Hello, yes, that's right, how can I help?"

"Hello Tom, it's Mark. We spoke on Skype, and I should be on my way to you now, but I didn't get the work permit."

"Oh, hello, yes, hello, how are you?" he says, clearly flustered.

"I'm really upset and disappointed not to get the work permit. I had been so excited and looking forward to coming to Grand Cayman and working with you."

"It's a shame, we were looking forward to having you," he says, sounding a little happier now. I have no doubt at one point this really was the case. But I smell a rat, hence the call to the immigration office and now this one.

"Listen, I knew something was not right so I called the immigration office." I pause and hear nothing but silence at the other end. "They never received an application for me. Can you explain that?" There is another pause.

"Yes, well, I can," he says, clearly flustered all over again.

"Did you submit it?"

"No," he says with some regret in his tone, but also a lot of embarrassment.

"I can't believe it, why not? I told you about my past and you said you understood and were fine with it," I say, glad to hear the truth but hurt nonetheless.

"I am fine with it, but someone at the immigration office said it might not get approved," he offers as way of explanation.

"Who said that?"

"One of the office workers." He sounds rather sheepish.

"Not an immigration officer?"

"No."

"Tom, that's crazy, it is no one else's decision to make." My heart sinks yet again. Not only have I not got the work permit, I don't have the official word. I want to scream and cry.

"Did you change your mind? Is that what this is about?"

"No, I didn't," he says, sounding sincere.

"So what is it then?"

"If the permit was not granted, I would have lost another week, and as you know, I need someone soon. I just couldn't afford to risk losing the time," he says.

"I can't believe it."

We go around in circles for a couple of minutes until there is nothing else to say except our good-byes.

"You know what I think?" says Robin as I hang up the phone.

"What," I say, not sure if I want to hear it.

"This is a case of Wilson honesty going against him."

"How so?"

"No one else would have told him they had a criminal record," Robin says, sounding absolutely sure of his words.

"They wouldn't?"

"No chance."

"So?"

"We don't know that Tom would have scoured through the application and found that page, do we?" says Robin.

"No," I have to admit, "we don't."

"Plus he said he was in a hurry, right?" Robin adds. I definitely know where this is going now.

"I am sure he would have submitted the application without looking at it, and at least now you would know the official outcome."

"Yeah, you're right Robin," I have to admit again. I am even more upset now. "When is being open and honest wrong?"

"It's not, but nobody else is," Robin offers. "Why didn't you apply for the work permit yourself anyway?"

"I can't, there has to be an offer of employment first, and then the employer submits it."

"I see," says Robin with a shrug.

"I didn't want to fool him, or have it come back and bite me later. I would rather have it out in the open, that's why I explained everything to him."

"You wouldn't have been misleading him. The information is on the form, that's all you had to do," Robin reassures me.

"But, oh I don't know, I just don't know."

I could scream again, at the record keepers and my prospective employer. I don't, but I do cry. If my record is irrelevant, then don't mention it at all, make it irrelevant. Is that too much to ask after twenty years? I guess the answer is yes, it is. A question I asked myself many years ago has been answered. I am indeed to be branded a thug and a criminal forever, and it hurts. Being kept in my place within the ranks of the immoral and unworthy, prevented from escaping my past indiscretions and moving on, hits me hard. I feel as miserable as I have ever felt. What's the point to any of this?

Everyone I speak to agrees with Robin, that I should have treated my record as irrelevant and not mentioned it to my prospective employer. Chances are Tom wouldn't have taken any notice of the form, my application would have been submitted, and at least I would know one way or the other what the authorities in Grand Cayman made of a twenty-year-old *irrelevant* record.

I am crushed and feel heavy all over again. Only one thing in life is certain, that one day it will end. Yet I don't have the courage to bring that about. I only fantasise about it. I am trying to be strong and think that perhaps feeling this way is just part of being depressed when something hurts to the core. Maybe thinking about mortality and the meaning of life is actually not uncommon, and perhaps everyone has times in their lives when they feel this way. The hours, the days, and the weeks pass, and I think about Irma, until one day months later something hits me.

The storm was a truly terrifying experience. It was bizarre to accept that I was going to end my days on a beautiful Caribbean island being dashed to pieces by a hurricane. I had truly accepted it. But in addition to acceptance of my fate, I clearly remember thinking, *Bloody hell, I haven't seen a tiger shark,* and it annoyed me.

I felt robbed. Irma had the power to rob me of experiences I hadn't had yet. In a text to Ian, I said we were fighting for our lives. This was speaking metaphorically, of course, as we were actually cowering helplessly, but you don't fight for something you don't want, either physically or metaphorically.

So when I answered Jenn's question with "I hope not"—despite not knowing where it came from at the time—I realise now, as I sit here writing in February 2018, that my answer did mean something. It has taken time and a combination of circumstances for me to understand what. I want more experiences, I do have something to offer, and I do have value. There is something else too, and terrible cliché or not, I have come to the conclusion that life is simply a journey, and just like any good road trip, the point of the journey is the journey. There will be twists and turns, there will be forks in the road and decisions to make, sometimes difficult ones. Here we cannot stand still but must make a decision for better or for worse, and we must live with our decisions. I don't hate Reese anymore; it is with a calm acceptance that I acknowledge I acted alone, and I made my own decision in Exmouth those many years ago. Our decisions, as well as the circumstances and experiences we have no control over, will affect our journeys through life, but regardless of what happens, we must keep moving.

This journey is about enjoying and collecting rainbow moments along the way and, perhaps more importantly, creating them for others. It is also about doing all you can to get to know yourself and being true to that self. It is about doing your best to bounce back from the knockdowns and finding ways around obstacles and being alert to the warning signs and the eyes lurking in the darkness at the roadside.

I will do my best to find and to know the Mum who was kidnapped by aliens and wasn't angry. The Mum who despite everything always put food on the table. The Mum who on occasion sent Paul, Ian, and me off to the movies on Sunday afternoons. The Mum who took us to the beach on weekends and during school holidays, when I would gather crabs in a bucket from rock pools, sit and stare at the anemones, and watch and wait for a blenny to poke its head out of a crevice in the rock. Where I would try and always fail to pull an unsuspecting limpet from what I would later learn is its scar upon the high and dry rocks. I will get to know Natalie and my nieces. Perhaps one day I can take them snorkeling or, even better, diving in some exotic location and watch their faces light up when they see all the colourful reef fish for the first time.

Like that unreachable horizon on the endless blue ocean highway, life's horizon or ultimate prize is perhaps reaching the end of it. Thinking of life in this way is not as negative as it might sound, and it does come with a caveat. We are all on our individual journeys through life, and we have an obligation to do all we can to make sure we and those dear to us reach its horizon contented. So we must all race along life's highway with purpose, vigour, and the tenacity with which I once pushed and pulled weights in the gym, because one day, perhaps when we least expect it, our horizon will come to us.

Epilogue

I now understand that, more than anywhere else in life, contentment will be found within the journey, not in the fulfillment of a dream or the winning of an ultimate prize. I have Irma to thank for that. Throughout our journeys, along with the good there will inevitably be some bad, some pleasure and some pain, successes and failure. The truth is that we need both. We need stark contrasts in our lives. How can we appreciate the light if we don't have the dark, the highs without the lows? How else would we recognise them when they came?

So I cannot deny that despite being hard at times, it has been an exciting, enlightening, incredible, and memorable journey, full of many great people, places, sights, sounds, and experiences.

But … I would risk them all for the chance to say yes to that movie.

Acknowledgments

T hanks to Cess, AKA Martin Searle, for all those deep conversations at the Lodge; they helped a lot. Thanks to Jenn for keeping me strong through all the craziness on Saint Martin and for feedback on early drafts of this book. Thanks to Jenn's mum for reading and commenting on early drafts. Thanks also to Lee and Melissa for reading and providing feedback on early drafts. Thanks again to Lee and Menno for coordinating and attempting to get us off the island. Thanks to Melissa for the website. Thanks to Imogen for her editing advice on early chapters. Thanks to Brooke, Krissa, Jennifer and Chris for the initial assessment, and for encouragement, editing, and continued support. Thanks to Tabitha for the cover and interior design. Thanks to Graeme for igniting the spark of an idea. Thanks to Ian for coordinating and communicating with everyone during the aftermath of Irma. Thanks to Paul for finding the Canadian flight, even though we didn't catch it, but we did get the flight to Martinique instead. Thanks to Natalie for communicating with Chris and for getting in touch with me in the first place. Thanks to everyone in the story and to everyone not in the book who had a role to play in my journey. Last of all and by no means least, thanks to all the French authorities and personnel involved in our evacuation from Saint Martin. Thanks also to all on those on Martinique and to those waiting for us on our arrival in France.

Most of the material came from memory, while some came from talking to people who were there, some from Julia's diary, and some from my own short diary from Tofo.

References

Steinbeck, John, 1902-1968. *The Log from the Sea of Cortez: the Narrative Portion of the Book, Sea of Cortez,* by John Steinbeck and E.F. Ricketts, 1941, Here Reissued with a Profile "About Ed Ricketts." New York, NY:Penguin Books, 1986.

Printed in Great Britain
by Amazon

73343800R00156